MIS-READING
THE
CREATIVE IMPULSE

MIS-READING THE CREATIVE IMPULSE

The Poetic Subject in Rimbaud and Claudel, Restaged

Adrianna M. Paliyenko

SOUTHERN ILLINOIS UNIVERSITY PRESS

Carbondale and Edwardsville

Copyright © 1997 by the Board of Trustees,
Southern Illinois University
All rights reserved
Printed in the United States of America
00 99 98 97   4 3 2 1

Library of Congress Cataloging-in-Publication Data
Paliyenko, Adrianna M., 1956–
Mis-reading the creative impulse : the poetic subject in Rimbaud and Claudel, restaged / Adrianna M. Paliyenko.
    p. cm.
Includes bibliographical references and index.
1. Claudel, Paul, 1868–1955—Criticism and interpretation.
2. Rimbaud, Arthur, 1854–1891—Criticism and interpretation.
3. Rimbaud, Arthur, 1854–1891—Influence. I. Title.
    PQ2605.L2Z82732   1997
841′.912—dc20   96-35091
    ISBN 0-8093-2122-X (cloth : alk. paper)   CIP

The paper used in this publication meets the minimum requirements of American National Standard for Information Sciences—Permanence of Paper for Printed Library Materials, ANSI Z39.48-1984. ♾

I DEDICATE THIS BOOK
TO MY HUSBAND, LEV.

"Je finis par trouver sacré le désordre de mon esprit."
—Rimbaud, *Alchimie du verbe*

CONTENTS

PREFACE

xi

ACKNOWLEDGMENTS

xv

ONE

Poetic Subjects and Their Double: Claudel's Map of Mis-reading Rimbaud

1

TWO

Principles of Mis-reading, Strategies of Metaphor

20

THREE

Revisioning the Self, Creating the Subject

35

FOUR

Illuminating the Discourse of the Other

62

FIVE

Revising the Poetic Subject, Repeating the Creative Word

93

SIX

Revealing Divine Order: Poesis Perennis

111

APPENDIX

Critical Turns of Metaphor

135

NOTES

141

WORKS CONSULTED

185

INDEX

199

PREFACE

Creative writers defend themselves and us against the "death of literature" by resurrecting their predecessors. The quest for originality provokes the specter of precursors toward and against whom aspiring authors turn to discover their own voice. This reckoning with the literary past does not overcome it but rather inspires the revisionist relations of earlier and later poets that in turn construct poetic history. Reading the impulse to create after Sigmund Freud, with Harold Bloom we understand that "strong poets make [poetic] history by misreading one another, so as to clear imaginative space for themselves" (1973, 5). This theory of misprision—that is, willfully taking something the wrong way—enables us to explore sites of revisionism in Western poetry that studies of influence have overlooked, if not altogether concealed. It is the past that, casting its shadow through the impulse to create, enlivens the future of poetic history.

Particularly compelling is the case of French poets Arthur Rimbaud (1854–91) and Paul Claudel (1868–1955). Various critical plots to pair them on the basis of spiritual and literary affinities have yet to uncover the revisionist impulse of Claudel's poetic writing in the shadow of Rimbaud. This book restages the poetic subject in Rimbaud and Claudel by uncovering the divergent strategies of metaphor at play in their respective stances. Relating these strong poets in the light of *misreading* the creative impulse illuminates more fully the shadow of Rimbaud in Claudel.

The case of Rimbaud and Claudel challenges the traditional approach to influence, which narrowly relates the similar in artists who, by virtue of the effects of their creative impulses, aim to make a difference. Themes and images at the surface of the text may corroborate Claudel's well-known myth of a Christian Rimbaud. Yet "Rimbaud's unsurpassed influence on Apollinaire and Jacob, Reverdy and Char, the Dada and Surrealist poets" (Perloff 4) contests the religious significance of his writing. Such mutually inconsistent readings expose the skewed treatment of influence that largely concentrates on *what* texts mean rather than on *how* they mean. To the contrary, a revisionist approach, which considers at various levels the textual play of convergence and divergence between creative artists, can indeed stage a poet's evolving stance. Reading Rimbaud and Claudel from this critical perspective follows their respective creative impulses as they emerge in, through, and between their texts.

In *Mis-reading the Creative Impulse*, I claim that poets, like other artists, *create* their precursors while seeking their own voices. Creative writers struggle against an initial identification with their literary fathers to project their *own* voice. Bloom's paradigm of influence, developed with the tools of literary analysis that Jacques Lacan's return to Freud provides, enables us to consider the psychical strife operative in literary relations. Various revisionary strategies or *ratios* (e.g., antithesis and repression) play a predominant role in the textual struggle with precursors. *Ratio*, in the etymological sense of a relation, also a reckoning, here suggests that writers relate to forerunners by making an account of their literary debts. This accounting of influence involves oppositional reading by the later author who aims to overshadow precursors while projecting his or her own originality. A Bloomian approach counters traditional studies of influence by objectifying the relation of precursors and aspiring poets in terms of texts (1975, 3). Aspiring poets' writings revise those of prior creative artists. These mis-readings, through which poets take up new stances, make poetic history.

Claudel's writings profess Rimbaud as his primary spiritual and literary influence and suggest a profound affinity between them. Yet Claudel's poetics of mimesis diverges sharply from Rimbaud's conception of poiesis or creative production. Mystical lyricism re-presents a Catholic worldview in Claudel, whereas the free production of signs in Rimbaud refuses the unifying power of a system per se. It is precisely this divergence that, viewed in light of the convergence with Rimbaud repeatedly claimed by Claudel, invites a revisionist approach to their relation.

Differing from previous critical treatments of spiritual and literary affinities that link Rimbaud and Claudel (MacCombie; Morisot; Nagy), in this study I consider how Claudel *mis-reads* Rimbaud. Claudel appropriates Rimbaud to his own religious cause, notably the Catholic renaissance in French literature in the early decades of the twentieth century. The pretension to totalization underlying Claudel's project transcends any particular religious outlook. In the broader light of diametrically opposed creative impulses, we shall see that Claudel reduces Rimbaud's postmodernist poetry to a modernist poetry. What comes sharply into focus through the course of this study is the theoretical debate about the relation of subjectivity and language that continues to reshape the history of Western poetry.

Preface

Translations for quoted primary and secondary sources in the text and in the notes aim to broaden this study's audience; I assume, however, the specialized reader's knowledge of the French texts cited in the appendix. In the first chapter, we read closely Claudel's mis-reading Rimbaud as his creative double to trace the various sites of this revisionism that up to now have remained unexplored. In chapter 2, I develop divergent strategies of metaphor that twist and turn from mimesis to poiesis; this is the critical maneuver that illuminates Claudel's revision of the unbounded production of *metaphora* in Rimbaud. Deviating from the postmodern subject of language in Rimbaud, Claudel returns to a largely classical paradigm where metaphor serves a mimetic function. By the postmodern, we understand a heterogeneous conception of discourse that challenges the authority of a binding system and thus subverts the structures of language. Claudel's "revolt" against his literary past thus takes an ironic turn back to a mimetic relation between rhetoric and language. With the belief that God revealed language to humankind, Claudel's poetic discourse repeats the divine voice at its center and thereby analogically represents the preexistent order of the universe. Claudel assumes the cognitive import of metaphor with specific reference to the representation of meaning, whereas Rimbaud links the creative work of *metaphora* to the construction of the subject and the production of meaning at the level of the signifier.

Rimbaud's metaphoric practice of *dreamwork* suggests more precisely the play of the unconscious in conscious discourse. *Metaphora* thus remarks the emergence of the speaking subject into language and becomes, by extension, the poietic functioning of discourse. Friedrich Nietzsche, Rimbaud's contemporary, maps out this metaphoric plot, which now reads in the poststructuralist terms that discourse is always already *metaphora*:

> It is language which has worked originally at the construction of ideas. ... That impulse towards the formation of metaphors, that fundamental impulse of man, which we cannot reason away for one moment—for thereby we should reason away man himself—is in truth not defeated nor even subdued by the fact that out of its evaporated products, the ideas, a regular and rigid new world has been built as a stronghold for it. (187–88)

We shall follow that creative "impulse toward the formation of metaphors" in the evolving stances of Rimbaud and Claudel, which mutually illuminate Claudel's map of mis-reading Rimbaud.

In chapter 3, I disclose a postmodern stance in Rimbaud in which the subject that poetic language constructs illuminates the discourse of the unconscious Other within the self. In short, Rimbaud endorses an autonomous creative impulse over the poet-as-self-willed-creator. His theory of the poetic speaking subject, notably *I is an Other*, which positions creative voice on the boundary of self and Other, prefigures Lacanian terms. My elaboration of this split subjectivity in Rimbaud works from Emile Benveniste's strictly linguistic treatment of the subject toward Mikhail Bakhtin's theory of dialogism, in which language happens at once inside and outside the person. A postmodern reading resituates the inside-outside duality in the context of an individual subject and opens up the unitary subject in Benveniste to the deep structures of language developed from Bakhtin.

In addition to a careful demonstration of this dialogic voice, in chapter 4 I present, through several close readings, the production of meaning at the level of the signifier in Rimbaud's *Illuminations*. This poetic writing, which we shall relate to Lacan's elaboration of the Freudian dreamwork, moves well beyond the modern rhetorical practice we find, for example, in the later Charles Baudelaire. Metaphoric practice in Rimbaud, as in dreams, proliferates images that resist analogical structure and creates signifying pathways at the level of the signifier alone.

In striking contrast to Rimbaud's postmodern stance, Claudel turns to mystical lyricism based on his acceptance of a transcendent divine hierarchy that the created world reflects. The poet assumes a God-like quality and the belief that the Divine Father speaks through poetic discourse. In chapter 5, I develop Claudel's theory of *connaissance*, or knowledge directed at centering self and world in universal harmony. Metaphor, in the classical mimetic view that Claudel derives from Aristotle, serves to mediate and express this relation at the level of the signified. In adopting a Catholic worldview, Claudel espouses the logocentric view that God guarantees the validity of language and, by extension, unequivocal meaning. His mimesis deviates significantly from the production of meaning at the level of the signifier in Rimbaud that gives voice to the unconscious Other within the self.

In a blind *return* to the subjective idealism refuted by Rimbaud's postromantic splitting of the subject in and through discourse, Claudel recenters the poetic subject by subjecting his willful creative urge to God. In chapter 6, I illustrate Claudel's turn from the unconscious Other in Rimbaud to the creative impulse outside the self. This positioning reconstructs in religious terms the illumination of a supernatural realm in Rimbaud's *voyance*. As we stage this scene of the anxiety of influence in French poetry, we look toward future sites of revisionism that the history of Western poetry has yet to reveal.

ACKNOWLEDGMENTS

The impulse to write this study, like many first books, emerged from the dense pages of my dissertation where I confronted the opposing poetics of metaphor in Rimbaud and Claudel. I thus acknowledge my "first" readers, including my director Carol Sherman, Yves de la Quérière, Sima Godfrey, Stirling Haig, Mallary Masters, and the late Edouard Morot-Sir, who encouraged me to pursue this line of thinking.

Intervening years of conference papers and published essays broadened my audience to include colleagues in nineteenth-century French studies whose rich insights have deepened my understanding of the poetic imagination. Of the many voices that inform *Mis-reading the Creative Impulse*, I extend special thanks to Scott Carpenter, Randa Duvick, André Guyaux, Edward K. Kaplan, Moses M. Nagy, Laurence M. Porter, Sergio Sacchi, Dianne Sadoff, and Charles Stivale. Fruitful dialogues with anonymous readers of various editorial boards have also shaped this project. I owe a special debt to Renée Kingcaid who carefully read an early version of the manuscript and helped me to think through critical turns of my writing.

I am also grateful to my colleagues in the French Department at Colby College, among others, who offered unwavering support while I completed this book. The entire staff of research librarians at Colby College, who filled countless requests for interlibrary loans, and Grace Von Tobel, who formatted the manuscript, freely gave crucial assistance. I am indeed indebted to Tracey Sobol-Hill and Carol Burns of Southern Illinois University Press and to Kathryn Koldehoff, an expert copy editor, who patiently encouraged me through various stages of preparing the manuscript for publication.

I gratefully acknowledge the following for permission to reprint selections from the work of Claudel and Rimbaud: Paul Claudel, *Five Great Odes*, trans. Edward Lucie-Smith (London: Andre Deutsch Ltd., 1967); *Arthur Rimbaud*: "Side Show" copyright © 1991 by Bertrand Mathieu. Reprinted from *A Season in Hell and Illuminations*, translated by Bertrand Mathieu, with the permission of BOA Editions, Ltd., 260 East Ave., Rochester, NY 14604; Arthur Rimbaud, *A Season in Hell* and *Illuminations*, translated by Louise Varèse, Copyright © 1945, 1946 by New Directions Publishing Corporation. Used by permission of New

Acknowledgments

Directions Publishing Corporation; Arthur Rimbaud, *Rimbaud: Complete Works, Selected Letters*, trans. Wallace Fowlie (Chicago: Univ. of Chicago Press), © 1966 by the University of Chicago. All rights reserved.

Portions of this study have appeared in earlier versions as follows: "Dreamwork in Rimbaud's *Illuminations*: The Scene of the Other in *Bottom*," *Romanic Review* 86.4 (Nov. 1995): 697–706; "The Dialogic *je* in Rimbaud's *Illuminations*: The Subject of Self and Other," *French Forum* 19 (Sept. 1994): 261–77; "Discourse of the Self and Rimbaud's *Lettres du voyant*: Alterity as a Creative Dialectic," *Nineteenth-Century French Studies* 21.3–4 (1993): 434–48. I thank the editors for permission to include revised versions of these articles.

I express heartfelt appreciation for my parents and my siblings, who have always cheered me on, and for my children Ludmila, Yuriy, and Natalia, whose boundless enthusiasm continues to liberate my own. My debt to my husband, Lev, who forever sustains my creative impulse, remains as always unspeakable.

MIS-READING
THE
CREATIVE IMPULSE

ONE

Poetic Subjects and Their Double
Claudel's Map of Mis-reading Rimbaud

> Rarement, en effet, lit-on sans aucune préoccupation, dans un état de parfaite disponibilité; le plus souvent chacun demande au texte qu'il a sous les yeux une réponse à ses angoisses, le sens de son aventure spirituelle, la solution de son drame: mais la vérité que chacun cherchait était déjà en lui.... Qu'y a-t-il donc d'étrange à ce que Claudel ait découvert dans le texte de Rimbaud ce que lui-même y avait mis?[1]
>
> —Franco Petralia, "Le Rimbaud de Claudel"

Who was Rimbaud for Claudel? To explore Franco Petralia's rhetoric, what does Claudel read into Rimbaud? Was Rimbaud all that his twentieth-century *successor* advanced, a great poet, an angelic spirit, an *untamed* mystic, a prophet, in short, "*l'illuminateur* de tous les chemins de l'art, de la religion et de la vie" (Berrichon 446)?[2] When read *au pied de la lettre*, Claudel's writings attribute a preponderant spiritual and literary influence to Rimbaud. Followed as a map of mis-reading, these writings disclose instead the revisionist relation of the two poets. Claudel, recreating Rimbaud in his own image, finds in and through this strong prior poet his own stance of mystical lyricism.

Some critics strictly uphold Claudel's reading of Rimbaud as a Christian poet who at once challenged and sought personal salvation (Lefèvre; MacCombie; Nagy, 1978, 1987); they maintain a deep spiritual and literary influence of Rimbaud upon Claudel. Others rightly question from various perspectives Claudel's claim that Rimbaud was his primary precursor (Blanchet; Bonnefoy, 1961; Morisot; Petralia; Suarès qtd. in Pinquet 93–104). Yet these analyses often skew the nature and site(s) of affinities that Claudel projects with Rimbaud.

Jean-Claude Morisot most closely suggests Claudel's response to Rimbaud's influence that we shall consider in revisionist terms: "il me semblait que Claudel n'avait pas tant subi une influence qu'il n'avait tenté de répondre, en effet, à l'oeuvre interrogative de Rimbaud" (29);

"[Claudel] interprète Rimbaud dans le sens de sa propre croissance" (61).³ The interplay of aesthetics and metaphysics that Claudel comes to interpret in accordance with a Catholic worldview informs his revision of Rimbaud. Claudel reads into Rimbaud, the poet-as-mystic, his own emergence as a Catholic writer.

TURNING AGAINST RIMBAUD, RETURNING TO GOD

The eighteen-year-old Claudel, who first read Rimbaud in June 1886, had abandoned the Catholic faith of his childhood and accepted the prevalent materialist worldview. Later that same year, on Christmas Eve, Claudel had a mystical conversion experience. His return to the church, however, was not immediate. Claudel struggled for four years before submitting himself to the Divine Father with a "second" communion in 1890. This chronology does not bear out the joining of Rimbaud and Catholicism that we repeatedly encounter in Claudel's writings. The interval between these events and Claudel's written account of them, however, provides the missing link.

Initially, Claudel does not claim that Rimbaud inspired his return to God. Rather, reading the *Illuminations* in 1886 shed light on a supernatural realm, which transformed Claudel's sense of reality. Claudel later adopts a religious sense of this other domain and revises accordingly the realm of the unknown in Rimbaud. His poetic project from 1895 to 1910, encompassing *Connaissance de l'Est*, *Art poétique*, and *Cinq grandes odes*, evolves a stance of mystical lyricism that sets the stage for mis-reading Rimbaud as a Christian poet. In his preface to Rimbaud's works published in 1912, Claudel insists upon his precursor's acceptance of God on his deathbed. Is the subsequent publication of his account of his own conversion in 1913 merely a coincidence? We can only speculate whether Claudel or his editor anticipated this ordering. These facts of publication nevertheless establish an intertextual relation between Rimbaud's alleged conversion and Claudel's return to the church, which in turn plays out Claudel's revision of Rimbaud.

Claudel's transformation of Rimbaud works out his own struggle with identity, notably priest versus poet. This personal debate targets broader questions of poetic voice and language. Aesthetic, psychological, and spiritual issues interpenetrate in Claudel's *coming to terms* with the role played by the poet. Self-surrender enables Claudel to create for God. Thus, instead of endorsing one vocation over the other, mystical lyricism marries the priest and the poet within him. Moreover, Claudel recenters the relation of self and world in God. His unequivocal discourse designed to communicate presupposed meaning diametrically opposes the opening up of poetic expression to unconscious mental activity that characterizes Rimbaud's postmodern expression. Misreading the creative impulse in Rimbaud in religious terms, Claudel projects instead his own poetic voice.

FROM INFLUENCE TO POETIC REVISIONISM

Influence, generally signifying power exerted over others, implies authority. Literary critics assuming this sense of the term limit influence to the transmission of themes, ideas, images, style, and so forth from earlier to later creative artists. Etymologically speaking, *influence* connotes a flowing in that we shall develop in psychopoetic terms. In the Bloomian scheme of poetic revisionism, which this reading of Rimbaud and Claudel develops, influence "cannot be reduced to source study, to the history of ideas, to the patterning of images" (1973, 7).[4] The *process* of literary influence entails the interiorization of a predecessor's voice, where we read with Bloom "the shadow cast by the precursor," which (in)forms the aspiring poet's sensibility (11). Inspiration in this sense leads in turn to revisionism.

Creative artists strive for originality, that is, to influence rather than to be influenced. Ironically, this drive for priority often has as its basis an initial identification with a strong prior poet. A precursor, or literary father, inspires yet enslaves the aspiring poet who is inhibited by the anxiety of imitation. Thus for Bloom, "every poet is a being caught up in a dialectical relationship with another poet or poets" (91). The literary past becomes the obstacle against which an aspiring poet, or ephebe, (un)consciously struggles in order to originate.

An ephebe deviates from a precursor through mis-reading and thus turns to a poetic stance of his or her own. Defending the creative self against influence is fundamentally what constructs poetic history. As Bloom writes, "poetic influence—when it involves two strong, authentic poets, —always proceeds by a misreading of the prior poet, an act of creative correction," that is, of poetic revisionism (30).[5] A 26 February 1896 statement to Maurice Pottecher indeed reveals the extent to which Claudel identifies himself with Rimbaud and thus mis-reads him while coming to terms with his own creativity:

> [J]e ne puis parler de Rimbaud avec sang-froid. Il a eu une telle influence sur moi sous tous les rapports que je me sens par l'esprit et les instincts

poétiques lié à lui par des communications si secrètes et si intimes qu'il me semble faire partie de moi-même. (Claudel, 1959, 101)[6]

Projected spiritual and literary affinity with Rimbaud enables Claudel to recognize *himself* as a mystical poet. From a Bloomian perspective, this identification prepares the site of misappropriation. Claudel transforms Rimbaud into a Catholic poet in consonance with his own mystical lyricism. This "creative correction" of Rimbaud parallels Claudel's primary goal of linking poiesis and theology.

CLAUDEL'S MAP OF MIS-READING: RIMBAUD AND CATHOLICISM

Claudel's writings on Rimbaud trace revisionist turns from the voice of the unconscious to God. In Bloomian terms, Claudel swerves away from a decentered speaking subject to unify self and world: "This appears as a corrective movement in his own poem, which implies that the precursor went accurately up to a certain point, but then should have swerved, precisely in the direction that the new poem moves" (1973, 14). Converting Rimbaud into a Christian poet projects instead the God-centered view of the world that Claudel assumes.[7] A preliminary link constructed between Rimbaud and Catholicism by Claudel appears in a letter to Stéphane Mallarmé (1897):

> Je me propose . . . de vous écrire un jour . . . à propos de certains sujets qui me tiennent à coeur comme: catholicisme et Arthur Rimbaud (envers qui vous semblez injuste). Depuis le coup de foudre initial dont m'a frappé la livraison de la *Vogue* où je lus pour la première fois les *Illuminations*, je puis dire que je dois à Rimbaud tout ce que je suis intellectuellement et moralement, et il y a je crois peu d'exemples d'un si intime hymen de deux esprits. (Qtd. in Petralia 217)[8]

Claudel proffers an intellectual and moral identification with Rimbaud, without, however, specifying his link with Catholicism. Edward Lucie-Smith suggests that "the point of contact between Rimbaud and Catholicism in Claudel's mind lay precisely in the idea of the symbolic" (83).[9] Indeed, both Rimbaud and Claudel open up the parameters of the real to the realm of the unknown. Yet they cast this occluded domain in diametrically opposed ways, notably the unconscious Other inside the self versus the transcendent Other outside the self.

Notwithstanding this symbolic difference, in a 12 March 1908 letter to Jacques Rivière (prior to the written account of his conversion),

Claudel affirms Rimbaud as the literary father who engendered his poetic sensibility and metaphysics:

> Rimbaud a été l'influence capitale que j'ai subie. D'autres, et principalement Shakespeare, Eschyle, Dante et Dostoïevsky ont été mes maîtres et m'ont montré les secrets de mon art. Mais Rimbaud seul a eu une action que j'appellerai *séminale* et *paternelle* et qui me fait réellement croire qu'il y a une génération dans l'ordre des esprits comme dans celle des corps. (Qtd. in Petralia 217; emphasis added)[10]

The inference of a similar generative principle in the mind and the body from Rimbaud relates to the revelation of the supernatural. In other instances, Claudel attributes his turn from positivist materialism to idealism to Mallarmé. Here, in the letter to Rivière, however, the shadow of Rimbaud eclipses Claudel's other literary debts:

> Je me rappellerai toujours cette matinée de juin 1886 où j'achètai cette petite livraison de *La Vogue* qui contenait le début des *Illuminations*. C'en fut vraiment une pour moi. Je sortais enfin de ce monde hideux de Taine, de Renan . . . de ce bagne, de cette affreuse mécanique entièrement gouvernée par des lois parfaitement inflexibles et pour comble d'horreur connaissables et enseignables. . . . J'avais la révélation du surnaturel. (Qtd. in Petralia 217–18)[11]

The sense of *surnaturel* here is not yet unequivocally religious.[12] What Rimbaud, along with Mallarmé, appears initially to inspire in Claudel is not in fact a Catholic worldview per se but rather a departure from materialism.[13] Claudel's allusion in the 12 March 1908 letter to Rivière to an autonomous creative impulse linked with the supernatural indeed coincides with idealist presuppositions: "Le génie se montre là sous sa forme la plus sublime et la plus pure, comme une inspiration réellement venue d'on ne sait où" (qtd. in Petralia 218).[14] Later writings specify Claudel's belief in a divine hierarchy that orders the world.

Various textual returns to Rimbaud move in the religious direction that Claudel takes. Claudel comes to misidentify the quest for the unknown in Rimbaud with his own return to God:

> Il n'y a pas d'homme . . . dont la mémoire me soit plus chère, à qui j'aie plus d'obligations et à qui j'aie voué un culte plus religieux, qu'Arthur Rimbaud. D'autres écrivains m'ont instruit, mais c'est Arthur Rimbaud seul qui m'a construit; il a été pour moi le révélateur dans un moment de profondes ténèbres, *l'illuminateur* de tous les chemins de l'art, de la reli-

gion et de la vie; de sorte qu'il m'est impossible d'imaginer ce que j'aurais pu être sans la rencontre de cet esprit angélique, certainement éclairé de la lumière d'en haut. Je me sens avec lui les liens qui peuvent nous rattacher à un ascendant spirituel. (Berrichon 445)[15]

Both the language of this avowal to Paterne Berrichon that expresses Claudel's interiorization of Rimbaud, to whom he devoted a *religious* cult, and the idea that Rimbaud *formed* Claudel corroborate the revisionist nature of their relation.[16] Claudel alters the impulse of the unconscious Other in Rimbaud that inspired the surrealists and mistakes his precursor's poetic voice for religious mysticism. Rimbaud thus illuminates for Claudel the path to God.

Surrealists, who vehemently denounced Claudel's hagiographic treatment, view the *surnaturel* in Rimbaud as an unconscious psychical reality. Claudel, to the contrary, comprehends the unknown in Rimbaud to illuminate the divine supernatural coterminous with the empirical world:

> C'est à Rimbaud que je dois humainement mon retour à la foi. Je pataugeais dans les marécages du rationalisme, et je pensais que le monde entier est aussi explicable qu'une machine à battre, quand la petite livraison de la *Vogue* du 13 mai 1886, est venue briser les murs de la prison infecte où j'étouffais et m'apporter la prodigieuse révélation du surnaturel partout présent autour de nous. Aucun livre ne m'a aidé plus que la *Saison en enfer* dans cette terrible agonie qu'est la reconquête de la vérité perdue. (Qtd. in Petralia 220)[17]

Claudel, reading into *Une saison en enfer* his own religious convictions, embraces in Rimbaud an agonizing spiritual struggle that ends with an affirmation of faith in God.[18] Thus, in Claudel's preface to Berrichon's 1912 edition of Rimbaud's works (Claudel, 1965, 514–21), Claudel revises the poetic subject in his precursor, staging instead his own conversion experience.[19]

REVISING THE CREATIVE IMPULSE IN RIMBAUD

From the outset, what Claudel's preface affirms about Rimbaud presents in turn Claudel's own spiritual journey:

> Arthur Rimbaud fut un mystique *à l'état sauvage*, une source perdue qui ressort d'un sol saturé. Sa vie, un *malentendu*, la tentative en vain par la fuite d'échapper à cette voix qui le sollicite et le relance, et qu'il ne veut

pas reconnaître: jusqu'à ce qu'enfin, réduit, la jambe tranchée, sur ce lit d'hôpital à Marseille, il sache! (1965, 514)[20]

Claudel reads several isolated affirmations from *Une saison en enfer* as evidence that prefigures Rimbaud's eleventh-hour conversion: " 'Nous ne sommes pas au monde!' — 'Par l'esprit on va à Dieu! . . . C'est cette minute d'éveil qui m'a donné la vision de la pureté . . . ' " (515).[21] On the basis of this scant textual proof, Claudel yokes the voice that solicited Rimbaud with "the call of God." André Blanchet suggests instead the missing revisionist *link* that this study uncovers between Rimbaud and Claudel: "Tout fait penser qu'en évoquant Rimbaud, Claudel a été obsédé par son propre cas" (771).[22]

Moreover, Claudel imagined Rimbaud's illumination according to his own (Blanchet 771), which occurred "in an instant," "in a single flash," as he later describes in *Ma conversion*:

En un instant mon coeur fut touché et je crus. . . . En essayant . . . de reconstituer les minutes qui suivirent cet instant extraordinaire, je retrouve les éléments suivants qui cependant ne formaient qu'un seul éclair . . . dont la Providence divine se servait pour atteindre et s'ouvrir enfin le coeur d'un pauvre enfant désespéré. (1965, 1010)[23]

Just as Claudel wavers following his encounter with the divine on 25 December 1886, so too Claudel's Rimbaud resists "the voice that solicits him and harasses him, and that he does not want to recognize . . . until finally he believes" (1965, 514).[24] We recognize with Blanchet that Claudel reveals his own spiritual crisis instead of elucidating the nature of Rimbaud's mysticism: "l'Arthur Rimbaud de l'article de 1912 est un double de Claudel lui-même en travail de conversion" (774).[25] To respond to the question of the Other voice in Rimbaud, Claudel marries the poet and the mystic and thus discovers his own creative identity.

Claudel asks what inspires Rimbaud: "Mais ce n'est pas une parole qu'il a entendue. Est-ce une voix?" (1965, 515).[26] His subsequent line of questioning debates the poet-as-willful-creator and the self-regulated creative process: "Est-il donc téméraire de penser que c'est une volonté supérieure qui le suscite?" (515).[27] The idea of a "superior will" that exceeds the boundaries of the subject echoes the autonomous impulse asserted in Rimbaud's seer letter, *on me pense* (an Other thinks me) and, by extension, *on m'inspire* (an Other inspires me). Rimbaud situates the creative Other inside the self. Claudel repositions this impulse outside the self, for only divine inspiration could account for genius at such an early age: "Est-ce un fait commun de voir un enfant de seize ans doué de facultés d'expression d'un homme de génie?" (1965, 515).[28]

Claudel's Rimbaud, divinely inspired, sees in and through the empirical world what remains otherwise obscure. This portrait of Rimbaud unwittingly retraces the emergence of poetic vision recounted in *Connaissance de l'Est*. Mis-reading the source of desire in Rimbaud writes in turn the transcendent urge of Claudel's poetic project:

> Il regarde avec une ardente et profonde curiosité, avec une mystérieuse sympathie qui ne peut plus être exprimée 'en paroles païennes' ces choses qui nous entourent et qu'il sait que nous ne voyons qu'en reflets et en énigmes. . . . Toute la vie n'est pas de trop pour faire la conquête spirituelle de cet univers ouvert par les explorateurs du siècle qui finit, pour épuiser la création, pour savoir quelque chose de ce qu'elle veut dire, pour douer de quelques mots enfin cette voix crucifiante au fond de lui-même. (1965, 516)[29]

The critical confrontation with an alien impulse within the self, which Claudel understands as *cette voix crucifiante*, configures Rimbaud's postmodern romantic subject.[30] Contrary to the transcendent origin of the poetic subject in Claudel, Rimbaud's poetic voice derives from an immanent source that I shall elaborate in the psychoanalytic terms of the interplay of conscious and unconscious signifying relations. His discourse moves against identification. Void of any transcendent properties, poetic writing in Rimbaud targets in a postmodern way the ongoing construction of self in and through language. The crucifying of voice that I shall consider in *Cinq grandes odes* connotes instead the sacrifice of the personal self to God, which enables the subject to speak in His name. Thus, Claudel misstates a progressive submission to divine inspiration in Rimbaud and relinks the boundless creative impulse in his precursor's early poetry to a God-centered voice.

WRITING STAGES OF CLAUDEL´S *VOYANCE:* MIS-READING RIMBAUD'S SUBJECT

At the time of Claudel's 1912 preface to Rimbaud's works, Henri de Bouillane de Lacoste had yet to publish his thesis that rightly questions the composition of the *Illuminations* prior to *Une saison en enfer*. It is doubtful, however, that Claudel would have altered his approach to Rimbaud on the basis of Bouillane de Lacoste's findings. For, as we shall see, Claudel skews the import of Rimbaud's experimentation with language in the *Illuminations* toward the spiritual *truth* of *Une saison en enfer*.

To outline how Rimbaud's poetic voice evolved, Claudel divides his precursor's work into three periods, the first of which he calls "celle de la violence, du mâle tout pur, du génie aveugle qui se fait jour comme un jet de sang, comme un cri qu'on ne peut pas retenir, en vers d'une force et d'une roideur inouïes" (1965, 516).³¹ The *Illuminations* constitute the second period. This *voyance*, in Claudel's account, moves from blind impulse to divinely enlightened poetic voice. Situating *Une saison en enfer* as the third and *final* literary work enables Claudel to mis-read Rimbaud in terms of a spiritual quest that culminates in a conversion experience (*Adieu*; i.e., à Dieu, to God) and the rejection of literature. These revised stages of the subject in Rimbaud unwittingly map out Claudel's return to the church and, moreover, his grounding of poetic voice in a Catholic world.

Claudel's map of *voyance* in Rimbaud follows in a religious sense the illumination of the supernatural. A retrospective statement underscores this misappropriated site/sight in Rimbaud: "[Les] *Illuminations* m'ont réveillé, révélé, pour ainsi dire, le surnaturel qui est l'accompagnement continuel du naturel" (Claudel et Amrouche 28).³² In other words, Claudel discerns that transcendent and visible realms coexist. What the surrealists read in Rimbaud in psychical terms Claudel comprehends instead in spiritual ones. Moreover, Claudel rewrites in his own terms of *connaissance* the evolution of poetic vision, voice, and language in Rimbaud.

Along with the Catholic worldview uniting all of creation in God, the metaphoric structure of poetic vision and voice articulated in *Art poétique* and perfected in *Cinq grandes odes* provides Claudel's model for Rimbaud's verbal practice of *voyance*. Bloom's term for the link that Claudel creates here with Rimbaud is *tessera*: "In the *tessera*, the later poet provides what his imagination tells him would complete the otherwise 'truncated' precursor poem and poet, a 'completion' that is as much [a] misprision as a revisionary swerve is" (1973, 66). Claudel, recentering self and world, antithetically completes his precursor in accordance with his own poetics of *connaissance*:

> Le matin, quand l'homme et ses souvenirs ne se sont pas réveillés en même temps, ou bien encore au cours d'une longue journée de marche sur les routes, entre l'âme et le corps assujetti à un desport rythmique se produit une solution de continuité; une espèce d'hypnose 'ouverte' s'établit, un état de réceptivité pure fort singulier. (1965, 517)³³

Here the sensory and intellectual contemplation of nature in *Connaissance de l'Est* takes the form of daydreaming ("hypnose 'ouverte' "). Moreover, Claudel reads into Rimbaud his own theory of *connaissance*, relating self and world, which possess an analogous constitutive rhythm. As Claudel's *voyant*, Rimbaud attains through psychical ascesis a state of pure receptivity and thus sees clearly otherwise obscured unity.[34] Differing from my inference of unconscious mental activity as the source of the creative impulse in Rimbaud, Claudel submits that such vision transfigures the poet-as-willful-creator into a poet-as-mystic. This revision of Rimbaud as a religious seer substantiates Claudel's broader goal of unifying poiesis and theology in mystical lyricism.

I shall develop from a Lacanian viewpoint the speaking unconscious in Rimbaud. It is precisely this inner voice that enables our postmodern way of reading poetry and of exploring the ever-emergent pathways of the creative impulse at the level of the signifier both in and between poets. Claudel, to the contrary, infers from the loosening of conscious ego control in Rimbaud the transformation of the poet into a mystic:

> Le langage en nous prend une valeur moins d'expression que de signe; les mots fortuits qui montent à la surface de l'esprit . . . forment une espèce d'incantation qui finit par coaguler la conscience, cependant que notre miroir intime est laissé, par rapport aux choses du dehors, dans un état de sensibilité presque matérielle. (1965, 517)[35]

Two views of language unwittingly overlap here in Claudel's review of the poetic subject in Rimbaud. The idea that poetic language reproduces meaning through symbols gives primacy to the signified. The suggestion that the poetic word arises spontaneously, which is to say unconsciously, highlights instead creative interplay through signifiers that we shall follow in Rimbaud. Yet an underlying belief in transcendence subverts the immanent source of creativity that Claudel seems to configure here.[36] Unlike the surrealists' view of Rimbaud, Claudel emphasizes a divine source of poetic inspiration in his forefather, at once the alien voice heard inside the self and the autonomous creative impulse outside the self that we shall observe in *Cinq grandes odes*.

Claudel supplants the unconscious Other in Rimbaud with the raw materiality of the created world. His terms of *connaissance* revise the "state of an almost material [i.e., physical] sensibility" in Rimbaud to prepare mystical communion and, by extension, poetic vision and voice:

Le poète trouve expression non plus en cherchant les mots, mais au contraire en se mettant dans un état de silence et en faisant passer sur lui la nature, les espèces sensibles 'qui accrochent et tirent.' Le monde et lui-même se découvrent l'un par l'autre. (1965, 517–18)[37]

Rimbaud envisions a new poetic language "de l'âme pour l'âme . . . de la pensée accrochant la pensée et tirant" at the level of the signifier. Claudel, paraphrasing this formula, replaces thought with "les espèces sensibles" and thereby substitutes the empirical world for mental peregrinations as the site/sight of Rimbaud's contemplation that leads to creative expression.

RIMBAUD´S POETIC LANGUAGE IN CLAUDEL´S RELIGIOUS LIGHT

In light of the religious quest I have sketched up to now in Claudel's reading of Rimbaud, this prefatory comment on the creative play of Rimbaud's discourse seems misplaced: "[d]es images désordonnées qui substituent à l'élaboration grammaticale, ainsi qu'à la logique extérieure, une espèce d'accouplement direct et métaphorique."[38] In fact, the idea of direct and metaphoric joining in Rimbaud's poetic discourse suggests more the postmodern approach to the metonymic grounding of *metaphora* that we shall take than Claudel's classical view of metaphor as analogy. Rather than serving mimetically to represent meaning, the signifier seems to supplant the signified in Rimbaud's verbal alchemy as Claudel describes it directly above.

Unlike his analogical use of metaphor to transpose a vision of universal harmony into discourse, here Claudel further states the extent to which Rimbaud liberates thought from logical relations by obfuscating the transfer of meaning intended in classical and neoclassical metaphor: "Chez ce puissant imaginatif, le mot 'comme' disparaissant, l'hallucination s'installe et les deux termes de la métaphore lui paraissent presque avoir le même degré de réalité" (1965, 518).[39] Claudel ostensibly understands the dreamlike work of metaphor by contiguity in this collection. Yet the sacred disorder that brings about fresh insight at the level of the signifier in Rimbaud for Claudel relates dissimilars at the level of the signified in universal harmony.

Notwithstanding these observations, which strike us as postmodern, Claudel moves immediately to a stance compatible with his mystical lyricism to recover Rimbaud's use of the metaphoric in "an extreme practice of a type of materialist mysticism." *Connaissance*, that is, knowledge of a transcendent unity relating self and world, thus restructures Rimbaud's poetic practice:

> Pratiques extrêmes, espèce de mystique 'matérialiste' qui aurait pu égarer ce cerveau pourtant solide et raisonnable. Mais il s'agissait d'aller à l'esprit, d'arracher le masque à cette nature 'absente,' de posséder enfin le texte accessible à tous les sens, 'la vérité dans une âme et un corps,' un monde adapté à notre âme personnelle. (1965, 518)[40]

The term *mais* marks a fundamental turn from Rimbaud. To quote Bloom on this revision, "a poet antithetically 'completes' his precursor, by so reading the parent-poem as to *retain its terms but to mean them in another sense*, as though the precursor had failed to go far enough" (1973, 14; emphasis added). By equating poetry with religious mysticism synonymous with the apprehension of divine truth, Claudel *corrects* the disintegration of communication in Rimbaud, where language escapes the circle of representation.[41] Rimbaud's modern split subject is precisely what Claudel unifies in order to recover meaning in a God-centered world.

Metaphysics and aesthetics overlap to restore logocentric discourse in Rimbaud so that metaphor functions to structure unequivocal meaning. The assumption of a Catholic universe analogically expressed through metaphor once again anchors the relation of self and world. Not only does metaphor function to disclose the unity of the material and the spiritual, it also illuminates the divine positioning of all creation. Metaphor for Claudel works to unify disparate phenomena by revealing their common structure. This grounding of metaphor deviates sharply from the metonymic joining of widely separate elements to form a poetic image in surrealism derived from Rimbaud (compare Morisot 522). In Claudel's poetic recovery of the presupposed divine design of the universe, metaphor functions not to create but rather to disclose or re-create the connections originally designed by God.

In Claudel's ordering, which runs counter to Verlaine's chronology (1873–75 [1972, 631]), what follows the second stage of the poetic subject in Rimbaud's *Illuminations* (1872–73) is the third and final period of *Une saison en enfer* (1873) in which the poet "attains full mastery of his art" (Claudel, 1965, 518). In the broad context of Claudel's map of mis-reading Rimbaud, not only does this order support the implicit conversion and rejection of literature in *Adieu* mentioned above but also the mission of a Christian mystic. As Franco Petralia puts it, "sa mission accomplie, Rimbaud s'exile et s'enferme dans le silence" (227).[42]

Poetic Subjects and Their Double

Along with a spiritual quest, Claudel focuses on aesthetics in *Une saison en enfer* where "la marche de la pensée aussi qui procède non plus par développement logique, mais, comme chez un musicien, par dessins mélodiques et le rapport de notes juxtaposées" (1965, 519).[43] The analogy with music that Claudel reads here as emblematic of the harmony underlying *Une saison en enfer* recalls the principle that structures *Cinq grandes odes*. Claudel misinterprets in Rimbaud his own aesthetics and metaphysics and thus emphasizes the joining of disparate elements at the level of the signified rather than at the level of the signifier.

The concluding statement of Claudel's 1912 preface to Rimbaud's works responds in part to testimony by Isabelle Rimbaud about her brother's final days and his concern that no one believed him: "Je suis un de ceux qui l'ont cru sur parole, un de ceux qui ont eu confiance en lui" (1965, 521).[44] Instead of saying that he understands Rimbaud, Claudel asserts that he has *faith* in him. Once more, this avowal casts a religious light on Rimbaud. The textual conversion of Rimbaud into a Christian poet recovers, in the conjoining senses of conceals and reveals, Claudel's affirmation of God; for Claudel's account of his turning back to religion, published in 1913, appears in the shadow of his 1912 preface to Rimbaud's complete works.

From the 12 March 1908 letter to Rivière considered earlier (qtd. in Petralia), we recall that Claudel's reading of Rimbaud was pivotal in revealing a supernatural domain coexistent with external reality. The missive discusses the supernatural in opposition to materialism and in connection with a symbolic realm coexistent with empirical reality.[45] *Ma conversion*, however, directs this illumination toward the return to religious truth. The *surnaturel* that Claudel mis-reads in spiritual terms in Rimbaud reveals God:

> *La première lueur de vérité* me fut donnée par la rencontre des livres d'un grand poète, à qui je dois une éternelle reconnaissance, et qui a eu dans la formation de ma pensée une part prépondérante, Arthur Rimbaud. La lecture des *Illuminations*, puis, quelques mois après, d'*Une Saison en enfer*, fut pour moi un événement capital. Pour la première fois, ces livres ouvraient une fissure dans mon bagne matérialiste et me donnaient l'impression vivante et presque physique du surnaturel. Mais mon état habituel d'asphyxie et de désespoir restait le même. (1965, 1009)[46]

The discovery of the supernatural was for Claudel instantaneous: "J'avais eu tout à coup le sentiment déchirant de l'innocence, l'éternelle enfance de Dieu, une révélation ineffable" (1010).[47] Yet he vacillated for four years after his conversion experience before submitting to divine will once and for all. This conflict informs Claudel's revision of reference to God in Rimbaud. We shall observe that these allusions disavow through ironic distancing the existence of the divine, whereas for Claudel they affirm God.

In fact, in the published account of his conversion, Claudel compares his spiritual crisis and wavering acceptance of Catholicism with that of Rimbaud. This resemblance does not derive from historical fact but rather from hearsay traced to Isabelle Rimbaud who claimed that her brother converted on his deathbed:

> Cette résistance a duré quatre ans. . . . Ce fut la grande crise de mon existence, cette agonie de pensée dont Arthur Rimbaud a écrit: 'Le combat spirituel est aussi brutal que la bataille d'hommes. . . . ' C'est vrai, je l'avouais . . . oui, Jésus était le Fils de Dieu. C'est à moi, Paul, entre tous, qu'il s'adressait et il me promettait son amour. Mais en même temps, si je ne le suivais pas, il ne me laissait d'autre alternative que la damnation. Ah, je n'avais pas besoin qu'on m'expliquât ce qu'était l'Enfer et j'y avais fait ma Saison. (1965, 1011)[48]

Reference here to *Une saison en enfer* exemplifies how Claudel skews allusions to Christianity in his precursor's writings on the questionable basis of a rumored conversion.[49] In *Une saison en enfer*, Rimbaud systematically negates each affirmation of God.[50]

The simultaneous genesis of metaphysics and aesthetics underscored in Claudel's account of his conversion obliquely restages his joining of Catholicism and Rimbaud: "L'éveil de l'âme et celui des facultés poétiques se faisait chez moi en même temps" (1012). "Peu à peu, lentement et péniblement, se faisait jour dans mon coeur cette idée que l'art et la poésie sont aussi des choses divines" (1013).[51] Claudel's misappropriation of Rimbaud coincides with his own submission to divine inspiration.

In revisionist terms, Claudel transforms a *poète maudit* into a *mystique à l'état sauvage*. This religious myth of Rimbaud maps out the resolution of the conflict between poet-as-willful-creator and poet-as-mystic that we find in Claudel's *Cinq grandes odes*.[52] Spiritual strife pervades Claudel's revision of Rimbaud. Claudel's *Parabole d'Animus et d'Anima pour faire comprendre certaines poésies d'Arthur Rimbaud* (1925; see Claudel, 1965, 27–28) configures in turn a psychological encounter with which Claudel identifies and, moreover, assimilates in his own struggle with poetic voice.

REVISITING RIMBAUD'S SUBJECT, HEARING CLAUDEL'S POETIC VOICE

Both the title and the first line of *Parabole d'Animus et d'Anima* allude to *Délires I* and thus announce Rimbaud as the explicit topic of Claudel's essay: "Tout ne va pas bien dans le ménage d'Animus et d'Anima, l'esprit et l'âme" (1965, 27).[53] The reading of two conflicting *voices* in Rimbaud rewrites Claudel's dialogue with *La Muse qui est la Grâce* in *Cinq grandes odes*. The dialogic relation of unconscious and conscious mental dispositions in the precursor inspires the aspiring artist's debate about the poet-as-willful-creator versus divine inspiration.

The relation of *animus* and *anima* in Claudel's reading I shall consider instead to present the Lacanian split subject in Rimbaud. Ideally speaking, animus and anima (i.e., the mind and the soul, reason and imagination, conscious and unconscious) work in harmony in the creative process. In this way, animus transposes inspiration received from anima into expression. Claudel notes a tension between these two capacities in Rimbaud, since both appear to contend for primacy in creation:

> Le temps est loin, la lune de miel a été bientôt finie, pendant lequel Anima avait le droit de parler tout à son aise et Animus l'écoutait avec ravissement. Après tout, n'est-ce pas Anima qui a apporté la dot et qui fait vivre le ménage? Mais Animus ne s'est pas laissé longtemps réduire à cette position subalterne et bientôt il a révélé sa vériable nature, vaniteuse, pédantesque, et tyrannique. (1965, 28)[54]

Here animus, aiming to reassert his authority, signifies the poet-as-willful-creator. In another sense, the nature of the conflict that Claudel highlights in Rimbaud involves the dominance of reason versus imagination and, by extension, consciousness versus the unconscious:

> Maintenant Anima n'a plus le droit de dire un mot, il lui ôte comme on dit les mots de la bouche, il sait mieux qu'elle ce qu'elle veut dire et au moyen de ses théories et réminiscences il roule tout ça, il arrange ça si bien que la pauvre simple n'y reconnaît plus rien. Animus n'est pas fidèle, mais cela ne l'empêche pas d'être jaloux, car dans le fond il sait bien que c'est Anima qui a toute la fortune, lui est un gueux et ne vit que de ce qu'elle lui donne. (1965, 27)[55]

With reference to Claudel's explicit rejection of dreams as a source of creative inspiration, the problem of voice in Rimbaud may stem in part from the loss of the artist's conscious control of poetic expression. By asserting that animus "knows better than anima what she wishes to say," Claudel underscores his own assumption of a cohesive speaking subject. The primary difficulty in Rimbaud involves more precisely a lack of submission to divine inspiration, that is, to anima. A biblical intertext identifies anima with Wisdom (*sagesse*) who proclaims her primacy in the creative work of God.[56] As repeatedly noted, Claudel's poet is subject to God. It is precisely this religious key that would free poetic voice in Rimbaud from the divisive effects of the unconscious Other.

A loss of voice that leaves the subject uncertain of his or her authority recurs throughout *Une saison en enfer*. *Délires I* attributes this dissolution to a lack of wisdom: "Mais moi qui ai perdu la sagesse ... Je ne sais même plus parler" (Rimbaud, 1972, 102).[57] Finding oneself speechless, unable to say what one thinks or think what one is saying, exposes Rimbaud's insightfully modern subject to the voice of the unconscious Other within the self. Claudel's parable, however, blindly links the lack of inspiration to the insistence of the poet's ego-self and attempt to control the creative impulse, that is, *La Muse qui est la Grâce*:

> Un jour qu'Animus rentrait à l'improviste ... il a entendu Anima qui chantait toute seule, derrière la porte fermée: une curieuse chanson, quelque chose qu'il ne connaissait pas, pas un moyen de trouver les notes ou les paroles ou la clef, une étrange et merveilleuse chanson. Depuis, il a essayé sournoisement de la lui faire répéter, mais Anima fait celle qui ne comprend pas. Elle se tait dès qu'il la regarde. L'âme se tait dès que l'esprit la regarde. (Claudel, 1965, 28)[58]

My reading of Rimbaud will associate *l'âme* with the unconscious. From this perspective, *l'âme se tait dès que l'esprit la regarde* signifies that we cannot *know* the unconscious directly; we *know* the unconscious only metaphorically, that is, through its effects on conscious discourse. In psychoanalytic terms, then, the unconscious Other within the self speaks Rimbaud's discourse and yet does not fully reveal the signifying pathways of its creative impulse.

Claudel understands instead a conflict between the poet-as-willful-creator and the autonomous onset of divine inspiration in Rimbaud. Again, he revises in his precursor his own wrestling with an alien, inner voice in the ode to *Les Muses* and *La Muse qui est la Grâce*:

> Alors Animus a trouvé un truc, il va s'arranger pour lui faire croire qu'il n'y est pas. Il va dehors, il cause bruyamment avec ses amis, il siffle, il tou-

che du luth, il scie du bois, il chante des refrains idiots. Peu à peu Anima se rassure, elle regarde, elle écoute, elle respire, elle se croit seule, et sans bruit elle va ouvrir la porte à son amant divin. (1965, 28)[59]

Claudel seems to identify with Rimbaud's coming to terms with the role played by the self in creativity.[60] Both artists indeed consider the status of the subject, although they advance divergent views of the poetic self.

The modern poetic subject in Rimbaud now reads in the Lacanian terms of *I is an Other*. In his revisionist turn from Rimbaud, Claudel safeguards an indivisible poetic subject by submitting the self and what reads as a Promethean aspiration to God:

> [J]e ne dirai pas, comme Rimbaud, que 'Je' est un autre; ce qu'il y a de terrible et parfois de cruel, c'est que 'Je' précisément n'est pas un autre, c'est qu'il est lui-même, c'est qu'il est . . . 'plus moi-même que moi' et c'est à ce 'moi-même' que sous le 'Je' superficiel s'adresse la vocation, le commandement de Dieu qui a besoin de lui, et qui lui demande un effort souvent inattendu et auquel il n'est pas préparé. 'Je' n'est pas un autre, il est 'lui-même,' mais un lui-même non encore abouti, non encore parvenu à l'état adulte. (Claudel et Amrouche 332)[61]

These lines come close to what Carl G. Jung calls the ongoing process of individuation. Human beings develop a sense of personal identity while coming to terms with their shadow.[62]

In Jung's paradigm, the archetypal figures anima and animus are function complexes that involve the hidden aspect of the personality. In a man, these are feminine characteristics (anima); in a woman, masculine (animus). For Jung, it is not a question of *realizing* our identity but rather of *integrating* the disparate aspects of our personality, since individuation is continual.

> The psyche not being a unity, but a contradictory multiplicity of complexes, the dissociation required for our dialectics with the anima is not so terribly difficult. The art of it only consists in allowing our invisible opponent to make herself heard, in putting the mechanism of expression momentarily at her disposal, without being overcome . . . by doubts as to the genuineness of the voice of one's interlocutor. (1953, 199–200)

Claudel, paralleling Jung's scheme up to a point, uses the figures anima and animus within the psyche of the poet to express the dialogic nature of the creative process. The masculine principle, associated with animus, voices anima, the feminine aspect synonymous with divine inspiration. Contrary to the dialogic subjectivity that we shall explore in Rimbaud, Claudel unifies the self. Thus, poetic voice, enlivened by the dialogue of mind and soul, relates all of creation in harmony. This mystical lyricism illuminates Claudel's map of misprision, which we conclude in *Un dernier salut à Arthur Rimbaud* (written in 1942; see 1965).

Claudel's final tribute highlights not the literary debt to his forerunner underscored in earlier writings but the spiritual role played by Rimbaud. He re-creates his precursor as a *voyant* in the biblical sense of prophet:

> Arthur Rimbaud n'est pas un poète, il n'est pas un homme de lettres. C'est un *prophète* sur qui l'esprit est tombé . . . comme sur Saül. . . . Il a plu à la Providence de donner à ce 'poète de seize ans' les facultés d'expression d'un homme de génie. Voici le phénomène de cet innocent monstrueux, chargé tout à coup d'un message auquel il ne comprend rien, comment s'étonner qu'il n'ait pas su l'arracher des entrailles sans toutes sortes de spasmes, de hoquets, de contorsions et de pleurs! (1965, 522)[63]

This portrayal of Rimbaud as an unwitting divine messenger indirectly clarifies the *mystique à l'état sauvage* at the outset of Claudel's 1912 preface, which recounts his own poetic evolution. The unenlightened mystic is none other than Claudel himself.

In the Bible, the prophet envisions and foretells what otherwise escapes humankind's notice. Notwithstanding an attempt to distinguish Rimbaud from the biblical *voyant*, we read between the lines of *Un Dernier salut à Rimbaud* the pathway of Claudel's own salvation:

> Je voudrais expliquer ce mot de 'prophète.' *Il s'agit de tout autre chose que de sainteté ou de vertu.* . . . Cet esprit de prophétie, l'Inspiration, la gratia gratis data n'a jamais à aucun moment cessé de souffler sur l'Humanité. C'est lui qui a suscité tant d'artistes, tant de poètes, tant d'initiateurs de toutes sortes. . . . Son accent est inimitable, aucune espèce de talent et d'artifice ne saurait en tenir la place, nous le reconnaissons aussitôt au fond de notre coeur. (1965, 522–23; emphasis added)[64]

If, as Marie-Joséphine Whitaker contends (1987, 19), here Claudel intends *prophète* in a strictly secular sense, why is the associated term *Inspiration* capitalized? Moreover, this Rimbaud-as-prophet recognizes Inspiration in the depths of his heart; this is precisely the source of poetic rhythm and, by extension, divine design that we find in Claudel's

Art poétique. The Word thus informs this creative impulse, so too the joining of religion and poiesis in Claudel's own mystical lyricism. Emphasis in this final tribute to Rimbaud on his break with materialism affirms in religious terms an idealistic worldview where Claudel finds "le message de la Pureté édénique, au milieu d'un monde abruti, vautré dans le matérialisme" (1965, 523).[65] Whereas the surrealists read the message in Rimbaud in aesthetic terms, Claudel hears in his precursor the voice of God.

Claudel's early accounts of Rimbaud's influence underscore the revelation of the supernatural in the *Illuminations*. His later statements make negligible mention of this collection and focus nearly exclusively on *Une saison en enfer*. Indeed *Un dernier salut à Arthur Rimbaud* presents this altered map of reading: "Au *Christus venit*! C'est ce mot... qui fait la liaison entre Les *Illuminations* et la *Saison en enfer*" (525).[66] Claudel isolates in a lengthy citation references to the divine throughout the *Saison* in a manner that underscores his religious revision of Rimbaud (525–26). Along with the discovery of a cross surrounded by rays on the writing table where Rimbaud composed the *Saison*, Claudel also upholds as proof Isabelle Rimbaud's account of "the crucifying death and final conversion of her brother" (527).

Once again by testifying to the influence (i.e., the interiorization) of his primary precursor, Claudel maps out his own poetic stance, all the while revising the creative impulse in Rimbaud. Claudel turns from the unconscious Other in Rimbaud's writing to a transcendent source of creativity. This striking case of misprision in French poetic history involves an ancient plot of metaphor that modern theory enables us to transport from linguistics to psychoanalysis while expanding the critical treatment of subjectivity in language.

TWO

Principles of Mis-reading, Strategies of Metaphor

Metaphoric practice turns from the production of meaning in Rimbaud at the level of the signifier (poiesis) to the representation of meaning at the level of the signified (mimesis) in Claudel.[1] This fundamental difference raises an important question concerning the nature of metaphor. Does metaphor pose a linguistic problem or a cognitive one?[2] Put another way, is metaphor a structure of language or of thought? Taking the question a step further with poststructuralists, do discourse and cognition originate simultaneously through the agency of metaphor?[3] Critical linguistic twists and cognitive turns from mimesis to poiesis in Aristotle show that from a linguistic perspective metaphor, at once poetic form and creative functioning, pervades the structure of language and thought alike. This expanded metaphoric plot sketches the pivotal turns that I shall follow to distinguish the psychopoetics of *metaphora* in Rimbaud from Claudel's mimetic strategy of metaphor.[4]

THE CREATIVE PROCESS OF *METAPHORA* IN ARISTOTLE

Aristotle's *Poetics* and his *Rhetoric* alike configure metaphor in the double terms of semantic properties and cognitive processes. Aristotle's theory of metaphor thus juxtaposes the representation through analogy of presupposed meaning with a means of achieving new insight. This collation links metaphor with both mimesis and poiesis. With the term *poiesis*, we recover the creative or productive process of *metaphora* in Aristotle that critics still largely focused on the rhetorical form of metaphor tend to ignore.[5]

Aristotle valorizes a mimetic aim of poetry "since its statements are of the nature . . . of universals" (*Poetics* 1451b). It is precisely this view that Claudel derives from Aristotle to structure analogically a unifying relation of God, self, and world.[6] As a "maker of likenesses," a poet re-presents presupposed truths through metaphor.

Principles of Mis-reading, Strategies of Metaphor

> The poet, being an imitator just like the painter or other maker of likenesses, must necessarily . . . *represent* things . . . either as they were or are, or as they are said or thought to be or to have been, or as they ought to be. All this he does with an admixture . . . of strange words and metaphors . . . since the use of these is conceded in poetry. (*Poetics* 1460b; emphasis added)

Here, metaphor, as a linguistic sign of poetry, deviates from ordinary words. Semantic deviation purportedly sets forth an opposition between the language of poetry and that of prose (*Poetics* 1404a:28–29, 1404b). Yet a subsequent assertion blurs this opposition in Aristotle's scheme by situating metaphor in both poetic discourse and quotidian language.

Aristotle indeed positions metaphorical expression in all discourse: "The proper or regular and the metaphorical are used by everybody in conversation; . . . metaphor is of great value both in poetry and in prose" (*Rhetoric* 1404b, 1405a).[7] Here *metaphorical* designates figurative language in general. The *metaphorical* expresses something in terms that usually denote something else but with which it may be regarded as analogous. We see that metaphor as poetic form crosses the boundary between poetry and prose and thus collapses the strict division between a figurative discourse and a literal one. This collapse of the metaphoric split between poetry and prose implicitly broadens the cognitive role played by *metaphora* in Aristotle's poetics.

A process of transference informs the linguistic structure of metaphor, which for Aristotle "consists in giving the thing a name that belongs to something else; the transference being either from genus to species, or from species to genus, or from species to species, or on grounds of analogy" (*Poetics* 1457b). From the perspective of a strictly mimetic aim traditionally assumed in Aristotle, we would understand that substitutive transference achieves referential adequation between language and the empirical world. "The production of [transference] from analogy is possible whenever there are four terms so related that the second (B) is to the first (A), as the fourth (D) to the third (C); for one may then metaphorically put D in lieu of B, and B in lieu of D" (1457b). A classical Aristotelean would argue that seeing the similar (i.e., A is to B, as C is to D) presents anew presupposed meaning.[8] Notwithstanding this mimetic strategy of metaphor, we can also understand that Aristotelean metaphor functions poietically (creatively) to produce meaning.

Key to this shift from mimesis to poiesis in Aristotle is the positioning of the transfer that *metaphora* performs. The following distinction between metaphor as poetic (decorative) form and as poietic (creative) process illuminates the cognitive role played by metaphor:

> It is a great thing, indeed, to make a proper use of the poetical forms. . . . But the greatest thing by far is to be a master of metaphor. It is the thing that cannot be learnt from others; and it is also a sign of genius, since good metaphor implies an intuitive perception of the similarity in dissimilars. (*Poetics* 1459a)

Metaphor for Aristotle involves "intuitive perception," an immediate knowing of something without the use of reason. This apprehension, unbounded from logic, suggests that the joining of disparate elements may indeed follow analogical structure without, however, recording an antecedent analogy. By situating the structuring and signifying work of metaphor in thought, we begin to see that metaphor does not strictly re-present meaning, as a classical Aristotelean would uphold, but rather produces meaning. Aristotle's rhetoric so casts the creative role that *metaphora* plays in cognition.

In *Rhetoric*, metaphor yields fresh insight: "Liveliness is specially conveyed by metaphor, and by the further power of surprising the hearer; because the hearer expected something different, his acquisition of the new idea impresses him all the more. His mind seems to say, 'Yes, to be sure, I never thought of that' " (1412a). Metaphor brings about through its cognitive functioning the discovery of the unknown. We shall see that the mimetic strategy of metaphor in Claudel overlaps with a poietic role in construal. Claudel links the conceptual use of metaphor, conceiving the unknown in terms of the known, to the revelation of divine order. Novel associations in Rimbaud target instead the revelation of the psychically unknown; this poietic plot of *metaphora* suggests the principal strategy of psychoanalysis aimed at investigating unconscious mental activity.[9]

The poietic aspect of metaphor in Aristotle entails fresh perception of the similar in the dissimilar. This cognition constructs new relations that expand our knowledge of the hitherto unknown. *Rhetoric* makes explicit the creative role played by metaphor that brings about such insight: "Ordinary words convey only what we already know; it is from metaphor that we can best get hold of something fresh" (1410b). The process informing *metaphora*, shaped by the imagination, illustrates the act of making sense of the world. As metaphorical words set the scene

Principles of Mis-reading, Strategies of Metaphor

before our eyes, the mind's eye comprehends or "perceiv[es] resemblances in things far apart" (1410b, 1412a).

Aristotle's view of the poietic role played by *metaphora* in *yielding insight* implies to a certain extent the strategy of Rimbaud's metaphoric practice. However, apprehension through the play of the creative imagination in Rimbaud positions *metaphora* in the mind, more precisely in unconscious mental activity, without linking its impulse to stimuli actually present in the external world. Moreover, the nondiscursive principle of metaphor practiced in Rimbaud refuses the discursive, analogical principle of metaphor traditionally derived from Aristotle. Meaning becomes for Rimbaud an effect of metaphor at the level of the signifier.

Such production of meaning challenges the notion of a knowing subject constituted outside language. Rimbaud's postmodern subject, constructed in and through discourse, becomes an effect of language. This positioning of the "I" discloses the Other voice of the speaking subject that emerges metaphorically through the discourse of conscious and unconscious mental activity. Clearly, this poietic strategy of metaphor exceeds Aristotle's largely linguistic perspective. Centuries later, Giambattista Vico suggests a critical yoking of verbal structures and mental processes that we shall follow in modern linguistics and poststructuralist psychoanalysis to map out Rimbaud's psychopoetics of *metaphora*.[10]

SAPIENZA POETICA: TOWARD A PSYCHOPOETICS OF *METAPHORA*

The emphasis in Aristotle on the cognitive import of metaphor lays the critical groundwork for our reading of the poietic impulse of metaphor in Vico's *New Science*. Vico postulates an inherent poetic faculty—a *sapienza poetica*—to account for humankind's earliest linguistic response to the natural world (104). Language was originally metaphoric in form, for example, *the river's mouth*, and poietic in its functioning. As Vico writes, "[I]n those first times all things necessary to human life had to be invented, and invention is the property of genius" (150). Vico's view of a poetic faculty that initially enabled humans to think and speak *metaphorically* implicitly disputes the suggestion in Aristotle that metaphor, as the distinct language of the poet, is a sign of genius that cannot be imparted. In the Vichian scheme, all early peoples spoke in and through metaphor since language *first* functioned metaphorically to transpose images into expression.

Once conventional signs were established because of humankind's increased power of reasoning, a *vulgar* language evolved that was less imagistic and more denotative than the metaphoric speech that had preceded it (62). Vico's scheme thus revises the narrowly derived Aristotelean notion of the metaphoric as a semantic deviation from an established norm. For Vico quotidian discourse departs instead from an original figurative mode:

> All the tropes . . . which have hitherto been considered ingenious inventions of writers, were necessary modes of expression of all the first poetic nations, and had originally their full native propriety. But these expressions . . . later became figurative when, with the further development of the human mind, words were invented which signified abstract forms or genera comprising their species of relating parts with their wholes. And here begins the overthrow of two common errors of the grammarians: that prose speech is proper speech and poetic speech improper; and that prose speech came first, and afterwards speech in verse. (118)

We see that Vico positions *metaphora* at the origins of linguistic activity as the cognitive process through which language first develops to mediate poetically between self and world.

The Vichian paradigm offers a protopsychoanalytic account of the unconscious work of *metaphora*—the cognitive and linguistically primordial process that constitutes us as speaking subjects while structuring our speech.[11] This creative aspect of metaphor, in the broader association with cognitive processes that modern linguistics suggests and psychoanalytic poststructuralism illuminates, takes pivotal turns in Rimbaud and Claudel. Rimbaud's postmodern discourse freely produces meaning by juxtaposing disparate elements at the level of the signifier, whereas Claudel assumes the unifying power of metaphor at the level of the signified.

CROSSING VERBAL AND MENTAL BOUNDARIES: THE METAPHORIC SPLIT

Metaphor, in the structural linguistics of Roman Jakobson, serves as the distinctive sign of poetry per se. Notwithstanding this metaphoric split between the figurative and the literal, Jakobson advances that the poetic function of language is not limited to poetry. Thus, as in Aristotle and in subsequent neoclassical and romantic elaborations, Jakobson's treatment of metaphor collapses the *classical* figurative/proper division.[12] This blurring of mimesis and poiesis provides a fruitful paradigm for distinguishing Rimbaud's poetics of the metaphoric split from that of Claudel.

Metaphoric and metonymic modes cooperate to comprise the bipolar structure of language; in this early configuration, Jakobson makes similarity the strategy of the metaphoric and contiguity the principle of the metonymic (1956, 76, 81–82). Yet later, Jakobson (1960) turns to the view that poetic utterances are an integral part of *all* discourse and so blurs the metaphoric gap between poetry and prose.

> Any attempt to reduce the sphere of poetic function to poetry or to confine poetry to poetic function would be a delusive oversimplification. Poetic function is not the sole function of verbal art but only its dominant, determining function, whereas in all other verbal activities it acts as a subsidiary, accessory constituent. This function, by promoting the palpability of signs, deepens the fundamental dichotomy of signs and objects. (1960, 356)

Moreover, Jakobson prefigures what will be the poststructuralist interpenetration of the metaphoric and the metonymic modes. They overlap for Jakobson "in poetry where similarity is superinduced upon contiguity, any metonymy is slightly metaphoric and any metaphor has a metonymical tint" (1960, 370). A comparable blurring in Jakobson's poetic function shows how similarity admits difference.

The constitutive principle of the poetic function formulated by Jakobson informs the way that all language works. This principle has its basis in metaphor construed as a cognitive process of transfer that has at the same time a semantic effect: "The poetic function projects the principle of *equivalence* from the axis of selection into the axis of combination" (Jakobson, 1960, 358; emphasis added). *Equivalence* implies a relation motivated by resemblance. However, the principle of similarity has difference as its basis. Instead of polarizing opposite categories (similar/dissimilar, metaphoric/metonymic), Jakobson provocatively outlines their interpenetration.[13] It is precisely this blurring of the metaphoric and the metonymic in the structuration of thought and language that outlines the poetic practice that I shall follow in Rimbaud. Claudel, to the contrary, turns to a mimetic strategy of *metaphora* in attempting to unify the relation of self and world.

Jakobson opens up the poetic functioning of language to mental processes with the statement that "competition between both devices, metonymic and metaphoric, is manifest in any symbolic process, either intrapersonal or social" (1956, 80–81). The following reference to

Freud's theory of dreamwork associates *intrapersonal symbolic process* with unconscious mental activity:

> Thus in an inquiry into the structure of dreams, the decisive question is whether the symbols and the temporal sequences are based on contiguity (Freud's metonymic "displacement" and synecdochic "condensation") or on similarity (Freud's "identification and symbolism"). (81)

In other words, Jakobson asks whether the metaphoricity of conscious discourse also characterizes the structure of unconscious mental processes formulated in the Freudian dreamwork.

Freud infers the existence and structure of the unconscious from instances of discursive discontinuity exemplified by dreams, parapraxes, symptoms, and obsessions (14:166-67). This structuring of the unconscious in terms of *gaps* has recourse to tropes—to transference. Gaps, which mark nondiscursive discourse, trace the transferential work of *metaphora* that underlies the organization and the effects of unconscious mental activity. Freud indeed prepares the psychopoetic path that leads us to the Lacanian joining of mental and verbal processes. For Lacan, unconscious mental activity, structured like a language, traces its effects in conscious discourse; this is the basis of my psychopoetics of *metaphora* in Rimbaud.

THE FREUDIAN DREAMWORK: TOWARD POIESIS IN RIMBAUD

The Freudian dreamwork provides a protolinguistic model for the metonymic grounding of metaphoric transposition in what Jean Laplanche and Serge Leclaire call "that vertiginous layer of language which certain poets occasionally allow us to glimpse" (177).[14] For the metonymic transfer through displacement of affect from one representation to another and the metaphoric compression of elements in dreamwork involves association by both contiguity and similarity. Elaborating Freud's dreamwork as a postmodern way of reading Rimbaud's later poetic language warrants an initial clarification.

Freud states that, "when the work of interpretation has been completed, we perceive that a dream is the fulfilment of a wish" (4:121). The inference of a metaphoric relation based on analogy between manifest and latent dream texts may invite our reading a literal text behind the figurative one.[15] Put another way, we might understand that Freud aims to symbolically discern dreams on the basis of a one-to-one correspondence of sign to meaning. Yet Freud does not support a strict replacement scheme that might allow for the definitive discernment of the literal from the figurative, since "it is never possible to be sure that a dream has been completely interpreted" (4:279). Having recourse to symbols may unravel some paths of the dreamwork, but analyzing a dream text does not produce *unequivocal* meaning.[16] Free association, which also informs the work of interpretation, constructs signifying networks between elements of manifest dreams. It is specifically this production of meaning at the level of the signifier that provides a paradigm for reading postmodern poetic texts like Rimbaud's *Illuminations*.[17]

The Freudian analysis of dream formation draws our attention to the protolinguistic strategy of dreamwork. The transfer, which displacement and condensation bring about, models itself upon *metaphora* in the broader etymological sense of transference, a carrying over and, by extension, displacement.[18] To read the metaphoric *writing* of dreams, the Freudian interpretation explores the "relations between the manifest content of dreams and the latent dream-thoughts" and "traces out the processes by which the latter have been changed into the former" (4:277). Freud's tracing of dreamwork as a signifying process that creates new forms is implicitly semiotic and thus prepares the Lacanian reading of dreamwork as a writing system that has the structure of poetic language.

The Freudian dreamwork offers insight into the mind's way of imaging, framing the psychic transfer from dream thoughts to dream content, from idea to image, in linguistic terms. We distinguish psychic images, as in dreams that are materially unrealizable, from sensorial images understood as copies of fading perceptions. The transfer through dreamwork between modes of expression is in fact troping, although the effect is not semantic but rather semiotic:

> The dream-thoughts and the dream-content are presented to us like two versions of the same subject-matter in two different *languages*. . . . The [manifest] dream-content seems like a *transcript* of the [latent] dream-thoughts into another *mode of expression*. . . . The dream-content . . . is expressed as it were in a pictographic *script*, the characters of which have to be *transposed* individually into the *language* of the dream-thoughts. (4:277; emphasis added)

The explicit linguistic frame of this psychic transfer between "two different languages" recalls Aristotle's definition of the metaphoric process in *Poetics*: "giving the thing a name that belongs to something else"

(1457b). At the outset of Freud's passage, because *transcript* implies the translation of presupposed meaning from one language into another, we might understand semantic deviation as the basis of this transfer. To the contrary, *script*, the characters of which one must transpose individually into the language of the dream thoughts, introduces the domain of the signifier (see Thom 3). When read with an emphasis on semiotics, rather than on semantics, Freud's subsequent caveat makes explicit the shift in his scheme from inferring the signified to reading the signifying relations between dream elements: "If we attempted to read these characters according to their pictorial value instead of according to their symbolic relation, we should clearly be led into error" (4:277).[19] Here the *symbolic* intends the semiotic work of what Lacan later calls the Symbolic order of language. The network of relations that links the elements of manifest dreams produces an effect of meaning at the level of the signifier and has the tropic (i.e., transferential) structure of discourse. The structure of dreams, as Freud configures it, suggests a writing system that is fundamentally *poietic*. I shall relate this strategy of *metaphora* to Rimbaud's *Illuminations*.

Freud sketches the relation between manifest dream content and dream thoughts in the linguistic terms of a difference *between* texts and thus tropically configures their relation on the basis of metaphoric transposition. He writes that "a *transference* and *displacement* of psychical intensities occurs in the process of dream-formation, and it is as a result of these that the difference between the *text* of the dream-content and the dream-thoughts comes about" (4:308; emphasis added). Reading *transference* in semiotic terms further illustrates the metaphoric plot of dreamwork.[20] The difference for Freud between the text of manifest content and latent thought is, above all, a signifying difference.[21] Dream elements signify only through their textual interplay at the level of the signifier. Dreams, read through free association as the *writing* of signifying relations, combine and select elements along the syntagm to evoke new forms. This is the postmodern way of reading nondiscursive texts for which Rimbaud's discovery of "a language of the psyche" lays the dreamwork.

Dreamwork assists in the production of signs (poiesis) without, however, relating them in terms of a signification (mimesis).[22] Here we distinguish *signification*, which connotes the meaning that a term, symbol, or character regularly conveys, from the act or process of signifying by signs or other symbolic means. To narrate or write a series of associations based on contiguous dream elements, the work informing dreams does not think analogically the way that the logical brain does. Rather, it tropes, condensing and displacing elements (psychic images) along signifying chains with the sole aim of giving things a new form without relating them to each other. As Freud states in *The Interpretation of Dreams*, "[W]hat is reproduced by the ostensible thinking in the dream is the *subject-matter* of the dream-thoughts and not the *mutual relations between them*, the assertion of which constitutes thinking" (4:312–13). Dreamwork constructs novel combinations: "It does not think, calculate or judge in any way at all; it restricts itself to giving things a new *form*" (5:507).[23] Here the term *form* means the production of a psychic image that facilitates the emergence into consciousness of what was unconscious.

The construal of the unknown on the boundary of the known in dreamwork recalls the poietic work of *metaphora*. Dreamwork, grounded in the interdependent metaphoric and metonymic modalities of displacement and condensation, sets preverbal imagistic elements in novel combinations before the mind's eye and sparks insight. The primary process of condensation collaborates with displacement in this poietic work of metaphoric transference. Associative links through which condensation and displacement achieve their poietic effects are not solely predicated on similarity and contiguity, respectively.[24] Rather, just as condensation selects while combining, so too displacement combines while selecting.[25] For the *relation* of *similarity* that dream formation favors is the syntagmatic joining of one signifying element with another.

From our semiotic perspective, dreamwork involves a paratactic mode of narrating, which selects and juxtaposes a series of elements without showing connections between them. This strategy of not relating casts a different light on the principle of *metaphora* that structures the dreamwork. The relation of similarity in the Freudian dreamwork does not operate at the level of the signified, as in traditional structuralist views of metaphor; rather, *metaphora* produces its effects at the level of the signifier by coupling—yet not relating—the *dis*similar. Moreover, contiguous elements are associated at an unknown level of similarity or dissimilarity in dreams (Ragland-Sullivan 237). *Unknown* connotes what we do not recognize from a conscious outlook because it is unconscious. Dreamwork, however, brings about creative insight and resonates in this respect with Rimbaud's *voyance* aimed at revealing through poetic work the unknown within the self.

The poietic strategy of the Freudian dreamwork models itself upon the process of *metaphora*. Seeing the similar in dissimilars does not operate at the level of the signified. Rather, in dreams, as in other prerational expression, associative links by displacement and condensation function at the level of the signifier. Moreover, dreamwork, which ignores cognitive relationships and makes even the rationally dissimilar equivalent, creates combinations that are not rationally recognizable. To illustrate this point in linguisitic terms, *A*, though the rational opposite of *B*, is its poietic equivalent in the writing of the dream.[26] So, while we may know *A*, it is unknown to us in the poietic sense produced in the dream. At bottom, then, the poietic strategy of the Freudian dreamwork favors poiesis over analogy.

Novel combinations in dreams derive from treating affinity as the basis for absolute identification. To read these odd alliances, we uncover through free association their grounding in a network of difference without which we could not relate signifying elements to each other. The relation of similarity that dreams favor opens up a gap. *Similarity* does not mean *the same as*; what we perceive as analogous is necessarily different. In other words, metaphoric association by similarity does not erase difference. For *metaphora* underlies "the figure of speech in which a name or descriptive term is transferred to some object different from, but analogous to, that to which it is properly applicable" (*Oxford English Dictionary* 9:676). Highlighting the emphasis on cognition in Aristotle's poetics, *metaphora* allows us to see the similar *in* the dissimilar.

Seeing the similar in this light also casts the shadow of the dissimilar, or the other. This conception of *metaphora*, extended to the poetics of the subject and of language in Lacan, enables us to read the metaphoric strategy of Rimbaud's postmodern discourse, which assumes that *I is an Other*.[27] Lacan's paradigm expands the structuring effects of *metaphora* from the one-word trope to the entire Symbolic order of language. This unconscious realm, structured according to linguistic laws of functioning, combining, and displacing, supports the work of the signifier. *Metaphora*, the transferring process distinguished from the rhetorical trope, structures the dreamwork of language that forms the subject in the *image* of, that is, in the terms of, the unconscious Other.

Lacan extends the tropic (transferential) grounding that constitutes the subject in and through discourse to the structuring of the unconscious and of subjectivity. In other words, to read psyche as text, as Lacan does, with the view that the unconscious has the structure of language is also to see text as psyche with the view that the unconscious is always already operative in language. The shift from linguistic explanations to semiotic mechanisms in Lacan's psychoanalytic account of subjectivity in discourse provides a critical opening for reading modern poets like Rimbaud.

Principles of Mis-reading, Strategies of Metaphor

LACAN'S LINGUISTIC RETURN TO THE FREUDIAN DREAMWORK

The linguistic parameters we have traced in the Freudian dreamwork become explicit in Lacan's view that "dans *la Science des rêves*, il ne s'agit à toutes les pages que de ce que nous appelons la lettre du discours, dans sa texture, dans ses emplois, dans son immanence à la matière en cause. Car cet ouvrage ouvre avec l'oeuvre sa route royale à l'inconscient" (1966, 267).[28] By "the letter of the discourse," we understand the signifier, which forms the basis for Lacan's reading of the unconscious in the Freudian dreamwork as a signifying process. In a critical shift away from the one-to-one symbolic correspondence to the free association method of dream interpretation, the principal strategy of dreamwork in the Lacanian elaboration becomes explicitly linguistic (1966, 268).[29] Thus, Lacan reconfigures the primary processes of displacement and condensation in semiotic terms as metaphoric and metonymic signifying formations at the level of the signifier.[30] Developing the interpenetration of the Freudian displacement and condensation, Lacan provides a semiotic turn of *metaphora* that prepares our critical strategy for reading nondiscursive poetic discourse in the later Rimbaud, where metonymy structures metaphor as a relation between signifiers.

Metonymy for Lacan functions semiotically. Association by contiguity, which connects one signifier to another, structures the groundwork of metaphor as the other signifying formation (1966, 263). This poststructuralist paradigm challenges the reduction of metaphor as a relation of motivated substitution formulated in opposition to metonymy in structural linguistics. The Lacanian scheme anchors metaphor to metonymy and demonstrates their interdependence as signifying formations, that is, as semiotic categories. The metonymic structuring of metaphor that Lacan intends as displacement takes the surrealist notion of the poetic image a step further (264). For Lacan, "l'étincelle créatrice de la métaphore ne jaillit pas de la mise en présence de deux images, c'est-à-dire de deux signifiants également actualisés" (1966, 265).[31] Rather, *metaphora* operates vertically, or paradigmatically, to link two signifiers, one of which is occluded yet present in its metonymic connection with an underlying signifying chain.

Lacan illustrates his formula for metaphor as a signifying formation, "un mot pour un autre [mot]," with an example from Victor Hugo's *Booz endormi*, "Sa gerbe n'était point avare ni haineuse" (264–65).[32] When read literally as a metaphor (*A* is *B*) to connote a presupposed analogy, this verse is nonsensical. Lacan makes the signifying connection between the repressed signifier *Booz* and the displaced *gerbe*. Drawing on the interpenetration of the metonymic and metaphoric modes in discourses like poetry and dreams, we can follow different pathways in the signifying network that underlies Hugo's verse. The relation of *gerbe* to *Booz* can be viewed in terms of both displacement and condensation: the representation of elements transferred or displaced from *Booz* to *gerbe* (metonymic) or the attributes of *Booz* condensed in *gerbe* (metaphoric). We shall adopt a similar strategy for reading Rimbaud's psychopoetics of *metaphora* in the *Illuminations*.

The interaction of an actual and an eclipsed signifier demonstrates in various ways the metaphoric effects of the unconscious (i.e., Lacan's Symbolic order of language) on conscious discourse. The occluded signifier fundamental to the operation of *metaphora* in the Lacanian scheme derives from a process of displacement linked with metonymy. Lacan, however, modifies the structural linguistic view of this mode of association by contiguity to signify the evocation of an unstated referent. To quote Ragland-Sullivan on this salient point, for Lacan "meaning emerges from the combination of ideas *inferred* between the two contiguous signifiers in play" (250). Lacan's return to the Freudian dreamwork makes explicit the linguistic parameters of the unconscious and clearly transposes psychic processes into semiotic mechanisms to configure the poietic functioning of unconscious mental activity.

Lacan thus elaborates Freud's intuition that the laws of the dream are the same as those of poetry: "c'est dans la substitution du signifiant au signifiant que se produit un effet de signification qui est de poésie ou de création, autrement dit d'avènement de la signification en question" (1966, 274).[33] John Forrester rightly asserts this primacy of the signifier in Lacan's scheme, which, as in Freud, endorses poiesis over analogy:

> What poetry and psychoanalysis have in common is a bracketing off of the real, or of the signified. Both poetry and psychoanalysis are linguistic practices in which signifiers replace other signifiers in an autonomous play of words; a mode of linguistic operation which is analogous to Lacan's definition of the unconscious: structured like a language, it is restricted in its activity to linguistic operations upon signifiers. (1981, 172)

Freudian dreamwork in its Lacanian development offers us a model for analyzing Rimbaud's poetic discourse that resists both the symbolic mode of analogical correspondences and the mimetic mode of representation.[34]

Instead of serving to express presupposed meaning, Lacan's metaphoric-metonymic dyad, which underlies dreams and nondiscursive poetic utterance alike, functions semiotically to produce signs that express the as yet unnamed. In "look[ing] beyond the substantive or metaphorical characteristics of the dream to its referential or metonymic functioning," Lacan "render[s] Freud's concept of overdetermination equivalent to the polysemous property of language itself and its infinite combinatory or generative capacity" (Ragland-Sullivan 241).[35] This poiesis, which gives form, repeats the metaphoric origins of language.[36] It is indeed a sign of our creative impulse, which would remain unknowable if not for the poietic functioning of our speech.

MIS-READING THE CREATIVE IMPULSE IN RIMBAUD AND CLAUDEL

Baudelaire's well-known call to poetic arms, "to the depths of the unknown to find the new," inspired Rimbaud to investigate his *âme* (soul/psyche) and thus give voice to the psychically unknown. Rimbaldian *voyance* seeks to transpose the unknown into language. His poetic project, which traces through writing the creative impulse of the unconscious Other, presents a protopsychoanalysis. Rimbaud situates his quest for poetic revelation within the self and voices through the dreamwork of language the unconscious Other in terms in which we construct ourselves as speaking subjects.

Traditionally, metaphoric construal, which proceeds from the known to the unknown, positions the unknown outside of the perceiving subject.[37] To the contrary, Freud, like his *poetic* precursor Rimbaud, locates the unknown within the subject.[38] This positioning of the subject now reads in the postmodern terms that all knowledge, based on the transposition of cognition into language, is metaphoric. *Metaphora*, then, structures the boundary of the unknown and the known inside and outside the self. In other words, *metaphora* crosses the border that it constructs between mental processes and verbal structures. Working from Freud in a different context, Kaja Silverman lucidly restates this point: "Language defines the limits of what the human subject can know both about the world and itself, since phenomenal and psychic experiences [that] are denied linguistic expression remain unknowable" (72).

Rimbaud's postromantic discourse explores unconscious mental activity as a source of creativity that illuminates the unknown, whereas Claudel construes a religious sense of the unknown. Diametrically opposed to Rimbaud's reading of Baudelaire, Claudel understands that "le but de la poésie n'est pas comme dit Baudelaire, de plonger 'au fond de l'Infini pour trouver du nouveau,' mais au fond du défini pour y trouver de l'inépuisable" (1965, 424).[39] In short, Claudel seeks to know God.

His poetic project presents a Catholic view of self and world created in God's image, where the poet's voice repeats the divine order at its center.

Rimbaud and Claudel may converge in their desire to discover the *unknown*. Notwithstanding this convergence, their poetics of subject and of language ultimately diverge and so illustrate discontinuity rather than affinity as the basis of their history of influence. My revisionist approach shows that Rimbaud and Claudel form the boundary between the known and the unknown in significantly opposing ways, psychical versus religious, respectively. Rimbaud metaphorically positions poetic voice on the border of the self and the unconscious Other. Claudel revises this positioning by assuming a knowing poetic subject, since he aspires to re-create through metaphor as analogy the unknown divine in the empirical world.

THREE

Revisioning the Self, Creating the Subject

I is an Other. Rimbaud's fragmented subject sets the stage for the postmodern expression of the romantic self—a subject divided in and through language. This revision of poetic voice turns against lyrical investment in an authorial "I" that insists upon the personal self conceived as a biographical entity. French romantic poetry, beginning with Marceline Desbordes-Valmore, Alphonse de Lamartine, and Hugo, assumes a centered speaking subject, anchored by a transcendent unity relating self and world. Such a conception of literary subjectivity links creativity with transcendence by identifying the voice of the poet with God, the Divine Creator. The poetic subject, so bounded with a structure that bestows identity and meaning, may overcome divisions within the individual or between the microcosm and the macrocosm. Shifts from a transcendent source of the creative impulse to an immanent dialogue on the boundary of unconscious and conscious mental activity in Rimbaud's predecessors destabilize the idealist romantic vision, without detaching the self from a cosmology. Rimbaud, however, severs such ties to configure this psychic mobility in what now reads in postmodern terms as the divisive effects of language upon the subject.[1]

The integral revision of romantic subjectivity that I shall map out in Rimbaud discloses more precisely the dialogic nature of language that alienates the self in and through its discourse.[2] The development of romanticism, for which Lucas's *The Decline and Fall of the Romantic Ideal* enumerates 11,396 definitions, clearly exceeds the parameters of this discussion. To clarify the evolving sense of Rimbaud's use of the term with relation to his revisionist strategies, I shall first distinguish the historical period labeled French romanticism that begins with François-René de Chateaubriand's *René* (1802) and Germaine de Staël's *De L'Allemagne* (1813). In Rimbaud's scheme, French romantic poetry appears with Lamartine's *Méditations poétiques* (1820) and develops through 1850 or so with the personal lyricism of Hugo and Alfred de Musset. Second, I shall maintain that romanticism, as an aesthetic, stems from "a change occurring in European sensibility toward the end of the 18th c[entury], and extending into the present" with the symbolist and surrealist stress on unconscious mental activity.³ My reading of Rimbaud as a modern romantic focuses on the divided subject that he positions against his predecessors' subjective idealism. Rimbaud's poetic discourse constructs the self in relation to the unconscious Other while exposing in turn the linguistic site of the creative impulse.

REREADING THE ROMANTIC SUBJECT

By the end of his career, Rimbaud had achieved the status of a strong prior poet, a precursor against whom aspiring poets struggled to develop their own voice. In the beginning, however, like any creative artist, Rimbaud had to confront his own literary past. For, as Bloom says in *Poetry and Repression*, "even the strongest poet must take up his stance *within* literary language" (1976, 4). The *Lettres du voyant* (written in 1871) reread the notion of the self in earlier French romantic poets with specific attention to the role played by the artist in creativity. Rimbaud aims to deviate from his forerunners' subject-centered poetic language and elaborate what he calls "objective poetry." Yet his poetic discourse retains throughout the lyric voice that he purportedly overcomes. What may initially strike one as a contradiction in fact demonstrates Rimbaud's originality. In a 24 May 1870 letter to Théodore Banville (Rimbaud, 1972, 236–37), Rimbaud projects himself as a "vrai romantique." As a *truly* modern romantic, he opens up subjectivity to the speaking unconscious.

To displace the creative artist's subjectivity as the central source of creativity, Rimbaud proposes a *poésie objective* that transposes into discourse what the "mind's eye/'I'" perceives. The notion of an autonomous creative impulse endorses poiesis over mimesis. Coming to poetic writing with the intuition that *Je est un autre*, Rimbaud discovers that his creative voice is not, so to speak, his own and that the creativeness of mind is not subject to conscious censorship. His poetic practice moves toward a modern romantic discourse that structures the self "always already" in relation to the nonself. *Voyance*, read in terms of this *split* romantic subject, implicitly prefigures the Freudian re(dis)covery and elaboration of unconscious mental activity some twenty years later.[4]

Critics have suggested that Rimbaud explores irrational mental activity, but they do not explicitly demonstrate its trace in his writing (Bodenham 1984; Frohock). Nathaniel Wing's early study on the *Illuminations*, however, considers Rimbaud's "recognition of the multiple levels of man's consciousness and a declaration that the Poet will focus on the irrational functions of the psyche" (1974, 15). More to the point, Wing's thematic analysis of a poetics of hallucination in these prose poems begins to open up Rimbaud's poetic expression to the play of the unconscious that I shall follow. Our postmodern map of reading enables us to position the role played by unconscious mental activity at the core of Rimbaud's psychopoetics of *metaphora*. Revising the poetic subject presents the impulse of the Other in Rimbaud's poetic writing.

RIMBAUD´S ANXIETY OF INFLUENCE: *JE VEUX ÊTRE POÈTE*

In theory and in practice, Rimbaud engages in an ambivalent relation with the romantic tradition before him through revisionist maneuvers that map out his anxiety of influence. Bloom's theory of mis-reading elucidates this ambivalence. The revisionist defends him- or herself against forerunners, that is, against imitating them. In other words, the aspiring poet represses his or her indebtedness to the literary past. The repressed, however, as Freud argues in *Beyond the Pleasure Principle*, returns. Just as unconscious psychical contents continue to affect conscious ideation and behavior, so too a poet compulsively repeats former literary stances through the twists and turns of creative misprision. From the viewpoint of poetic revisionism, I bring to light the shadow of early French romanticism in Rimbaud's evolving poetics of the subject.

In the letter to Banville (24 mai 1870) mentioned above, Rimbaud declares his goal to become "un vrai romantique." With the adjective *vrai*, he disputes false notions in his French predecessors, notably the romantic self. Indeed, a year later, the *lettre du voyant* to Paul Demeny makes explicit Rimbaud's project to redefine the speaking subject of poetic discourse: "Si les vieux imbéciles n'avaient pas trouvé du moi que la signification fausse, nous n'aurions pas à balayer ces millions de squelettes qui . . . ont accumulé les produits de leur intelligence borgnesse" (Rimbaud, 1972, 250).[5] This statement nominally perpetuates the characteristically romantic *culte du moi*, while announcing Rimbaud's revisionism.

Rimbaud's epistolary manifestoes set forth a poetics of alterity to challenge the unequivocal relation between self and creative expression promulgated by prior romantic poets. Yet his turn against various aspects of French romanticism in the *Lettres du voyant* stems from the stance he implicitly takes within this tradition as set forth in the letter to Banville in 1870. In a theoretical move that calls to mind the revisionist relation, for example, of structuralism and poststructuralism, Rimbaud structures the romantic self in terms of the unconscious Other. He thus demonstrates the discursive construction of the *modern* speaking subject.

Writing to persuade Banville to include his verses in a subsequent issue of *Le Parnasse contemporain*, Rimbaud underscores an identification with him: "Que si je vous envoie quelques-uns de ces vers . . . c'est que j'aime tous les poètes, tous les bons Parnassiens, —épris de la beauté idéale; c'est que j'aime en vous, bien naïvement, un descendant de Ronsard, un frère de nos maîtres de 1830, un vrai romantique, un vrai poète. . . . [Moi aussi], messieurs du journal, je serai Parnassien" (24 mai 1870; 1972, 236).[6] Along with a political motive in Rimbaud's missive aimed at having his poems published, here we also understand a revisionist strategy. Not only does Rimbaud identify with Banville but also with his literary paternity ("nos maîtres"), all the while projecting his own poetic identity as "un descendant de Ronsard, un frère de nos maîtres de 1830, un vrai romantique, un vrai poète, . . . [un] Parnassien." Just as Rimbaud turns toward preceding French romantics to situate his poetic project, so too he turns away from his predecessors with tactics that play out his anxiety of influence.

The *lettre du voyant* to Demeny (1871) departs from the identification with Banville in 1870. Although poetic history traditionally links Banville with Parnassianism, Rimbaud's revisionist scheme discusses Banville as one of the "seconds romantiques" who were "très voyants" but whose poetic form lacked innovation. This association of romanticism and Parnassianism has theoretical significance for the evolving poetic subject in Rimbaud to which I shall return. The seer letter implicitly mocks the Parnassian poets and turns from the former identification with Banville and company to prepare Rimbaud's original poetic vision and voice.

The enumerated attributes, "a descendant of Ronsard, a brother of our masters of 1830, a real romantic, a real poet," which constitute the poetic identity that Rimbaud seeks, refer on the one hand to romanticism. Rimbaud traces French romanticism to Pierre de Ronsard, implicitly named the father of the French lyric. Lyricism à la Ronsard is not equaled until the nineteenth-century French romantics, or as Rimbaud writes, "nos maîtres de 1830." On the other hand, the poet for Rimbaud is a Parnassian devoted to formal beauty, an aesthetics that traditional criticism usually opposes to romanticism. How are we to understand this association of romanticism and Parnassianism, of subjectivity and objectivity?

Revisioning the Self, Creating the Subject

In the first *lettre du voyant* to Georges Izambard (13 mai 1871), Rimbaud argues against a *poésie subjective* in favor of a *poésie objective*. His turn toward objectivity does suggest a rejection of the personal lyricism of romantics, such as Lamartine and Musset. Yet *poésie objective* does not simply mean for Rimbaud the impassive or impersonal expression traditionally associated with Parnassianism. Why would we equate *poésie objective* with Parnassian aesthetics in view of Rimbaud's statement above on Banville, which announces an aim to supersede his predecessor? We discover the key to the theoretical shift toward a *poésie objective* in Rimbaud's rereading of poetic history.

The second seer letter, reviewing the romantic tradition, presents the Parnassian poets as a second stage of French romanticism. Rimbaud recognizes only three eras of poetry: "Toute poésie antique aboutit à la poésie grecque ... De la Grèce au movement romantique" (15 mai 1871; 1972, 250).[7] To infer from this statement that Parnassianism for Rimbaud is a stage through which romanticism evolves blurs the distinction generally made between subjective and objective poetic modes. Rather than opposing romanticism and Parnassianism, the *lettres du voyant* situate poetic voice on the boundary of subjectivity and objectivity. In the psychoanalytic terms introduced in chapter 2, we understand a split or dialogic subjectivity constructed by the interaction of conscious and unconscious mental activity. *Voyance*, which theoretically recasts the poetic subject with relation to the unconscious Other, becomes the modern expression of romanticism, or what Rimbaud calls "le vrai romantisme."

The poet-as-seer gives voice to the creative impulse. Such *voyance* is inextricably linked with psychical ascesis. To cultivate the self beyond the expression of conscious feelings opens up contact with the unknown or unconscious (1972, 251). This delving into a poet's mental activity assumes the immanent source of the discourse of self rendered manifest or objectified through the creative process. Taking up the call to poetic arms in Baudelaire, the provocative shift in Rimbaud's *voyance* from the *connu* to the *inconnu*, from conscious ego to unconscious mental activity as the source of the creative impulse, demands in turn new poetic forms to express formless psychical material. Maneuvers against both the exaggerated personal sentiment à la Musset and the impassive formal precision of the Parnassian poets, whom Rimbaud calls the "seconds romantiques," clear a space for *voyance* or "le vrai romantisme," in Rimbaud's idiosyncratic use of the term.

For Rimbaud, "les premiers romantiques ont été voyants sans trop bien s'en rendre compte: la culture de leurs âmes s'est commencée aux accidents" (1972, 253).[8] Parnassianism too misses the visionary mark: "les seconds romantiques sont très voyants, mais inspecter l'invisible et entendre l'inouï [est] autre chose que reprendre l'esprit des choses mortes" (253).[9] Just as Rimbaud turns toward and from these predecessors, so too he relates to Baudelaire.

On the one hand, Baudelaire, "le premier voyant, roi des poètes, un vrai Dieu," is a true romantic in Rimbaud's idiosyncratic terms, a modern romantic.[10] On the other hand, he adds concerning this predecessor, "encore a-t-il vécu dans un milieu trop artiste, et la forme si vantée en lui est mesquine" (253–54).[11] Rimbaud so breaks with a strict identification with Baudelaire, and makes explicit his objective to bring romanticism to its fullest expression of the modern poetic subject.

A revisionist strategy moves Rimbaud toward discontinuity with the literary past; he purports to retain romantic aesthetics, but he rereads its terms. The seer letter to Demeny claims that Rimbaud's predecessors misread romanticism: both critics, who viewed it purely intellectually, and creative artists, who understood it to express pure sentiment (1972, 250). The relation between the creative artist and his or her expression in Rimbaud rejects the romantic identification of the personal self with the speaking subject. From a Lacanian perspective, we can understand Rimbaud's *split subject* in these terms: signifying relations, which construct the self, also objectify it and thus alienate the subject of being from the speaking subject. So too the creative impulse can no longer be identified solely with the poet-as-speaker once an unconscious Other appropriates the discourse of the "I." Various divisions within the speaking subject from Lamartine to Baudelaire become for Rimbaud the modern romantic self, constructed in and through discourse with relation to the nonself.

SEEING THE SELF OTHERWISE

The *voyant* letters, commonly read as Rimbaud's nascent *art poétique*, propose an objective poetry derived from a new conception of the poet-as-seer that I shall consider in psychical terms rather than in religious or social ones.[12] The *prophetic* role of the poet in Rimbaud discloses the unknown psyche. This poetic sight clearly differs from the romantic view derived from the biblical *voyant*-as-prophet who reveals the Divine Word to humankind (which we find in Claudel) and from the illuminist view that the *voyant* contributes to social progress.

Aspiring to transpose visions derived from the unknown or unconscious into discourse, Rimbaud, to objectify poetic language, renounces the self-centered discourse of his romantic predecessors. I shall explore how Rimbaud revises creativity with relation to its source. As the key to understanding the genesis of the creative act in Rimbaldian aesthetics and, moreover, to the sense of *objective* poetry, the celebrated dictum *Je est un autre* shifts the source of inspiration from outside (transcendent) to inside (immanent) the self. *I is an Other* becomes a statement about the unconscious origins of the creative process and a figure for the heterogeneous voice of the poetic text.[13] Unlike a transcendent mystical experience, the path of immanence that Rimbaud follows reveals a self that is perpetually divided in and through language. In his scheme of creativity, alterity defers identity and enunciation is no longer ascribed to an unequivocal empirical speaker.[14]

The heterogeneous speaking subject formulated in the *voyant* letters has elicited numerous critical responses that generally presuppose an opposition between subjective and objective poetry. These modes of discourse, however, overlap in Rimbaud's notion of the subject with relation to poetic creation. Rimbaldian critics, such as Enid Starkie, Marc Eigeldinger (1975; "Notes") and C. A. Hackett (1981), have emphasized the repudiation of romantic aesthetics in the 1871 *voyant* letters to Georges Izambard and to Paul Demeny. Others, including Atle Kittang, Lionel Ray, Karin Dillman, Antoine Raybaud, and Benjamin Fondane, have underscored from various theoretical perspectives modern conceptions of the speaking subject and of poetic discourse adumbrated within Rimbaud's critique of subjective idealism.

The psychoanalytic approach to the heterogeneous subject that I shall develop here, with particular attention to the creative process, exposes the Other in linguistic treatments of subjectivity. For example, Dillman conceptualizes the objectification of Rimbaud's speaking subject in these terms: "the subject *je* is objectified by and through [the pronoun] *on*, but its presence as referent continues to exist" (38). Construed as a grammatical subject that "makes sense in context only" (41), *je* functions textually to guide the narrative and to create the illusion of a speaking voice while disrupting the latter at the same time (117–18). Dillman would have us attempt to ascribe meaning to each narrative instance of *je*, that is, to assign an identity to a functioning that cannot be named.

How can we name the Rimbaldian *sujet* when, as we shall discover, *je* does not say what it means or mean what it says? To paraphrase Rimbaud, *je* is thought and spoken by an Other. The term *Other* specifically intends the Lacanian notion of unconscious mental activity continuous with the Symbolic order of language, whereas *other* signifies the commonplace sense of what is different or additional, existing in opposition to or excluded by something else. In Rimbaldian poetics evolving from the *voyant* letters to the *Illuminations, je* is no longer solely *a* persona, *a* narrator, or *a* voice; rather, "I" is a dialogic signifying relation that blurs the antinomy between self and Other by positioning poetic voice on the boundary of the subject and the object.

Rimbaud's struggle against the personal lyricism of his romantic heritage aims to develop an *objective* poetry that I have already distinguished from the impassive expression of the Parnassian poets. In the 13 May 1871 seer letter to his mentor Izambard, Rimbaud takes to task the subjective principle, that is, the source, of prior French romantic poetry and declares his intention to write objective poetry:

> Au fond, vous ne voyez en votre principe que poésie subjective: votre obstination à regagner le râtelier universitaire—pardon!—le prouve. Mais vous finirez toujours comme un satisfait qui n'a rien fait, n'ayant rien voulu faire. Sans compter que votre poésie subjective sera toujours horriblement fadasse. Un jour, —bien d'autres espèrent la même chose—je verrai dans votre principe la poésie objective, je la verrai plus sincèrement que vous ne le feriez! (1972, 248)[15]

It is not obvious from these comments to Izambard what Rimbaud understands by *objective* poetry. Is he simply opposing objective to subjective poetry and thus proposing to replace individual bias with a detached discourse?

A thematic view of the pair subjective and objective reduces Rimbaud's poetic expression to repressed obsessions. Although Rimbaud proposes to write objective poetry, what Starkie calls "a literature of ideas," in her view, his discourse remains *subjective* and expresses hidden aspects of the self. Starkie advances that "[Rimbaud] wrote, without knowing it, only of what went on in himself and was hidden from his conscious mind" (147–48). Mistaking content for process, as Starkie does, limits the critical opening provided by her allusion to an unconscious aspect of creativity in Rimbaud. From a postmodern critical perspective, *poésie objective* challenges the notion that a creative artist's thoughts and feelings determine poetic expression. Instead, the unconscious Other within the self becomes the source of poiesis.

The poetic subject that evolves from the seer letters to the *Illuminations* dialogically voices the creative impulse of which the poet is otherwise unaware. Since the second letter to Demeny does not further define the idea of *poésie objective*, we infer the sense of this term from both Rimbaud's statements on the speaking subject and his poetic practice. *Objective* does not qualify the form, theme, or referent of poetry. Rather, as I shall remark, this term highlights in Rimbaud the functioning of poetic discourse with relation to its unconscious psychical source.[16] In other words, *poésie objective* voices the creative impulse that an artist sees or hears unconsciously.[17] I next follow the visionary map of objective poetry to prepare stages of the *sujet en procès* of *Une saison en enfer* and the dialogic *sujet* that narrates the *Illuminations*.

AU FOND DE L'INCONNU POUR TROUVER L'AUTRE

We recall that the seer letters dispute the earlier French romantic conception of self as both the (speaking) subject and object of the creative process, since "les romantiques . . . prouvent si bien que la chanson est si peu souvent l'oeuvre, c'est-à-dire la pensée chantée et *comprise* du chanteur" (15 mai 1871; 1972, 250).[18] Rimbaud, in the same letter, dismisses an unequivocal relation of the self and language and asserts with regard to poetic "voice" that *I is an Other*: "Si le cuivre s'éveille clairon, il n'y a rien de sa faute. Cela m'est évident: j'assiste à l'éclosion de ma pensée: je la regarde, je l'écoute" (250).[19] When Rimbaud postulates the role played by the self in the creative process and asserts that "Je est un autre," he is no longer saying "je pense, donc je suis."[20] Nor does he mean in Benvenistian terms, "je dis, donc je suis," a supposition shared by critics like Dillman who view *je* exclusively as a grammatical or textual subject.[21] By unseating the ego-self, the "I"-as-creator, to elaborate creativity in terms of an impersonal impulse, Rimbaud advances a modern notion of the poetic subject that a Lacanian perspective illuminates. Consonant with Lacan's view of misapprehending the self as the speaking subject, Rimbaud implicitly challenges the identification of the *moi du sujet* (self of the subject) with the *je de son discours* (I of its discourse).[22] Moreover, Rimbaud's poet, dissociated from his or her language, prefigures Lacan's theory of the discourse of the self. Psychical ascesis reveals a split self.

The configuration of poetic voice in and through discourse objectifies the Rimbaldian speaking subject. This dialogism informing subjectivity divides the subject of being from the speaking subject. So too an "Other" appropriating the discourse of the "I" dissociates the creative impulse and the poet-as-speaker. Rimbaud's subversion of the Cartesian cogito signals the decentering of subjectivism through the refusal to ground poetic practice in an empirical subject.[23] Statements about the speaking subject in the seer letters asking "what is I?" and postulating the role played by an Other invite a Lacanian reading of the dialogue between unconscious and conscious psychical activity that constitutes the modern romantic subject in Rimbaud.[24]

THE OTHER WITHIN THE SELF

In the Rimbaldian scheme, "I," at once the subject of enunciation and the subject of statement, is always other than "I" rather than another "I." As Lacan asserts, one is unconsciously Other: "je pense où je ne suis pas, donc je suis où je ne pense pas" (1966, 277).[25] The various guises and postures attributed to *je* throughout the texts of the *Saison en enfer* and the *Illuminations* demonstrate the inability to articulate a stable, unified identity. Lacan argues on an analogous basis that an inherent ignorance or *lack* of knowledge structures the self as perpetually Other: "Ce qu'il faut dire, c'est: je ne suis pas, là où je suis le jouet de ma pensée; je pense à ce que je suis, là où je ne pense pas penser" (277).[26] Displacing the self-centered discourse of the romantics, Rimbaud cultivates a new sensibility that expands poetic vision to the unknown. What Rimbaud discovers through sensory displacement shows from a Lacanian perspective the poietic way that language works, that is, without thinking as the logical brain does.

In the seer letters, Rimbaud considers how an individual transforms him- or herself into a visionary. Transfiguration into a creative artist involves a disordering of the senses linked with the exploration of the unknown (unconscious) mind. Writing to Izambard 13 May 1871, Rimbaud states, "Je veux être poète, et je travaille à me rendre *Voyant*. . . . Il s'agit d'arriver à l'inconnu par le dérèglement de *tous les sens*" (1972, 248).[27] To become a poet, a seer in the sense of a creator, one must engage in mental "work" to explore the *âme*, or psyche, as the provenance of the creative urge.

Georges Poulet rightly infers from the psychological work in Rimbaud a query concerning the creative process: "Mais ce moi autre, étranger à moi-même et qui jaillit pourtant de ma pensée créatrice, ne puis-je le reconnaître comme mien, comme identique à moi? (1980, 120).[28] Yet Poulet misconstrues Rimbaud's response in the 13 May 1871 letter, "c'est faux de dire: je pense. On devrait dire: On me pense." He also oversimplifies the speaking subject of Rimbaud's discourse: "De la sorte se trouve affirmé par Rimbaud le grand principe de l'altérité du moi par rapport à lui-même. Cela signifie: je puis me penser autre que je suis ou que j'étais . . . je puis me créer (ou me recréer) autre que je n'étais" (120).[29] The alterity of self that Rimbaud reveals through the creative process in fact supplants the conscious ability to think oneself to be other than one is. What challenges unequivocal identity is the voice of the unconscious.

Rimbaud's 15 May 1871 letter to Demeny details the psychical ascesis that objectifies the self in terms of the Other:

> La première étude de l'homme qui veut être poète est sa propre connaissance entière; il cherche son âme, il l'inspecte, il la tente, l'apprend. Dès qu'il la sait, il doit la cultiver; cela semble simple; en tout cerveau s'accomplit un développement naturel; tant d'*égoïstes* se proclament auteurs; il en est bien d'autres qui *s'*attribuent leur progrès intellectuel! (1972, 251)[30]

Egoists who call themselves "authors," like those who attribute their intellectual progress to themselves, to their ego-self, conflate the subject of being with the speaking subject of poetic discourse. Such "poets" are essentially un(self)conscious and psychically insensitive to the nature of the creative process. It is precisely the ego-self that psychical ascesis displaces as the assumed speaking subject of poetic creation. The plunge into the unknown self described above suggests an identification with the legendary Orpheus, who has embodied various myths of the poet through centuries of literary history.

The tripartite Orphic story offers two distinct myths of the poet's vision as transcendent and immanent. We recall that Orpheus transcends the chaos of the physical world, moving rocks and trees and subduing animals with his voice. Orpheus later descends into the underworld after the death of his wife, Eurydice, in an attempt to rescue her; he loses her a second time by looking back at her before reemerging from Hades. Reading the Orphic descent emblematically as an exploration of the unconscious, the loss of Eurydice suggests that unconscious psychical contents can be known, that is, can be expressed, only indirectly. Again in a symbolic sense, after Orpheus is killed by the Maenads, his voice transcends death as his severed head, still singing, floats down the river.

The Orphic myth metaphorically relates the poet to his or her language. The first and third figures of Orpheus above focus on the transcendent power of his song, whereas the second figure involves a descent into the depths. This descent symbolically relocates the path to creation within the psyche. So too Rimbaldian *voyance* overlaps an immanent source with the transcendent power of the poet's language. Although the *voyant* letters clearly turn from the transcendent role played by the romantic self in the creative process, they assert divergent schemes of psychical ascesis leading to inspiration.

An Orphic descent into the personal self and, by extension into unconscious mental activity, versus a mystical ascent into the realm of an impersonal transcendent order set forth alternate paths to creativity.[31] From the critical perspective of dialogism, however, the coexistent Orphic and Promethean myths of the poet in the seer letters do not present a strict contradiction. Rather, they cast in different terms the interpenetration of the subjective and the objective in the construction of the Rimbaldian subject that I have already suggested.

FROM ORPHIC IMMANENCE TO TRANSCENDENCE

The theory of the speaking subject and of discourse in the seer letters forefronts an inner source of creativity in Rimbaud. Transposing visions of the unknown into discourse precludes absolute immanence; a strictly immanent act is one performed entirely within the mind of the subject and produces no external effect. Thus, reference to unconscious mental activity in this discussion takes a Freudian view of its putative origins and situates the latter within the mind of the subject.[32] Moreover, the transposition of unconscious psychical contents into discourse adheres to the idea that, again postulated by Freud, we *know* the unconscious only indirectly through its effects.[33] Read emblematically, the paradox of Orphic and Promethean myths of the poet in the *voyant* letter to Demeny equivocates the subject of poeisis in Rimbaud, at once the poet-as-willful-creator and creativity as autonomous.[34] This ambivalence relates the dialogic construction and expression of the Rimbaldian *sujet* to the unconscious Other.

A "new" poetic language, alluding to a self-willed creator, announces a Promethean gesture. Yet in the 15 May 1871 letter, Rimbaud situates the quest for the unknown in an Orphic manner, "*là-bas*" ("down there"):

> Donc le poète est vraiment voleur de feu.
> Il est chargé de l'humanité; . . . il devra faire sentir, palper, écouter ses inventions; si ce qu'il rapporte de *là-bas* a forme, il donne forme; si c'est informe, il donne de l'informe. Trouver une langue. (1972, 252)[35]

Framed in Bloom's terms of revisionism, a poet quests for fire in an attempt "to burn through the very content that the precursors created or themselves accepted" (1975, 17). The Prometheus complex involves

Revisioning the Self, Creating the Subject

a creative defense against the literary past. Along with a revisionary quest, the allusion to Prometheus links poetry and transcendence. From this perspective, the creative act embodies a totalizing power through which the poet re-creates cosmic harmony. The poetic word thus unites humankind with nature and consciousness with matter.

Reference to a universal mind and to a universal soul in the letter to Demeny implies a Promethean strategy of transcendence in Rimbaldian *voyance*:

> L'intelligence universelle a toujours jeté ses idées, naturellement; les hommes ramassaient une partie de ces fruits du cerveau: on agissait par, on en écrivait des livres: telle allait la marche, l'homme ne se travaillant pas, n'étant pas encore éveillé, ou pas encore dans la plénitude du grand songe. Des fonctionnaires, des écrivains: auteur, créateur, poète, cet homme n'a jamais existé! (1972, 250–51)

"Le poète définirait la quantité d'inconnu s'éveillant en son temps dans l'âme universelle: il donnerait plus—que la formule de sa pensée, que la notation de *sa marche au Progrès*" (252).[36] The recurrent term *universelle* suggests Eastern mysticism to Rolland de Renéville and the collective unconscious to Eigeldinger.[37] Both critics nonetheless note an overlapping quest for unity of self through immanence that we reread with Houston (1986) to redirect the creative impulse in Rimbaud to the individual unconscious.

L'âme universelle in Rimbaud has a psychical sense distinct from the divine in Western mysticism and the collective unconscious in Eastern mysticism. As Houston cogently remarks, the "universal soul is . . . a religiously subversive term for it designates an impersonal reserve of power utterly different from the Christian God" (13). Moreover, the poet's Orphic descent into the unknown, *là-bas* (down below), contrasts with "*là-haut* [up above] of the traditional realm of God" (13). This underconsciousness, or unconsciousness, rejects unity through immanence as conceived by Renéville and Eigeldinger or transcendence à la Claudel, since "the idea of union with the One, so characteristic of mysticism, is lacking in [Rimbaud's] thought" (Houston, 1986, 44).

An Orphic exploration of the inner self in Rimbaud turns against the religious mystical tradition in Western thought connected to the quest for unity of the self in God. His nondiscursive poetic language also deviates from the other mystical discourses of the nineteenth century based on a coherent system of correspondences, as in Emanuel Swedenborg and the early Baudelaire, where a universal soul centralizes self and world.[38] How, then, are we to read in the Demeny letter the allusion to a universal language?

Rimbaud's poetics of the fragmented subject refutes the principle of transcendence.[39] Thus, we read the adjective *universelle* to connote what is common to all (Littré 4:2396). The universal language that Rimbaud seeks relates to humankind's inherent *sapienza poetica*, that is, to poiesis or creative production. Moreover, "finding a language" targets specifically giving voice to the creative impulse within the individual self. A seer poet, we recall, "devra faire sentir, palper, écouter ses inventions" (Rimbaud, 1972, 252). Such poetic language transposes into discourse the previously unknown that the mind's eye sees without de-forming the formed or forming the formless. How is it that poetic discourse, a visible written text, does not give form to the formless?

Informe, in strict opposition to *forme*, connotes something without form. The term *informe* also implies "ce dont on ne peut définir la forme," "ce dont la forme n'est pas achevée ou à demi consciente," and "[là] où rien ne se manifeste encore" (Littré 3:736).[40] When Rimbaud writes "si ce que [le poète] rapporte de là-bas a forme, il donne forme; si c'est informe, il donne de l'informe," he is not necessarily opposing *forme* to *informe*. Here *informe* describes fleeting psychical images that bear no resemblance to empirical reality and consequently escape recognition from a conscious outlook.[41] Rimbaldian *voyance*, viewed as a protopsychoanalysis, voices unconscious mental activity and images the cognitively unknown through the metaphoric functioning of language.

SEEING THE UNKNOWN, VOICING THE OTHER

The creative artist, in Rimbaud's scheme, retraces the psychical impression of the formless without being able to name or render the latter in a manner analogous to an empirically perceivable form. Poetic creation, like dreaming, images what we see in a realm fully accessible only to the mind's eye:

> Le Poète se fait *voyant* par un long, immense et raisonné *dérèglement* de *tous les sens* . . . il cherche lui-même, il épuise en lui tous les poisons, pour n'en garder que les quintessences. . . . Car il arrive à *l'inconnu!* Puisqu'il a cultivé son âme, déjà riche, plus qu'aucun! Il arrive à l'inconnu, et quand, affolé, il finirait par perdre l'intelligence de ses visions, il les a vues! (15 mai 1871; Rimbaud, 1972, 251)[42]

Revisioning the Self, Creating the Subject

These mental visions generally elude comprehension with reference to the empirical world. To make sense of them without having amply *seen* them, Rimbaud's poet follows the linguistic impulse of the creative voice within the psyche. This inner poiesis implies the genesis of discourse at the level of thought: "toute parole étant idée, le temps d'un langage universel viendra. . . . Cette langue sera de l'âme pour l'âme, résumant tout, parfums, sons, couleurs, de la pensée accrochant la pensée et tirant" (252).[43] Different from a coherent system of correspondences, here the sense of *universel*, with relation to the *sapienza poetica* that I have already discussed, suggests language embodying the fullest expression of the psyche. In other words, Rimbaud endeavors to expand to the unconscious Other within the self the expressive capacity of language.

Whereas Baudelaire, Gérard de Nerval, and Comte du Lautréamont may invite thematic readings of a divided subject, Rimbaud makes an original move by constructing the subject in terms of the alienating structures of language. His maneuver unwittingly opens up poetic discourse to the impulse of what Freud later elaborates as unconscious mental activity. Equating *idée* with psychical image in Rimbaud, we understand primary process ideation where "la pensée accroch[e] la pensée et tir[e]."[44] This language "of the psyche for the psyche," best exemplified by the *Illuminations*, constructs signifying relations that suggest an affinity with the Freudian dreamwork. Association by resemblance and contiguity overlap in Rimbaud's psychopoetics, where the modes of metaphor and metonymy condense and displace signifiers. Poetic voice thus becomes the instrument of an unconscious poiesis, the creative Other heard, or seen, or both within the self.

ON THE BOUNDARY OF SUBJECTIVITY AND OBJECTIVITY

The seer letters of 1871 theorize a heterogeneous speaking subject that supplants the ego-self of French romantic subjectivism. In practice, however, Rimbaud retains a *lyrical* voice to narrate *Une saison en enfer* (published in 1873). The persistence of a first-person narrator *after* the objective poetry projected in the *voyant* letters supports the view that Rimbaud does not define *objective* (*non-je*) in opposition to *subjective* (*je*). Rather, he redefines the lyric speaker; dissociating *je* from an individual ego, Rimbaud positions poetic voice on the border of self and Other.[45] This split or dialogic subjectivity exceeds strictly linguistic parameters. A psychoanalytic paradigm informed by dialogism enables us critically to map out *je* as a discursive *autre* (Other). From this perspective, the impulse of the unconscious Other that splits the subject also traces its primary process effects at the level of the signifier. Having considered the theoretical stage of the poetic subject in the *voyant* letters, I shall now move toward Rimbaud's modern romantic subject constructed *in* and *through* discourse. *Une saison en enfer* puts into play a multiplicity of voices that intermittently dialogizes the explicit first-person narrator. This prepares the configuration of the dialogic subject of the *Illuminations* on the margins of self and Other.[46]

Taking the view that the *Saison* serves as a transition piece from subjective to objective poetry, I shall consider questions raised in this collection as a whole on the relation of self to language and the source of creativity. Framed by the quest for poetic voice set forth in the seer letters, *Une saison en enfer* stages the psychical ascesis that prepares the dialogized voice and metaphoric mode of the *Illuminations*.[47] A closer look at the first-person narrator of *Une saison en enfer* will reveal, in psychoanalytic terms, a subject-in-process that thwarts a nostalgic search for unity. This configuration of the subject also questions the role played by the poet in creativity. References to having insight, yet being speechless, implicitly debate the poet-as-willful-creator versus the autonomous creative process. The evolving subject in *Une saison en enfer* endorses poiesis over mimesis. Rimbaud's poetic practice thus moves toward the free production of signs in the *Illuminations*.

The title *Une saison en enfer* connotes a passage through or within; we read it metaphorically as an Orphic descent into the self. Both explicit and implicit references to this psychical probing in *Une saison en enfer* recall the *là-bas* of the seer manifesto: "Je ne suis plus au monde"; "Il n'y a personne ici et il y a a quelqu'un"; "Décidément, nous sommes hors du monde" (*Nuit de l'enfer*; 1972, 101); "La vraie vie est absente. Nous ne sommes pas au monde" (*Délires I*; 1972, 103); "Je suis au plus profond de l'abîme et je ne sais plus prier" (105).[48] Instead of unity, however, in exploring the source and expression of the creative impulse, Rimbaud affirms a split self alienated in and through the complex structuring of language. As Monique Jutrin rightly observes, this ascesis prefigures the object of psychoanalysis:

> La métaphore de la 'descente en enfer' est une espèce d'archétype profondément ancré dans le psychisme humain; fort répandu dans la tradition alchimique, il a été repris par la psychanalyse, et continue à nourrir la littérature. C'est qu'il traduit une expérience psychique menant à la décou-

verte de soi, il représente une aspiration de l'être à se saisir, à se comprendre comme unité. (9)⁴⁹

The untitled prologue of *Une saison en enfer* projects a return to an anterior plenitude: "Jadis, *si je me souviens bien*, ma vie était un festin. . . . A cette [période, c'était] ma vie éternelle, non écrite, non chantée, —quelque chose comme la Providence . . . à laquelle on croit . . . et qui ne chante pas" (Rimbaud, 1972, 169; emphasis added).⁵⁰ At the same time, the term *si* prepares the narrator's ironic distance, which configures an introspective stance and, by extension, a split subject. The psychical drama unwittingly staged in *Une saison en enfer* plays out the desire for an untenable state of wholeness.

Our reading of the nostalgic quest for *ma vie . . . non écrite, non chantée* in *Une saison en enfer* underscores with Jutrin "la nostalgie d'un état antérieur à la parole . . . l'état d'*infans*, de celui qui ne parle pas" (12).⁵¹ Psychical ascesis interjects through ironic distancing a religious accent. As I shall later discuss, Claudel will literally "mistake" references to religion in Rimbaud as a quest for personal salvation and unity in God. *Infans* may call to mind the mystic's silence. Whereas the mystic awaits divine inspiration, Rimbaud aims to discover the source of poetic speech with the individual psyche.

Only by ignoring the narrator's ironic stance could we read the religious scheme in *Mauvais sang* with unequivocal reference to an original state of innocence and of oneness preceding humanity's fall. Rather, the narrating subject (*je*) submits an identification with profane predecessors that prevents personal salvation per se.

> J'ai de mes ancêtres gaulois . . . l'idolâtrie et l'amour du sacrilège. . . .
> . . . Je me rappelle l'histoire de la France fille aînée de l'Eglise. . . . Je ne me vois jamais dans les conseils du Christ; ni dans les conseils des Seigneurs, —représentants du Christ. (1972, 94–95)⁵²

In an ironic light, we see that *Mauvais sang* dethrones God-as-origin. The human psyche thus becomes the source of knowledge. Once science replaces religion, rationalism becomes for the narrating subject the means to ultimate knowledge: "Nous allons à *l'Esprit*. C'est très certain, c'est oracle, ce que je dis. Je comprends, et ne sachant m'expliquer sans paroles païennes, je voudrais me taire" (95).⁵³ Language, which plays a fundamental role in constructing the modern speaking subject in Rimbaud, nevertheless defers knowledge and identity. This first of many allusions in *Une saison en enfer* to speechlessness expresses an inability to say what one means. Finding oneself speechless presents more precisely the loss of narrative authority, credibility, or both, since *I is an Other*. This lack, moreover, configures *je* as *un autre*, that is, the noncoincidence of the subject of enunciation (*énonciation*) and the subject of statement (*énoncé*).

The debated relation of self, language, and knowledge in *Mauvais sang* alternates an implicit psychological scheme ("ne sachant m'expliquer") and a religious one ("païennes"). Ironic allusions to religion overlapping with references to a psychical realm implicitly dispute the source of creativity, transcendent versus immanent, that we observed in the seer letters. *Une saison en enfer* does not sustain a religious reading of humanity's fall. Rather, the quest for voice advances a psychological exploration that enables us to read the *fall* in Rimbaud's scheme to signify the subject's accession to the alienating structures of language.

Reading from this psychoanalytic perspective, we can follow Jutrin's comment that for Rimbaud "the *fall* of human beings is tied to the emergence of language" (12). Her remark echoes Lacan's theory of the simultaneous advent of the unconscious and consciousness through language that inaugurates the irreversibly split subject.[54] We reread references to Christianity in *Une saison en enfer* with relation to the supremacy of the Word. More precisely, the Word in Rimbaud relates to Lacan's Symbolic order in terms of which the subject is constituted and subsequently *subjected* to speak.

Mauvais sang intermittently casts the search for unity in religious terms, only to consistently refute allusion to God through ironic reversals: "Le sang païen revient. L'Esprit est proche, pourquoi Christ ne m'aide-t-il pas, en donnant à mon âme noblesse et liberté. Hélas! L'Evangile a passé . . . ! J'attends Dieu avec gourmandise" (95). "Oui j'ai les yeux fermés à votre lumière. . . . Mais je puis être sauvé" (97). "J'ai reçu au coeur *le coup de la grâce*" (98).[55] The concluding lines of *Mauvais sang* reject salvation per se and thus support a *false conversion*, or a refusal of religion, in *Une saison en enfer:* "*Je ne me crois pas embarqué pour une noce avec Jésus-Christ pour beau-père*" (99; emphasis added):

> Je ne suis pas prisonnier de ma raison. J'ai dit: Dieu. Je veux la liberté dans le salut? comment la poursuivre . . . ? *Plus besoin de dévouement ni d'amour divin. Je ne regrette pas le siècle des coeurs sensibles.* . . . Je retiens ma place au sommet de cette angélique échelle de bon sens. (99; emphasis added)[56]

Mauvais sang repudiates God-as-origin. Moreover, the decentered relation of self and world therein precludes union through transcendence. Searching for wholeless within a psychical realm (*la nostalgie de l'infans*) brings about, nonetheless, a similar estrangement of the subject in Rimbaud.

RIMBAUD´S *SUJET EN PROCÈS*

"This language . . . of the psyche for the psyche" described in the seer manifesto blindly asserts in the shadow of Rimbaud's romantic predecessors the subject's quest for plenitude in language. In a Lacanian light, this putative desire to recapture an anterior state of unconsciousness targets in fact the impossible—a discourse that would overcome the divisive effect of language on the self by transforming the relation of discourse and speaking subject into a nondifferentiated, unmediated state. Rimbaud discovers that a speaking subject cannot surpass the aporia at its origins.

Lacanian terms develop Rimbaud's modern romantic stance. For Lacan, the state of an *infans* precedes the advent of language and the unconscious that simultaneously establishes a speaking subject. Through entry into the Symbolic order and the attendant coming to consciousness, the subject becomes estranged and loses "any image of an 'original' self . . . in the hole of the unconscious" and yet forever "desir[es] presumptive unity with the m(other)" (Mellard 19). Becoming *self* conscious alienates the speaking subject from the unconscious Other within the self and creates through repression a gap in our knowledge of ourselves.

Rimbaud's search for poetic voice, and by extension for a language, implicitly re-presents the quest for a unitary self. Wing rightly observes this search for wholeness in Rimbaud's *Impossible* in these terms: "[T]he subject could exist outside of the constraints of any discourse whatsoever, be identical to its own undivided psychical components . . . or outside of any articulation between the subject and its relation to a lack" (1984, 47). The lack *of* voice often expressed in *Une saison en enfer* parallels the lack *in* expression that reconfigures the split at the origination of the speaking subject, as in *Matin*: "Moi, je ne puis plus m'expliquer que le mendiant avec ses continuels *Pater et Ave Maria. Je ne sais plus parler!*" (Rimbaud, 1972, 115).[57] Read emblematically, the prayer to Father and M/other alternates the nostalgia for totality outside and inside the self (*Pater, Ave Maria*, respectively). Neither positioning, however, achieves the desired plenitude of identity and expression. For the evolving poetic subject in Rimbaud is in theory and practice alienated in and through discourse. We can indeed follow with Wing the discovery in Rimbaud that "each utterance of the first-person pronoun produces a division of the self at the very instant that it is posited" (44).[58]

Taking a step further the psychic estrangement of the poet that Nerval, Baudelaire, and Lautréamont thematically portray, Rimbaud discloses in *L'Impossible* the alienating structuration of discourse that "con-figures," or splits, the subject on the boundary of self and other: "M'étant retrouvé deux sous de raison—ça passe vite—je vois que mes malaises viennent de ne *m'être pas figuré* assez tôt que nous sommes à l'Occident" (1972, 113; emphasis added).[59] Wing insightfully remarks that the expression *se figurer* suggests "the acknowledgment that the self can take its 'place' only in the figures, in the language, of the West." Indeed, language mediates the subject's understanding (as I shall now show), dialogically constructing narrative voice on the margins of subjectivity and objectivity.[60] Thus, blurred boundaries of immanence and transcendence, which we observed in the *lettres du voyant* through the interpenetration of Orphic and Promethean myths of the poet, set the stage for the specifically dialogic scheme of the evolving poetic subject in *Une saison en enfer*.

The texts of *Une saison en enfer* largely represent first-person narratives where an explicit "I" (*je*) prevails, whether in self-address or in dialogue with an interlocutor. For example, in the prologue, an exchange between the narrator and *Satan*, self and Other, follows a recognizable pattern of address between an "I" and a "you":

"Tu resteras hyène, etc . . . ", se récrie le démon qui me couronna de si aimables pavots. . . .
   . . . —Mais, cher Satan, je vous en conjure, une prunelle moins irritée . . . ! vous qui aimez dans l'écrivain l'absence des facultés descriptives ou instructives, je vous détache ces quelques hideux feuillets de mon carnet de damné. (1972, 93)[61]

The *Saison* is replete with narrative instances in which an "I" converses with an implicit or explicit "you." The interlocutor is within or without the self (*Alchimie du verbe, L'Eclair, Matin, Adieu*) and in other instances is a third person, usually an *il* (*Délires: Vierge Folle, L'Impossible*). I now turn from this apparent dialogue to shifts in first-person voice that dialogize the speaking subject (*Mauvais sang*) and others that displace the primacy of the "I" (*Nuit de l'enfer*).

Revisioning the Self, Creating the Subject

IL FAUT ÊTRE ABSOLUMENT MODERNE:
TOWARD DIALOGIC VOICE

Along with the *je* that first enunciates *Mauvais sang,* the narrating subject alternately assumes the voice of *on* (one, someone, we) or *nous* (we or us). Both of these pronouns nevertheless imply, and thus maintain, the *I* that narrates most of the text. In this sense, the move from *I* to *we* (*on* or *nous*) dialogically frames the speaking subject without putting into question the first-person narrative role: "*On* ne part pas. — *Reprenons* les chemins d'ici, chargé de *mon* vice" (Rimbaud, 1972, 96; emphasis added).[62] To the contrary, *Nuit de l'enfer* foreshadows the dialogic voice of the *Illuminations.* The change from an explicit or implicit first-person to a third-person narrator objectifies the "I" in and through discourse. Moreover, this objectification displaces the narrative role of the first-person speaking subject. Just as "I" becomes through dialogue the object of its interlocutor, so too the Other (interlocutor) takes the subject's place; this alternating narrative role dialogically constructs the speaker and the addressee.

The singular first-person subject of *Nuit de l'enfer* addresses an indefinite plural "you" (reader? unconscious Other?) then invokes a singular "you," subsequently identified with *Satan qui dit*: "Voyez comme le feu se relève! Je brûle comme il faut. Va, démon!" and "Tais-toi, mais tais-toi! . . . Satan qui dit que le feu est ignoble. . . . —Assez! . . . Des erreurs qu'on me souffle, magies, parfums faux, musiques puériles" (100).[63] How do we identify references to Satan here in *Nuit de l'enfer* and in other instances in the *Saison?* Rather than assuming that Satan signifies Paul Verlaine, as some critics argue, Rimbaud's Orphic stance (and, by extension, psychical ascesis) indeed supports our identifying Satan with the inner, alienated voice within the self. Jean Lacose upholds a similar view: "Le héros de la *Saison* ne parle à personne, ne se débat qu'avec lui-même, devenu pour soi l'autre de l'histoire" (Lacose et al. 9).[64]

From a poststructuralist psychoanalytic perspective, we read the speaking subject in *Nuit de l'enfer* in dialogic relation to this demon/Other within the self, that is, "you [Satan] who love in a writer the absence of instructive or descriptive faculties" quoted above. *On me souffle* echoes *on me pense,* which we now understand in the Lacanian terms of a split subject. Thus, *on me souffle* reinscribes the objectification of the subject's voice by the Other postulated in the seer letters.

From the broader perspective of dialogism that I shall develop in the *Illuminations, on me souffle* refers to the internal, alienated voice addressed as *tu* ([Satan] *me souffle*[*s*]). This locution also relates to a third person (i.e., reader) outside the dialogue between *je* and the unconscious Other within the self. Thus, we dialogically situate the poet's voice *in relation to* the Other(s). This positioning is also inferred from the textual marks of omission in the fragment of *Nuit de l'enfer* cited above.

In the text, dashes and elision marks indicate changes of topic, time, place, and speaker throughout *Une saison en enfer*. They proliferate shifts in *Nuit de l'enfer*, without, however, providing sufficient guideposts for the reader to identify who is speaking to whom about what.

> Que de malices dans l'attention dans la campagne . . . Satan, Ferdinand, court avec les graines sauvages . . . Jésus marche sur les ronces purpurines, sans les courber . . . Jésus marchait sur les eaux irritées. La lanterne nous le montra debout, blanc et des tresses brunes, au flanc d'une vague d'émeraude . . .
> Je vais dévoiler tous les mystères . . .
> Ecoutez! . . .
> J'ai tous les talents! —Il n'y a personne ici et il y a quelqu'un: je ne voudrais pas répandre mon trésor.
> —Veut-on des chants nègres, des danses de houris? (1972, 101)[65]

The narrating subject moves from *je* to *nous*, to *Ecoutez*, then to *on*, and finally back to *je* in the space of these short lines, followed by, "Fiez-vous donc à moi, la foi soulage, guide, guérit" (101).[66] Who is indeed speaking and to whom? Along with the ostensible allusion to God addressing the fallen (narrating) subject, we might infer from the term *foi* that the narrator ironically solicits the trust of the reader as his or her interlocutor. Claudel, however, has *faith* in Rimbaud and thus misconstrues the Other outside the self in a transcendent realm with God, the Divine Creator.

A Lacanian perspective of the debated relation of self, language, and knowledge in *Une saison en enfer* enables us to discern the poet implicitly questioning the self that he or she claims to know. Staging the scene of the unconscious Other within the self, both the *nous* of the ensuing line ("Et pensons à moi," 101) and a subsequent reference to *nous* imply self-address ("Décidément, nous sommes hors du monde," 101).[67] Rimbaud's psychodrama obliquely relates to Orpheus's failed attempts to recapture Eurydice. Whether implicit or explicit ("Je suis caché et je ne le suis pas," 102), the speaking subject, no longer identifiable with a stable, presupposed entity, has become an effect of writing that cannot fully capture what it desires or means to say.

DREAMING, CREATING: THE DISCOURSE OF THE OTHER

Statements throughout *Une saison en enfer* emphasize an inability to directly transpose insight into discourse. Rimbaud's creative artist sees what he or she can name only indirectly, that is, metaphorically. Images incongruous with reference to known empirical reality elude direct expression, as in *Mauvais sang*: "Dans les villes la boue m'apparaissait soudainement rouge et noire, comme une glace quand la lampe circule dans la chambre voisine, comme un trésor dans la forêt!" (Rimbaud, 1972, 97).[68] The term *comme* offers a comparison one remove from the insight itself, the agency of which is autonomous (*m'apparaissait*). Yet the use of a metaphoric mode by analogy becomes untenable for Rimbaud's creative artist.

Vertiginous visions present nondiscursive associations that do not make sense from a conscious outlook. Structured like unconscious mental activity, which we cannot directly apprehend and thus name, hallucinations are unspeakable ("*innom*brables"). From *Nuit de l'enfer*: "Puis-je décrire la vision. . . . Les hallucinations sont innombrables" (Rimbaud, 1972, 100). And from *Délires I: Vierge folle*: "A présent je suis au fond du monde! O mes amies! . . . non pas mes amies . . . Jamais délires ni tortures semblables . . . Je ne sais même plus parler" (102).[69] These allusions to hallucinations and delirium offer a basis for associating Rimbaud's poetic language with a pathological state of mental alienation, like that of a mad genius. Debating the view that Rimbaud was indeed mad exceeds our purposes here.[70] What is of particular interest is the analogous split subjectivity in Rimbaud's *psychic* writing and in the expression of the mentally alienated.

Rimbaud's poetic alienation presents for Dr. Jean Fretet a striking parallel with medical discourse on delirium. The impersonal or objective expression of the prose texts in the *Illuminations* speaks to the subject in a voice that the subject does not recognize. So too, Fretet remarks, the mentally alienated say that their voices are not their own, that "on les parle, qu'*on les pense*" (198).[71] Tzvetan Todorov similarly assumes an affinity between creating and hallucinating in the *Illuminations* (1978, 220). Liberated from its role of expressing and representing at the level of the signified, poetic discourse in Rimbaud produces an effect of meaning at the level of the signifier. What Todorov calls the "discours schizophrénique" that twentieth-century poetry inherits from Rimbaud opens up poetic language to the unconscious Other within the self. This is the creative impulse that speaks to Rimbaud's modern poetic subject.

Like the hallucinating or dreaming subject, Rimbaud's *voyant* hears and sees without thinking. Loss of conscious ego control gives precedence to primary processes that result in the nondiscursive and imagistic expression of hallucinations and dreams. As we observed in *Mauvais sang*, for example, the agency of poetic vision exceeds the speaking subject's authority. Unlike a hallucinating (neurotic or psychotic) subject, however, Rimbaud's poet possesses a strong ego and thus seeks a linguistic path back from fantasy to reality. Yet the poet does not achieve mastery of his or her voice. In fact, the narrating and creating subject of *Une saison en enfer* often finds language inadequate or lacking and thus is rendered speechless: "Connais-je encore la nature? me connais-je? —*Plus de mots*" (1972, 97).[72] Writing about not having words to write casts in different terms Rimbaud's modern romantic construction of the subject in and through discourse. Encountering lack while writing also unwittingly debates the autonomous impulse of creativity at the level of the signifier.

The tension between the poet-as-willful-creator and the autonomous impulse of creativity resurfaces in *Alchimie du verbe* in a retrospective critique of the seer's attempt to *find a language*. By the creative artist's own admission, "la vieillerie poétique avait une bonne part dans mon alchimie du verbe" (108):

> J'ai créé toutes les fêtes, tous les triomphes, tous les drames. J'ai essayé d'inventer de nouvelles fleurs, de nouveaux astres, de nouvelles chairs, de nouvelles langues. J'ai cru acquérir des pouvoirs surnaturels. Eh bien! Je dois enterrer mon imagination et mes souvenirs! Enfin je demanderai pardon pour m'être nourri de mensonge. (116)[73]

In other words, cultivating, that is, consciously creating, hallucinations blindly contests the role of the unconscious Other theorized in the seer letters. Thus, this retrospective insight underscores that, like his romantic predecessors from whom he aimed to deviate, Rimbaud intermittently attempted to assert his authority as the creating subject.

The modern romantic subject, which we have followed from the seer letters through *Une saison en enfer*, exposes a poetics of *cultivated* hallucinations refuted by Rimbaud in *Alchimie du verbe*. To cultivate or consciously create assumes the poet-as-willful-creator's mastery of his or her language. Purported authorial control of poetic expression contrasts sharply with episodes of speechlessness that I discussed above:

> J'inventai la couleur des voyelles. . . . Je réglai la forme et le mouvement de chaque consonne, et avec des rythmes instinctifs, je me flattai d'inventer un verbe poétique accessible un jour ou l'autre à tous les sens. Je réservais la traduction. (1972, 106)[74]

This primacy of the speaking subject indeed contradicts the scheme in the seer letters to liberate poetic discourse from the tyranny of reason that limited Rimbaud's romantic predecessors' poetic sight. Yet Rimbaud's temporary blindness leads to insight. The cultivated hallucinations of the early verse, for example, *Voyelles*, alluded to in *Alchimie du verbe*, prepare the metaphoric mode of the *Illuminations*. A psychiatric intertext in this poetics implies the effects of unconscious mental activity on conscious discourse.

We have yet to discover explicit reference made by Rimbaud to the emergent psychiatric discourse of his period. Nevertheless, the linguistic cultivation of hallucinations reviewed in *Alchimie du verbe* implicitly echoes the retracing of unconscious mental activity from dream accounts written immediately upon awakening by nineteenth-century French lay dream interpreters Alfred Maury and Hervey de Saint Denys. To observe and analyze mental activity, Rimbaud's creating subject first recorded the discontinuous discourse of this inner voice: "Ce fut d'abord une étude. J'écrivais des silences, des nuits, je notais l'inexprimable. Je fixais des vertiges."[75] *Silences* evokes both the white or blank space of the page and the idea of drawing (inscribing) a blank—here a gap in ideation. *Night* signifies the formless ink of the well that gives form to characters on the white page, transposing *idée* (idea) into *parole* (word or speech). The poet thus noted or inscribed the inexpressible (*in-* also signifying within), writing down thoughts without any apparent connection. This disorder, however, sparked creativity: "Je finis par trouver sacré le désordre de mon esprit."[76] Here the term *sacré* suggests the idea of inspiration (i.e., *feu sacré*).

According to the 1871 manifesto, transformation into a seer through the cultivation of the psyche would lead the poet to the unknown, an unknown we have been treating as unconscious mental activity.[77] Rimbaud's alchemy of the word recounted in *Une saison en enfer* calls to mind accounts of hallucinations in nineteenth-century French psychiatry, for example, those of François Leuret, Jean-Etienne Esquirol, and Jules Baillarger (see Paliyenko). Moreover, the nondiscursive discourse of this primary process ideation advances the psychopoetics of *metaphora* developed in chapter 2 from the Freudian dreamwork of condensation and displacement in its Lacanian elaboration:

> Je m'habituai à l'hallucination simple: je voyais très franchement une mosquée à la place d'une usine, une école de tambours faite par des anges, des calèches sur les routes du ciel, un salon au fond d'un lac. . . . Puis j'expliquai mes sophismes magiques avec l'hallucination des mots! (Rimbaud, 1972, 108)[78]

Read in linguistic terms, *mosquée* displaces *usine*. This superimposition of signifiers defines Lacan's metaphor. Like the psychical sight in dream, the linguistic site of this condensation embodies the metaphoric mode, *un mot pour un autre*. This mode interpenetrates with metonymy at the level of both the signifier *in praesentia* and of underlying signifying chains.[79] Such unexpected associations ("des calèches sur les routes du ciel, un salon au fond d'un lac") give rise to a vision comparable to an eidetic image, which "once seen (and stated) does not remain; it blurs and gives way to others until eventually the visionary, or hallucinative, experience wears out and comes to an end" (Frohock 130–31). This may explain in part Rimbaud's serious doubts concerning his early poetics of hallucination and, moreover, his critique and rejection of this method: "A moi. L'histoire d'une de mes folies" (Rimbaud, 1972, 106). "Aucun des sophismes de la folie, —la folie qu'on enferme, —n'a été oublié par moi: je pourrais les redire tous, je tiens le système" (111).[80] A broader issue, however, underlies this disputed linguistic alchemy, which ultimately upholds poiesis over mimesis.

By asserting his *author*ity or *subject*ivity ("je tiens le système"), Rimbaud's poet counters the recurrent claim in the seer letters that *I is an Other*. He also presupposes a fully retrievable meaning accessible to the writing subject and thus the ability to reproduce vision(s) of the unknown: "Puis j'expliquai mes sophismes magiques avec l'hallucination des mots." Despite the intensity of their impression, psychical imagistic contents cannot be integrally re-captured in language since we can know or name them only indirectly through *metaphora*. Language cannot provide direct reference to reality either inside or outside the subject. Poetic writing, as Rimbaud practices it in the *Illuminations*, is not reproductive (i.e., mimetic) like classical metaphor but rather productive (i.e., poietic). Instead of a hallucination per se, language produces, at best, a hallucinatory effect through its metaphoric functioning at the level of the signifier.

In contradistinction to the fundamental incompatibility of eidetic and linguistic modes that Rimbaud discovers, André Breton asserts that "l'écriture automatique . . . mène tout droit à l'hallucination visuelle . . . il suffit de se reporter à 'Alchimie du verbe' pour constater que Rimbaud l'avait faite bien avant moi" (1970, 187).[81] Although clearly different from Claudel's Catholic revision of Rimbaud's poetics, Breton too mis-reads Rimbaud by mistaking unconscious mental activity for a retrievable content. I position instead the effects of the unconscious at play in Rimbaud's discourse at the level of the signifier to follow the creative impulse of his psychopoetics of *metaphora*.[82]

Revising the limits of traditional poetic discourse, Rimbaud begins to see "language in and for itself, corresponding to no reality," neither outside nor inside the subject (Houston, 1986, 48–49).[83] In Rimbaud's psychopoetic writing, an impulse, at once self and Other, speaks through the lacunae, or speechless gaps, in the poet's expression. The poet may describe him- or her*self* as not having words to utter. Reading between the lines of such speechlessness, we understand the disruptive effects upon conscious discourse of the speaking unconscious having appropriated narrative authority to itself. Along with a dialogic construction of voice in the *Illuminations*, the production of meaning through the metaphoric mode becomes an effect of writing.

FOUR

Illuminating the Discourse of the Other

To read Rimbaud on his own terms as a poet aiming to be *absolutely* modern, we assume an impersonal subject in the *Illuminations*. Like Hugo Friedrich, then, we no longer identify the "I" speaker in Rimbaud with the romantic self: "*Les Illuminations* . . . is . . . a text without an 'I.' The 'I' that appears in a few of the pieces is the alien, artificial voice adumbrated in the *voyant* letters. . . . *Les Illuminations* is the first great monument of the modern imagination become absolute" (59). Yet "I" is not absolutely absent in the *Illuminations* but rather dialogically present as the unconscious Other theorized in the seer letters and nominally practiced in the *Saison*. As the full expression of the modern romantic subject, Rimbaud's *Illuminations* voice a fundamental autonomous creative impulse and thus shift the genesis of the creative act from personal self to Other, from subjective to objective. Rimbaud confronts an insurmountable ambivalence through the conception and practice of an objective poetry no longer informed by the subjectivity of the creative artist as speaking subject. The modern poetic subject in Rimbaud illustrates that creativity involves an ambiguous speaking subject, an inherently dialogic subject, at once I and Other, personal and impersonal, conscious and unconscious.

As discussed in chapter 3, Rimbaud's well-known 1871 epistolary manifestoes (see Rimbaud, 1972) postulate a depersonalized speaking subject and propose a *poésie objective* to revise the subjective discourse of romantic predecessors. The first-person voice narrating *Une saison en enfer* notably deviates from prior romantic poetic discourse, as in Lamartine and Hugo.[1] Different from his predecessors' subjective poetry that presupposes a speaking subject identified with a personal self, Rimbaud's poetic subject is objectified, that is, constructed, in and through discourse. The widely adopted chronology from Verlaine (1972, 631), which dates the majority of the *Illuminations* to 1874 and 1875, supports the following scheme for reading stages of the subject in Rimbaud: *le sujet en procès* of *Une saison en enfer*, which stems from the split subject sketched in the *Lettres du voyant*, culminates in the *poésie objective* of the *Illuminations*.

A shift from subjective to objective poetic discourse, which implies a move from first-person to third-person narrative voice, from personal to impersonal, ostensibly dissociates poetic discourse from the creative artist's subjectivity. Notwithstanding this theory of the poetic subject in the seer letters, in nearly all of the prose poems of the *Illuminations*, a *je* subject either explicitly persists as the narrator or plays the role of an implied narrator through multiple textual guises. This ambiguous first-person speaker, alternating personal and impersonal voice, prepares a modern poetic subject constructed in and through discourse that distinguishes Rimbaud's *poésie objective* from other nineteenth-century experimental poetic writing as in Nerval, Baudelaire, and Lautréamont. Recast in a postmodern light, the *Illuminations* are hybrid texts that blur the nineteenth-century opposition between subjective and objective by assuming the dialogized voice of narration as the speaking subject of poetic discourse. Instead of opposing subjective to objective, *je* to *un autre*, Rimbaud dialogically relates them. A postmodern reading illuminates this conjunction of self and the unconscious Other in and through discourse in the narrative stances of the *Illuminations*.

OBJECTIFYING THE SUBJECT, DIALOGIZING POETIC VOICE

To construct the poetic self in relation to its otherness ("Je est un autre"), Rimbaud divorces the speaking subject from a real biographical entity. His objectification of the subject deviates from nineteenth-century philosophical discourse that, as summarized by Emile Littré, diametrically opposes the terms *objectif* and *subjectif*: "On appelle *sujet*, l'esprit conscient, le moi; *objet*, la chose, quelle qu'elle soit, dont l'esprit a conscience. On entend par *subjectif* ce qui appartient au sujet pensant, au moi, et par *objectif* ce qui appartient à l'objet de la pensée, non-moi" (3:775).[2] Rimbaud's poetics of the speaking subject transforms this opposition between subjective and objective into a dialogic relation that we position at once outside and inside the subject.

Rimbaud's celebrated dictum quoted above presents a relationship between its terms *je* and *un autre*. The metaphorical copula posits an equivalent connection, where "*A* is *B*" and "*B* is *A*." *I is an Other* thus suggests that subject (*je*) is object (*autre*) and, conversely, that object is subject. From a Bakhtinian perspective, speech as an interactive construction presupposes an interlocutor and thus is oriented toward his or her answer.[3] According to this dialogic model, *je*, in playing the role of subject, relates to an interlocutor, an Other. Either internal (unconscious mental activity) or external (reader or text), this Other supplants the speaker through its responsive role and makes the subject its object. Such dialogic interaction at once dividing and objectifying the subject opens up literary subjectivity to the alienating structures of language.

Benveniste's linguistics of enunciation advance a unitary first-person voice. He nevertheless assumes the inherently responsive or dialogic notion of voice that we find in Bakhtin to construct subjectivity *through* discursive relations:

> La conscience de soi n'est possible que si elle s'éprouve par contraste. Je n'emploie *je* qu'en m'adressant à quelqu'un, qui sera dans mon allocution un *tu*. C'est cette condition du *dialogue* qui est constitutive de la *personne*, car elle implique en réciprocité que je deviens *tu* dans l'allocution de celui qui à son tour se désigne par *je*. (Benveniste, 1966, 259–60; emphasis added)[4]

Inevitable orientation toward the Other, toward the "non-I," dialogizes the grammatical (*je*) or personal (*moi*) subject. This dialogic play in Benveniste's scheme exposes the textual interplay of the "I" and the non-I in the *Illuminations*.

Rimbaud's subject split on the boundary of self and Other exceeds the dialogue that Bakhtin situates between self and other outside the subject (278). With Julia Kristeva, we extend dialogism to the deep structures of discourse by turning "to the psychic aspect of writing as [a] trace of a dialogue with oneself (with another), as a writer's distance from himself, as a splitting of the writer into subject of enunciation and subject of utterance" (1980, 74). The splitting of a locutor into *sujet de l'énonciation* and *sujet de l'énoncé* implies a dialogue with the Other within the self. We can follow the distinction between the capitalized and the noncapitalized *other* that Kristeva takes from Lacan: the term *other* has the sense of "what exists as an opposite of, or excluded by, something else"; whereas the capitalized *Other* "refers to a hypothetical place or space, that of the pure signifier, rather than to a physical entity or moral category" (1980, 17). Thus, for our purposes here, the *Other* largely intends Lacan's Symbolic order of language, although this term also extends to the Imaginary Other(s) within the self.

Construed, then, in terms of an inner dialogue, Bakhtin's scheme provides a model for the psychogenesis of the speaking subject in the *Illuminations* (see Schwab). We shall also observe textual indices of shifts in these texts from internal (unconscious mental activity) to external dialogue (text, reader) that position the other outside the speaking subject. Thus, while the site of dialogue may alternate in this analysis, I situate the splitting of the subject in the relation of the *sujet de l'énonciation* to the *sujet de l'énoncé* because of the inherent orientation of all discourse toward the other, even when that "Other" is part and parcel of the *sujet*.

Discursive relations are textually marked by pronouns. Implicit first-person narrative involves, first of all, the personal pronoun *nous*; although the narrator speaks as *nous*, *nous* implies *moi et vous* or *moi et vous et eux* and thus can be ascribed to a first-person narrative voice. Second, a *tu/vous* addressee necessarily presumes an "I" speaker. *On* can be read as a third textual guise implying first-person narrative. Whereas *on* suggests an omniscient, unintrusive narrator that we would label impersonal or objective, by virtue of its semantic ambiguity, *on* can also imply *nous* and, by extension, *je/moi*. Deictics represent a fourth manifestation of first-person narrative. A shifter, like *this* or *that*, textually erases a narrator speaking as "I" and yet intimates a narrative presence. For "deictic reference presupposes the existence of a speaker referred to as 'I,' a listener addressed as you, a[n] object indicated as this" (Elam 140).

Taking Benveniste's distinction of subjective versus objective discourse marked by the pronouns *je/tu* and *il*, respectively, as our starting point, we can identify two primary discursive relations in the *Illuminations*.⁵ We find both explicit first-person text, where the narrator speaks as "I," and multiple instances of an implied first-person narrator textually marked by the pronouns *nous*, *tu/vous*, *on*, and deictics. For Benveniste, these narrative stances typify subjective discourse. How does this practice relate to the theory of a modern subject considered at length in the *voyant* letters and in the *Saison*? Is the later Rimbaud finally turning to the objective poetry he proposed to write? Or is his revisionist project turning against, in the conjoining senses of making contact with and moving away from, previous romantic discourse?

The predominant first-person speaker in the *Illuminations* is a dialogic voice positioned on the boundary of subjectivity and objectivity, apart from four texts (*Fairy*, *Fête d'hiver*, *Marine*, and *Royauté*) that maintain a strictly third-person narrative throughout. In the majority of these prose poems from which *je* is textually absent, its narrative presence (*subject*ivity) is nonetheless invoked and inscribed through various discursive relations. Continuous alternation between explicit and implicit first-person narrative in this poetic writing textually configures a complex form of dialogism that both constitutes and appropriates to itself the "I." Either manifest or implied, "I" emerges dialogically, at once as subject and as object. Narrative voice, then, like discourse, is dialogically constructed and co-opted by an other, both inside and outside the word and the speaking subject, respectively.

THE DIALOGIC *JE* IN THE *ILLUMINATIONS*: *PARADE*

The explicit "I" of the *Illuminations* differs from a lyric speaker ascribed to a poet on the basis of autobiographical evidence in the text. As a grammatical subject, *je* is neither readily identified with a personal subject in the context of an individual prose poem nor stable throughout the collected texts.[6] Benveniste would have us assign meaning to each discursive instance of *je*. Such an approach, however, does not account for the heterogeneous narrator who speaks in the *Illuminations*, at once as "I" and as non-I.[7]

Inscriptions of dialogic, or split, subjectivity in the *Illuminations* explicitly narrated by "I" are multiform. In *Parade*, for example, the move from a third- to an explicit first-person narrator occurs at the end, where we observe the only textual instance of *je* in the piece.

> Des drôles très solides. Plusieurs ont exploité vos mondes. Sans besoins, et peu pressés de mettre en oeuvre leurs brillantes facultés et leur expérience de vos consciences. Quels hommes mûrs! Des yeux hébétés à la façon de la nuit d'été, rouges et noirs, tricolores, d'acier piqué d'étoiles d'or; des facies déformés, plombés, blêmis, incendiés; des enrouements folâtres! La démarche cruelle des oripeaux! —Il y a quelques jeunes, —comment regarderaient-ils Chérubin? —pourvus de voix effrayantes et de quelques ressources dangereuses. On les envoie prendre du dos en ville, affublés d'un *luxe* dégoûtant.
>
> Ô le plus violent Paradis de la grimace enragée! Pas de comparaison avec vos Fakirs et les autres bouffonneries scéniques. Dans des costumes improvisés avec le goût du mauvais rêve ils jouent des complaintes, des tragédies de malandrins et de demi-dieux spirituels comme l'histoire ou les religions ne l'ont jamais été. Chinois, Hottentots, bohémiens, niais, hyènes, Molochs, vieilles démences, démons sinistres, ils mêlent les tours populaires, maternels, avec les poses et les tendresses bestiales. Ils interpréteraient des pièces nouvelles et des chansons 'bonnes filles.' Maîtres jongleurs, ils transforment le lieu et les personnes et usent de la comédie magnétique. Les yeux flambent, le sang

chante, les os s'élargissent, les larmes et des filets rouges ruissellent. Leur raillerie ou leur terreur dure une minute, ou des mois entiers.

J'ai seul la clef de cette parade sauvage. (1972, 126)[8]

At first glance, *Parade* presents an objective discourse; the voice narrating the first line, "des drôles très solides," is conspicuously impersonal. Other textual evidence, albeit not immediately apparent, renders the narrative stance subjective.

Multiple instances of a "you/addressee," beginning with the second sentence, "Plusieurs ont exploité vos mondes," assume an "I" speaker as Benveniste has argued. Yet the textual sign of objectivity and attendant change in voice implied by *on* in the eighth sentence of the first paragraph distances the implicit first-person speaker from the narrated scene. How do we read this ambiguous narrative stance, at once subjective and objective? Is the anonymous narrative voice recollecting a performance once observed in an external space, a theater or circus? Or does the text re-present a scene played out on an inner stage? The grammatical subject *je*, which makes a single appearance to conclude the poem in an afterword set apart from the narrated text, offers a key to the voice of the other/Other in *Parade*.

Whereas vivid details indeed suggest a recollection authored by the narrator's subjectivity, the virtually absent speaking subject *je* implies instead an objective discourse, where *un autre est je*. Thus, *des drôles très solides* relates to an inner context or realm discontinuous with readily apprehended external reference. Read emblematically, the textual markers of voice in *Parade* imply in psychological terms the dissociation of the *sujet de l'énoncé* and the *sujet de l'énonciation*. Dissociation in psychiatry signifies the splitting off of certain mental processes from consciousness resulting in varying degrees of autonomy. From this perspective, the "you" addressed by Rimbaud's "I" speaker does not connote *la personne non-je* outside the speaker as Benveniste would argue but rather an inner non-I. *Parade* traces an unconscious scene of the Other within the self.[9] An autonomous creative impulse, postulated in the seer letters, exceeds the control of the poetic subject.

Freely associated streams of images and pronouns in *Parade* strongly suggest an internal kaleidoscopic vision that recombines day residues according to a dream logic.[10] The transposition of this unconscious mental activity into discourse, however, captures only the trace of the imaged scene.[11] In the seer letter to Demeny, Rimbaud makes an analogous claim concerning a creative artist's estrangement from what is envisaged. By seeking inspiration in the realm of the unknown, a poet "sees" unconsciously what would elude a conscious outlook: "Il arrive à l'inconnu, et quand, affolé, il finirait par perdre l'intelligence de ses visions, il les a vues" (1972, 251). Symbolizing a similar split, the perceiving I/eye textually separates itself from the enigmatic scene to which it ostensibly holds the key: "J'ai seul la clef de cette parade sauvage." Who is speaking to whom? Is Rimbaud speaking to his readers? To his text? Or perhaps the text is speaking to the poet-as-willful-creator?

If we were to conflate the implicit and explicit *je* with the poet, then the statement "I alone have the key to this barbarous procession" would address the reader and mock our lack of comprehension. However, we cannot be certain of the narrator's identity or credibility. Rimbaud's poetics of the split subject that I framed above with Lacan indeed questions the identification of the "I" speaker with the one holding narrative authority and, in turn, the semantic key to the text. In *Parade*, textual separation of the "I" from its narrative suggests an affinity for retelling dreams that escape the poet-as-dreamer's full apprehension. In this sense, the scene of the unconscious Other appropriates narrative authority to write the discourse of the self. This speaking unconscious seeks to establish its own credibility with the reader. Such co-optation of narrative authority by the Other, not exclusive to dreams by the way, characterizes for Lacan both the construction of the speaking subject in and through discourse and the alienation of the subject from itself.

In broader Lacanian terms, the *je* subject in *Parade* emblematically re-presents the psychical estrangement at the origins of the speaking subject. Coming to speech irremediably alienates the *sujet* in and through discourse. In other words, language both structures and mediates the subject's desire for the Other within the self. The textual separation of *je* from its narrative in *Parade* underscores that the I/eye holding the key does not coincide with the "I" of its discourse. The Other of the *énoncé*, that is, the act of *énonciation* that produces it, undermines the coincidence of *sujet de l'énoncé* and *sujet de l'énonciation*. Rimbaud's *je* is thus objectified in and through its discourse—the Other, the Symbolic order, that speaks in its place and holds with the self the fullest expression of the modern poetic subject. The equivocal identity of *je* in *Parade* dialogizes narrative authority, at once the poet-as-willful-creator and an autonomous creative impulse.

DIALOGIC VOICE AND FICTIONS OF THE SELF: *AUBE*

Some critics infer a projected autobiography from other first-person narratives of the *Illuminations*, as in *Aube*, *Enfance*, and *Bottom* (e.g., see Steinmetz, 1990, 43–58). I assume instead the ongoing construction of the self in and through discourse and liken these narratives of fictive selves to fictions of the self.[12] My reading of *Aube*, for example, shows the dialogic voice operative in the *Illuminations*. Alternation between first- and third-person narrative discloses the otherness in terms of which "I," construed either as a grammatical or a personal subject, is constituted.

Aube reverses the narrative shift we followed in *Parade*, changing from an apparently personal voice (*je*) to an impersonal one (*il*). Moreover, the site of the other alters from reader to text through the dynamics of this split subjectivity. An initial dialogue between poet-as-speaker and reader-as-interlocutor relates in turn to an inner scene that the text-as-speaker plays out for the poet-as-interlocutor:

> J'ai embrassé l'aube d'été.
>
> Rien ne bougeait encore au front du palais. L'eau était morte. Les camps d'ombres ne quittaient pas la route du bois. J'ai marché, réveillant les haleines vives et tièdes, et les pierreries regardèrent, et les ailes lèverent sans bruit.
>
> La première entreprise fut, dans le sentier déjà empli de frais et blêmes éclats, une fleur qui me dit son nom.
>
> Je ris au wasserfall blond qui s'échevela à travers les sapins: à la cime argentée je reconnus la déesse.
>
> Alors je levai un à un les voiles. Dans l'allée, en agitant les bras. Par la plaine, où je l'ai dénoncée au coq. A la grand'ville elle fuyait parmi les clochers et les dômes, et courant comme un mendiant sur les quais de marbre, je la chassais.
>
> En haut de la route, près d'un bois de lauriers, je l'ai entourée avec ses voiles amassés, et j'ai senti un peu son immense corps. L'aube et l'enfant tombèrent au bas du bois.
>
> Au réveil il était midi. (1972, 140)[13]

A personal speaker, an "I," introduces *Aube*. The reader may initially presume the credibility of this subjective voice to consider what resembles a dream experience. Read emblematically, the title, which signifies an intermediate state between darkness and light, positions the textual scene on the margins of the unconscious and consciousness. Thus framed, the verb *embrasser* implies embracing in the sense of seeing through the mind's eye. Moreover, a progression through time and space ("au front du palais"; "dans l'allée"; "par la plaine"; "à la grand'ville"; "en haut de la route"; "au bas du bois") calls to mind the primary process of displacement that results in incongruous relations. Along with these freely associated elements, textual markers indicate shifts in voice that trace, as in *Parade*, the appropriation of narrative authority by the Other.

Verb tenses, shifting from *histoire* to *discours*, mark the double role that the "I" speaker plays. At once author recounting and participant observing, subject and object, *je* is positioned both outside and inside the dreamlike scene.[14] While serving to identify the poet-as-dreamer (*sujet de l'énonciation*) with the dreaming subject (*sujet de l'énoncé*), this doubling introduces a gap that splits them. The coincidence between subject of narration and subject of utterance presumed by earlier romantics collapses. The "I" subject previously identified with the poet-as-speaker abruptly disappears from the narrated scene close to the text's end.

A third-person speaker, in Benveniste's terms a non-I, interjected in the penultimate line of the text ("L'aube et l'enfant tombèrent au bas du bois") that we identify with the unconscious Other within the self, co-opts the narrative role. The verb "tombèrent" remarks an objective mode of enunciation (Benveniste's *histoire*) that supplants the poet-as-dreamer's subjectivity. Discursive relations construct Rimbaud's poetic subject on the boundary of self and Other. *Aube* thus self-consciously demonstrates the dialogic activity that splits the speaking subject in and through discourse. Moreover, this text questions the relation of the "I" speaker and the narrated dream experience where an Other speaks in *je*'s place and dialogizes voice between the "I" and the non-I.

In the words of another nineteenth-century visionary, Gérard de Nerval, as scenes of the unconscious Other, dreams bear witness to the split self that *Aube* embodies: "Le Rêve est une seconde vie . . . ; un engourdissement nébuleux saisit notre pensée, et nous ne pouvons déterminer l'instant précis où le *moi*, sous une autre forme, continue l'oeuvre de l'existence" (359).[15] In *Aurélia*, Nerval attempted to separate dream discourse, like that of mental alienation in the clinical sense, by excluding the voice of a split self from the language of reason. Rimbaud, to the contrary, assumes this decenteredness as his voice to elaborate a *poésie objective*. Such a stance, however, does not succeed in totally divorcing discourse from the creative artist's subjectivity. Rather, it maintains the subject through the process of objectifying, or dialogizing, it as Kristeva observes,

The subject of narration is drawn in, and therefore reduced to a code, to a nonperson, to an anonymity (as writer, subject of enunciation) mediated by a third person, the he/she character, the subject of utterance. The writer is thus the subject of narration transformed by his having included himself within the narrative system; he is neither nothingness nor anybody, but the possibility of permutation ... from story to discourse and from discourse to story. (1980, 74)[16]

The dialogic voice exemplified in the *Illuminations* simultaneously inscribes subjectivity and objectivity.

In *Parade* and *Aube*, we may examine how discursive relations construct and dialogically appropriate the speaking subject. These texts blur the distinction between *je* and *un autre*. The "I," either implied or explicit, becomes in turn the "you" or the non-I. The role reversal that Benveniste articulates between *je* and *tu* typifies the structuring of narrative voice in *Parade*: "*je* et *tu* sont inversibles: celui que *je* définis par *tu* se pense et peut s'inverser en *je*, et *je* (moi) devient un *tu*" (Benveniste, 1966, 230).[17] In *Aube*, "the one who is absent," that is, a third-(non)person speaker preempts the explicit *je*'s narrative role and thus undermines an unequivocal identification of the *sujet de l'énonciation* and the *sujet de l'énoncé*.

THE SUBJECT OF SELF AND OTHER: *APRÈS LE DÉLUGE*

The second discursive relation in the *Illuminations* identified above involves texts in which *je* as a grammatical subject is textually absent and yet implicitly present in variants of *me*, *tu*, *on*, *nous*, *vous*, and deictics, for example, *this* and *here*. Keeping in mind Rimbaud's aim to write a *poésie objective*, we are again struck by the grammatical reinscription of subjectivity in a seemingly objective discourse. *Après le déluge*, for example, opens as a third-person narrative, unleashing a flood of discontinuous images:

> Aussitôt que l'idée du Déluge se fut rassise,
> Un lièvre s'arrêta dans les sainfoins et les
> clochettes mouvantes et dit sa prière à l'arc-en-ciel
> à travers la toile d'araignée.
>
> Oh! les pierres précieuses qui se cachaient, —
> les fleurs qui regardaient déjà.
>
> Dans la grande rue sale les étals se dressèrent,
> et l'on tira les barques vers la mer étagée là-haut
> comme sur les gravures.

Le sang coula, chez Barbe-Bleue, —aux abattoirs, —dans les cirques, où le sceau de Dieu blêmit les fenêtres.
Le sang et le lait coulèrent.
Les castors bâtirent. Les 'mazagrans' fumèrent dans les estaminets.
Dans la grande maison de vitres encore ruisselante les enfants en deuil regardèrent les merveilleuses images.
Une porte claqua, —et sur la place du hameau, l'enfant tourna ses bras, compris des girouettes et des coqs des clochers de partout, sous l'éclatante giboulée.
Madame*** établit un piano dans les Alpes. La messe et les premières communions se célébrèrent aux cent mille autels de la cathédrale.
Les caravanes partirent. Et le Splendide-Hôtel fut bâti dans le chaos de glaces et de nuit du pôle.
Depuis lors, la Lune entendit les chacals piaulant par les déserts de thym, —et les églogues en sabots grognant dans le verger. Puis, dans la futaie violette, bourgeonnante, Eucharis me dit que c'était le printemps.
—Sourds, étang, —Écume, roule sur le pont et pardessus les bois; —draps noirs et orgues, —éclairs et tonnerre, —montez et roulez; —Eaux et tristesses, montez et relevez les Déluges.
Car depuis qu'ils se sont dissipés, —oh les pierres précieuses s'enfouissant, et les fleurs ouvertes! —c'est un ennui! et la Reine, la Sorcière qui allume sa braise dans le pot de terre, ne voudra jamais *nous* raconter ce qu'elle sait, et que nous ignorons. (Rimbaud, 1972, 121–22; emphasis added)[18]

A subsequent inscription of subjectivity counters the third-person narrator. The lyric interjection *ô*, beginning the second paragraph and recurring as *oh* in the final paragraph of the text, invokes through apostrophe an implicit first-person voice. Just as the identity of this implicit narrative presence remains indeterminate, so the collective textual scene, in turn discontinuous with empirical reference, circumvents *normal* relations of logic. From the critical perspective of Freudian dream-work cast in semiotic terms, we would construct the signifying network in *Après le déluge*. My focus here involves the relational positioning of poetic voice in this text. This dialogism renders the narrator nameless, speaking in and through a multiplicity of voices, at once subjective and objective.[19]

Intervening paragraphs reassume a third-person narrative stance. In a single occurrence, the pronoun *me*, embedded in "Puis, dans la futaie violette, bourgeonnante, Eucharis *me* dit que c'était le printemps," ostensibly interjects a "personal" voice that recasts the narrative in a subjective mode. The narrative credibility of this "I," however, is conspicuously challenged by "Eucharis," a cliché of pastoral literature. Instead of presenting an individual vision, the narrator records a conventional view of a bucolic scene. The objective narrative presence that up to now played the role of a detached observer nevertheless comes to participate as an interlocutor in the scene described.

Moreover, to borrow Benveniste's term, the *je dilaté* (i.e., the *nous*) that closes the narrated text underscores this subjectivity: "Car depuis qu'ils se sont dissipés . . . c'est un ennui! et la Reine, la Sorcière qui allume sa braise dans le pot de terre, ne voudra jamais *nous* raconter ce qu'elle sait, et que *nous* ignorons" (emphasis added). At the same time, the relation between "I" and non-I that constructs *nous* objectifies the implicit *je*.[20] The poet-narrator becomes the interlocutor, that is, becomes the reader of the text. This role reversal dialogically inscribes narrative voice.

Further still, this split subjectivity contrasts with the primacy and *unicité* of *je* upon which Benveniste insists.[21] As Kristeva states, "by the very act of narrating, the subject of narration addresses an other; narration is structured in relation to this other" (1980, 74). How, then, do we identify narrator and interlocutor when the speaker shifts nearly imperceptibly from third to first person? Other textual evidence in *Après le déluge* demonstrates that objective and subjective discursive modes construct narrative voice in dialogic relation.

From the critical perspective of dialogic subjectivity and affinities linking dreams with other imaginative discourses, *Après le déluge* writes the text of the unconscious Other within the self that the poet-as-dreamer reads.[22] The mind's eye/I imagines what escapes the conscious control of the creating subject. The allusion to *la Reine* [*des facultés*] calls to mind Baudelaire's *imagination créatrice*, a nameless, autonomous creative impulse. At the outset of the text, I/poet-as-dreamer plays the role of observer-interlocutor, while the discourse of the Other narrates, speaking in the *je*'s textually marked absence. The "I" attempts to assert its narrative authority at the text's end and yet cannot fully possess the inner scene that escapes its voice: "la Reine, la Sorcière . . . ne voudra jamais nous raconter ce qu'elle sait, et que nous ignorons." This is indeed consonant with Rimbaud's description of the dialogism constituting poiesis (creativity) in the *voyant* letter to Demeny: "Cela m'est évident. J'assiste à l'éclosion de ma pensée: je la regarde, je l'écoute" (1972, 250).[23] Rimbaud's creative artist reads this mental activity by writing its trace as discourse where his or her voice becomes a text.

SUBJECTIVE AND OBJECTIVE NARRATIVE VOICE: *BARBARE*

Poetic vision narrates *Barbare*, in which, as in *Après le déluge*, its dialogic nature is highlighted by the juxtapositioning of subjective and objective modes of discourse:

Bien après les jours et les saisons, et les êtres et les pays,
Le pavillon en viande saignante sur la soie des mers et des fleurs arctiques; (elles n'existent pas.)
Remis des vieilles fanfares d'héroïsme—qui nous attaquent encore le coeur et la tête, —loin des anciens assassins—
Oh! Le pavillon en viande saignante sur la soie des mers et des fleurs arctiques; (elles n'existent pas.)
Douceurs!
Les brasiers, pleuvant aux rafales de givre, —Douceurs! —les feux à la pluie du vent de diamants jetée par le coeur terrestre éternellement carbonisé pour nous. —Ô monde! —
(Loin des vieilles retraites et des vieilles flammes, qu'on entend, qu'on sent,)
Les brasiers et les écumes. La musique, virement des gouffres et choc des glaçons aux astres.
Ô Douceurs, ô monde, ô musique! Et là, les formes, les sueurs, les chevelures et les yeux, flottant. Et les larmes blanches, bouillantes, —ô douceurs! —et la voix féminine arrivée au fond des volcans et des grottes arctiques.
Le pavillon . . . (1972, 144–45)[24]

Barbare lacks the textual indices of a first-person narrator that would syntactically occupy the place of the subject. At first glance, this text presents an objective mode of discourse narrated in the third person. A significant number of exclamations, beginning with the lyric interjection *Oh* in the fourth paragraph, then indicate, as in *Après le Déluge*, a subjective mode of discourse. Through responsive interaction, multiple apostrophes give voice to an autonomous creative impulse.

We can identify the implicit sign of subjectivity (*ô* or *Oh*) with the first-person plural pronoun *nous* in the third paragraph of *Barbare*.[25] This subjective voice, however, does not take the grammatical form of the *nous* subject. Instead, *nous* appears in paragraph three as a direct object and then, at the end of the sixth paragraph, as the object of a preposition. With this responsive position, *nous* demonstrates the interactive orientation at play in the text which alternates between subjective and objective modes of discourse. Thus, the first-person plural pronoun marks a multiplicity of voices speaking in dialogue, at once poet-as-author and poet-as-participant, reader-as-interlocutor and unconscious-mental-activity-as-text. Like *Aube*, *Barbare* self-consciously exhibits its dialogic narrative mode.

To further illustrate this dialogism in *Barbare*, an objective voice is inscribed as the speaking subject through the pronoun *on* (i.e., the "one who is absent"). This third-person speaker intermittently replaces the implied first-person narrator and thus enters into dialogue with the text from which it is set apart or alienated by parentheses. Syntactic and semantic parallels, for example, "loin des anciens assassins" and "(loin des vieilles retraites et des vieilles flammes, qu'on entend, qu'on sent)," echo the dialogic relation of the nonparenthetical and parenthetical texts.[26] Preceding occurrences of *nous* may predispose the reader to comprehend *on* in the final parenthetical phrase in *Barbare* with a first-person cast to it. The ambiguous identity of *on* nevertheless precludes unequivocal identification. Since there is no grammatical object form of *on*, it, along with *nous, les, eux,* and *elles,* can express *on* in an object position. As an indeterminate sign of narrative voice, at once personal (alluding to *je* and, by extension, *nous*) and impersonal (alluding to *non-je*), the pronoun *on* points to the dialogicity of the text. Deictics inscribe an implicit first-person narrative voice, while the parenthetical asides introduce a third-person narrator speaking in response to the text.

This dialogue in *Barbare* once again invites Kristeva's reading of the narrative: "The writer's interlocutor, then, is the writer himself but as reader of another text. The one who writes is the same one as the one who reads. Since his interlocutor is a text, he himself is no more than a text rereading itself as it writes itself" (1980, 86–87). Reading in Kristeva's terms the dialogic *je* in *Barbare,* an anonymous narrative voice writes in the first person while addressing the Other within the self in the third person. This Other co-opts in turn the speaker's role. As in other texts of the *Illuminations* considered above, *je* becomes *un autre* through this interaction, which positions the speaker on the boundary of self and Other. I shall return to *Barbare* to consider more specifically the creative impulse of the Other circulated through signifiers.

Rimbaud's elaboration of a *poésie objective* to overcome earlier romantic subjectivity moves well beyond the nineteenth-century investigation of the self that Littré describes: "Objectiver le subjectif, examiner comme un objet d'étude notre propre moi et chacune de ses impressions ou de ses opérations" (3:775).²⁷ The texts just read exemplify the modern discursive relations of the *Illuminations*. In these prose poems, "I" (as both grammatical and personal subject) interacts with an Other/other, construed as unconscious mental activity, text, or reader. An inner psychical dialogue makes the unconscious Other the constitutive boundary of the self. Shifting grammatical subjects, which alternately co-opt the narrative role, manifest this dialogue at the surface of the text. These signifying relations create the poetic subject in Rimbaud.

The dialogic voice that narrates the *Illuminations* dissolves the identity of *je* both as *sujet de l'énonciation* and *sujet de l'énonce*. This objectification of the subject(ive), through which an Other appropriates to itself the voice of the "I," suggests the mental alienation that plays a role in Rimbaud's poetic discourse, albeit not literally as Benveniste proposes:

> En effet une caractéristique des personnes 'je' et 'tu' est leur unicité spécifique: le 'je' qui énonce, le 'tu' auquel 'je' s'adresse sont chaque fois uniques. Mais 'il' peut être une infinité de sujets—ou aucun. C'est pourquoi *le 'je est un autre' de Rimbaud fournit l'expression typique de ce qui est proprement l'aliénation mentale où le moi est dépossédé de son identité constitutive*. (1966, 230; emphasis added)²⁸

Reading *je est un autre* as a literal sign of mental alienation that marginalizes heterogeneity, as in Nerval, enables Benveniste to safeguard a whole first-person subject. His view obliquely supports skewed readings of Rimbaud as a clinically *mad* poet who mis-read the source of the creative impulse in the *Illuminations*.

What distinguishes the poetic subject in Rimbaud is the heterogeneity that characterizes *il* in Benveniste's scheme ("mais 'il' peut être une

Illuminating the Discourse of the Other

infinité de sujets—ou aucun"). The *autre* of Rimbaud's dictum, read as metaphor for *je*, implies the dialogic functioning that we now understand constitutes the self *as* other. Rather than marginalizing alterity, dialogism opens up poetic voice to the excluded subject, the non-I that also speaks in *je*'s place. Revising the false primacy of the romantic self, Rimbaud as a modern romantic relates the self to the Other: "C'est faux de dire: Je pense. On devrait dire: On me pense" (1972, 249).[29] With the assumption that no one, that is, the one who is absent, speaks (*Un Autre est je*), Rimbaud's poetic discourse posits *énonciation* dialogically between conscious and unconscious, between self and Other.

DIALOGISM AND ONEIRIC WRITING

Reading "the absence of any coherent and durable subjectivity" (Bersani 230–58), "poetics of hallucination" (Wing, 1974, 112–33), "the discourse of schizophrenia" (Todorov, "Complication of Text," 223–37), and "poetics of indeterminacy" (Perloff 3–66) in the *Illuminations* presupposes a heterogeneous speaking subject, the subject that my study envisions, rather, in terms of dialogic subjectivity. As we now understand, Rimbaud situates the poetic subject on the border of subjectivity and objectivity. This positioning, like the split self characteristic of dreams, blurs the distinction between the desiring subject and the desired object, between self and other. Further still, as in dreams, indistinct spatial and temporal boundaries in many of the *Illuminations* superimpose disparate elements of the text instead of relating them. Indeterminate in voice, while disordered in structure, these texts highlight through the use of dashes and parataxis a dreamlike strategy.[30] Discontinuity at the level of the signifier traces the effects of the discourse of the unconscious Other upon the configuration of the speaking subject.

Recurrent dashes typographically inscribe discontinuity throughout the *Illuminations* with various effects. Some dashes introduce a change in interlocutor of indeterminate identity, as in *Parade, Conte, Ville, Veillées I*, and *Being Beauteous*, among others.[31] Read semiotically, these dashes interject through dialogism the voice of the unconscious Other speaking to the subject. Other texts in which dashes indicate an unnamed interlocutor include *Villes I, Vagabonds, H, Vies I, Angoisse, Solde, Jeunesse: Sonnet, Dévotion*, and *Démocratie*. Along with discontinuous narrative voice, other dashes trace disjunction through shifts from real phenomena to unreal ones, for example, in *Nocturne vulgaire, Soir historique, Phrases, Ornières, Mouvement, Promontoire, Fête d'hiver,*

Barbare, and *Fairy*.[32] Moreover, dashes in *Les Ponts, Mystique, Vingt ans*, and *Génie* effect dissolution through erasure, while those in *Départ, A une raison*, and *Barbare* underscore repeated elements.

Similarly, parataxis (placing clauses or phrases one after another without coordinating or subordinating connectives) presents dreamlike construction, for instance, in *Veillées* (parts one and two), *Phrases, A une raison, Après le déluge*, and *Enfance* (parts one, two, and three). Parataxis, like dashes, which superimpose rather than express relations, shows how images pile up in Rimbaud's text, which resists discursivity based on mimetic analogy. This textual strategy of juxtaposition, which characterizes a metonymic mode of discourse at the level of the signifier, exemplifies how the *Illuminations* subvert metaphoric relations, that is, how the *Illuminations* subvert association by resemblance at the level of the signified.[33] Rather than coalescing in the re-presentation of meaning, as in dreams, the metaphoric in Rimbaud resists such closure because of its metonymic grounding at the level of the signifier.

Part three of *Enfance* exemplifies parataxis through anaphoric construction, which sets forth a series of unrelated images that create an unreal landscape.

> Au bois il y a un oiseau, son chant vous arrête et vous fait rougir.
> Il y a une horloge qui ne sonne pas.
> Il y a une fondrière avec un nid de bêtes blanches.
> Il y a une cathédrale qui descend et un lac qui monte.
> Il y a une petite voiture abandonnée dans le taillis, ou qui descend le sentier en courant, enrubannée.
> Il y a une troupe de petits comédiens en costumes, aperçus sur la route à travers la lisière du bois.
> Il y a enfin, quand l'on a faim et soif quelqu'un qui vous chasse. (1972, 123)[34]

Although we can make "sense" of the individual elements, their purported "sequence" seems nonsensical and nondiscursive; the poem displays no readily apprehended relations based on resemblance or contiguity. We find other hallucinatory scenes (for example, in *Veillées, Nocturne vulgaire*, and *Soir historique*) that contradict the associative, mimetic function traditionally ascribed to metaphor at the level of both the statement and the text as a whole and block the referential function served by quotidian language. Are we to read these dreamlike texts, which often present the unreal as the real, as transcriptions of dreams (that Rimbaud perhaps had)? What role do dreams play in the *Illuminations*?

Todorov states that "le rêve n'est plus pour Rimbaud, comme il l'était pour Baudelaire par exemple, un élément thématique, mais plutôt un opérateur de lecture, une indication sur la manière dont on doit interpréter le texte qu'on a sous les yeux" (1978, 209).[35] Perhaps the eight occurrences of the word *rêve* (dream) in the *Illuminations* indeed serve to remind us not to read the surface incoherence of these texts with reference to external reality.[36] In an interiorized world such as that of dreams, the logic of rational order is abandoned. Dreamwork associates elements through primary process ideation, which "prevents cognition or re-cognition as much as it enables it" (Chase 214).

Just as dreamwork enables novel associations (i.e., cognition), so too dreamwork prevents our re-cognition by not relating elements as the logical brain does. Rimbaud's *metaphora*, the impulse of which is poietic (creative), becomes a way of knowing that illuminates without fully revealing the unknown. This metaphoric mode grounded in metonymy, where heterogeneous elements coexist without apparent connection, eludes discursive logic and analogical structure while allowing us to see the dissimilar in a new light. Claudel, as later discussion will show, turns to an opposing, mimetic view of cognition grounded in metaphor as analogy. His *co-naissance* (knowledge) relates the known and the unknown and thus anchors meaning to the orienting function of a transcendent order.

Taking the narrow stance that indeterminate associations in the *Illuminations* prevent interpretation, Todorov asserts that "vouloir découvrir ce qu'ils veulent dire, c'est les dépouiller de leur message essentiel, qui est précisément l'affirmation d'une impossibilité d'identifier le référent et de comprendre le sens, qui est manière et non matière" (1978, 220).[37] Since these texts literally block our access to their meaning, Todorov hastily concludes that "Rimbaud a découvert le langage dans son (dis)fonctionnement autonome, libéré de ses obligations expressive et représentative, où l'initiative est réellement cédée aux mots; il a . . . à la suite de [Friedrich] Hölderlin légué le discours schizophrénique comme modèle à la poésie du XXe siècle" (220).[38]

Todorov's comment that, in the later Rimbaud, "the initiative has been given to the words themselves" unwittingly suggests in fact how primary process structuring enables re-cognition in the *Illuminations*, notably at the level of the signifier alone. Dream discourse provides a semiotic model rather than a semantic one for many of these texts that disclose an autonomous creative impulse, which I have been treating as poiesis. A semiotic approach to Rimbaud's poetic discourse that resists metaphor per se brings to the fore the metonymic derivation of *metaphora* at play in the production of signs at the level of the signifier.[39]

The associative work of dream interpretation in Freud bears upon my semiotic treatment of poetic writing in Rimbaud. Reading the text of dreams maps out metonymic pathways that produce an effect of meaning. Recall that Rimbaud's creative artist, like a dreaming subject, participates as a spectator and as an interlocutor in an inner dialogue where thoughts interact (Rimbaud, 1972, 252). As a model for creative mental activity, "la pensée accrochant la pensée et tirant" implies association along a syntagmatic axis. This mode operates by contiguity, as dream construction does, selecting and combining significant day residues with memory representations into associative networks or signifying chains.[40] The imaginative writing of the *Illuminations* that corresponds neither to external reference nor to consistent psychological themes operates through signifiers, where metaphoric and metonymic modes interpenetrate.[41] Morever, this work of *metaphora*, like the interplay of condensation and displacement in the Freudian dreamwork, produces meaning through the poietic play of signifiers.[42] This creative strategy of dream construction informs the Other scene in *Bottom*.

ILLUMINATING THE DREAMWORK OF *METAPHORA* IN *BOTTOM*

Dreamlike writing that goes beyond metaphoric association by resemblance at the level of the signified traces the scene of the Other in *Bottom*. Shakespeare's character Bottom, often cited as an intertextual source for Rimbaud's text, poetically relates a dreamer's estrangement from the scene of the unconscious Other in which he or she unwittingly participates.[43] As dreamers, we observe ourselves in scenes staged in an inner psychical theater that we cannot fully recognize upon waking. Just as a dreaming subject is estranged from the psychical scene that he or she unconsciously desires, so too the self is constructed in relation to its otherness. Thus, either dreaming or speaking (especially in trying to speak the dream), the subject is alienated from desired identity in and through discourse. For discourse writes the self in terms of signifying relations that reveal the dialogic relation between the unconscious subject of identifications and the speaking subject. As Ellie Ragland-Sullivan rightly states, "the *moi reveals* itself in the present speaking through *je* by which it is not recognized" (46). Although Rimbaud erased the text's original title, *Métamorphoses*, its trace remains operative in *Bottom*. In this theater of the self, an unconscious play of signifying chains structured like dreamwork dialogically configures the desiring subject as the object of its desire.

Bottom calls to mind a dream text—not because we assume that Rimbaud transcribes an *actual* dream in the poem but because its writing follows closely the primary processes of dreamwork, displacement and condensation.[44] To read texts like *Bottom*, which exhibit affinities with Freudian dream construction, we may discern the metonymic network(s) of their writing without fully disclosing their meaning. As Freud argues, even if a reading seems satisfactory and without gaps, "the possibility always remains that the dream may have yet another meaning. Strictly speaking, then, it is impossible to determine the amount of condensation" (4:279). Dream interpretation thus comprises creative mental activity. To "interpret" dreams, like nondiscursive texts, we follow the signifying traces of dreamwork. These ever-emergent networks of associations by resemblance and contiguity overlap at the level of the signifier. Poietic selection and combination of disparate elements brings about an effect of meaning.

DREAMING THE SUBJECT, CREATING THE SELF

Bottom presents a series of incongruous transformations. Association by presupposed resemblance no longer obtains in this dreamlike writing.

> La réalité étant trop épineuse pour mon grand
> caractère, —je me trouvai néanmoins chez Madame, en gros
> oiseau gris bleu s'essorant vers les moulures du plafond et
> traînant l'aile dans les ombres de la soirée.
>   Je fus, au pied du baldaquin supportant ses bijoux
> adorés et ses chefs-d'oeuvre physiques, un gros ours aux
> gencives violettes et au poil chenu de chagrin, les yeux aux
> cristaux et aux argents des consoles.
>   Tout se fit ombre et aquarium ardent.
>   Au matin, —aube de juin batailleuse, —je courus
> aux champs, âne, claironnant et brandissant mon grief,
> jusqu'à ce que les Sabines de la banlieue vinrent se jeter à
> mon poitrail. (1972, 151)[45]

The introductory locution ("La réalité étant trop épineuse pour mon grand caractère") expresses a state of anxiety giving rise to a desire or wish to escape from reality. The textual dash thus marks the space of transformation from a conscious outlook to a fantasizing or dreaming subject's unconsciousness. A dreamlike scene ensues, staged by both an indeterminate person and place ("—je me trouvai néanmoins chez Madame") and a speaking subject's transformation from "en gros oiseau gris bleu" into "un gros ours," and then into an "âne."

An autonomous agency appropriates to itself the expression of the subject's desire. The conjunction *néanmoins* implies at once a lack of self-control and a compulsion to repeat, which from a psychoanalytic perspective signal the discourse of the unconscious Other within the self. Jan Kott, with a similar emphasis, rephrases the underlying voice of desire in the line "Love looks not with the eyes, but with the mind" (*A Midsummer Night's Dream* 1.1.234) to read "Does desire also look with 'the mind' and not with 'the eyes'?" (9). This discourse of desire operates its effects through the interplay of signifiers in Rimbaud's *Bottom*.

Different from the single transformation of Bottom into an ass in Shakespeare's play, in Rimbaud's text, there are multiple metamorphoses (bird-bear-*fish?*-ass).[46] Moreover, these changes occur in circumscribed yet indefinite places ("chez Madame"; "vers les moulures du plafond"; "au pied du baldaquin"; "Tout se fit . . . aquarium ardent"; "aux champs"). The person to whom *Madame* refers, and consequently the place *chez Madame*, is ambiguous. Does *Madame* refer to a particular mistress, Rimbaud's mother, or any female?[47] This indeterminacy blocks representation of an external referent. Successive actions ("je me trouvai"; "je fus"; "Tout se fit"; "je courus") during a specified and apparently progressive time ("de la soirée"; "au matin, —aube de juin batailleuse") nonetheless present a narrative; yet the surface sequence of this narrative does not cohere semantically. As in dreams, relations of the narrating subject *je* to *Madame* and to various identifications with bird, bear, and ass are not made explicit. Read from a conscious outlook, moreover, these dream relations do not make sense.

Critics have made much ado about the intertextual connection that links the final metamorphosis of the speaking subject into an ass in *Bottom* to *A Midsummer Night's Dream*.[48] Although this common thread may peripherally tie together Rimbaud's text and Shakespeare's play, this ostensible intertextual source does not elucidate intervening transformations of the speaking subject into a bird, bear, and fish. A more likely case can be made for this intertextual echo in terms of the displaced site of desire that Bottom's transformation into an ass embodies. With the body of a man and an ass's head, Shakespeare's Bottom can be seen to represent the discourse of the split self, where desire for and of the Other plays the primary role. Connected to the unconscious Other that Bottom's transformation brings to the fore, this intertextual key does open the veiled signifying chains of Rimbaud's text. Imaginative (poietic) writing in *Bottom* demonstrates an affinity with dream discourse that resists the transfer of presupposed meaning, as in classical metaphor, and produces instead an effect of meaning at the level of the signifier. Why not take Rimbaud at his word, insisting in another context that "ça veut dire littéralement et dans tous les sens"?[49] Let us then read this *unconscious* agency of the letter in *Bottom*.

THE SCENE OF THE OTHER IN *BOTTOM*

The English title of the poem, read literally, signifies the lowest or deepest part of anything, as distinguished from the top. In this sense, *Bottom* directs us to the bottom of the page to the signifier *âne*, which appears only once, close to the text's end. Colloquial language would support an anatomical meaning (bottom = *âne* = ass). Context suggests instead a zoological association and, by extension, a character type. In another sense, the signifying chain linking *Bottom* to *âne* draws our attention to both the textual surface and a covert interplay of signifiers that the title, which also connotes "the underside of something," invites us to read *dans tous les sens*. Various signifying chains operate within the metonymic network of *Bottom*, which, like dreamwork, overdetermines the elements at its surface.

The locution "la réalité étant trop épineuse pour mon grand caractère" qualifies reality as *épineuse*, an adjective used in literal reference to a thorny plant and, in figurative connotations, to signify a touchy, prickly character. In expressing the desire to flee from reality, the subject unwittingly discloses what he or she finds unbearable, notably his or her *self*. The odd attribution "la réalité . . . épineuse" thus displaces the underside of a lofty character that is, at bottom, very touchy. Extreme sensitivity, moreover, renders this character a thorn in one's side or, in both English and French slang, in one's *âne*. Projecting through displacement oneself elsewhere expresses a desire for transformation. Flight from reality in the sense of a current situation masks a flight from oneself, that is, a desire to become an Other. Yet the transformation of the speaking subject "en gros oiseau gris bleu," which implies the desire to escape from a confining space, whether inside or outside the self, has an inverse effect on the subject's desire.

Constricted space ("s'essorant vers les moulures du plafond") bears down upon the subject's wings ("traînant l'aile dans les ombres de la soirée"). A metonymic spatial move from the top to the bottom underscores the shift in identification from bird to bear: "Je fus, au pied du baldaquin . . . un gros ours." A psychoanalytic approach discloses the unconscious economy of *Bottom* by reading between the lines the related expression *se traîner aux pieds de quelqu'un*. This occluded signifying chain advances the transforming play of signifiers from bird "traînant l'aile" into bear "au pied du baldaquin," where metaphoric and metonymic modes overlap.

Ensuing associations motivated by the subject's desire weave the top (surface) of the text into its underside. The desiring subject grovels at the feet (bed) of the object of its desire, "au pied du baldaquin supportant ses bijoux adorés et ses chefs-d'oeuvre physiques." Read literally, the signifiers *bijoux* and *chefs-d'oeuvre physiques* intend *les bijoux d'une femme*, that is, of (perhaps) the elusive Madame. Yet in other senses, they evoke the physical sight/site, both the vision and the locus, of female sexuality. The purple gums and hoary fur of the bear ("un gros ours aux gencives violettes et au poil chenu") overdetermine through displacement the labia and hair of female genitalia, respectively.[50] The desired female object at once prevents and enables the subject's desire.

Prickly reality displaced from self to Other at the outset of the text now illuminates striking condensations. Attributes of the desiring subject and the desired object overlap both explicit and implicit identifications with "ours." "Madame," the inaccessible desired object who rejects the desiring subject, evokes an occluded signifying chain, "elle est un peu ours" ("she is a bit of a bear"). This expression, which connotes a misanthrope, recalls the narrating, desiring subject's wish to flee from an unbearable reality at the outset of the text. With the English title, we can entertain a bilingual pun; along with signifying *bear*, the French "ours" becomes a play on the possessive adjective *ours*. In short, the desiring subject projects its prickly character onto the desired female object. Although desired, the female object is unbearable because she refuses the subject's desire for her and remains out of the subject's reach. Her resistance puts into play and thus stimulates the subject's desire. Just as the dream does not think but rather desires, so too this text forms the desiring self in and through the desire of the Other. Desire *of* the subject thus becomes desire *for* the object.

The "ours aux gencives violettes et au poil chenu de chagrin" also produces traits of both the desiring subject and the desired object. Embedded in the purple (*violette*) of the feminine gums, at once the subject and object of desire, is the masculine *violet* which masks the otherwise unreadable *violer* (to rape). Chagrin ("au poil chenu de chagrin") implies rejected amorous advances, which is to say the lack of the desired object, and therefore deflates the violent thrust of the desiring subject ("aux gencives violettes"). "Au poil chenu de chagrin" exemplifies at the level of the signifier the metonymic-metaphoric mode or comparison by superimposition that characterizes many images in the *Illuminations*.[51]

Two signifying chains interact here. Displaced and condensed in "au poil chenu de chagrin," we read, in one sense, the desiring subject evoked by hoary fur. In another sense, combined, "gencives violettes et au poil chenu de chagrin" metonymically designate female genitalia and allude to the desired object. This unreal image again underscores the dreamlike writing of *Bottom* and, moreover, the dialogicity of the text. The gaze of the desiring subject ("les yeux aux cristaux et aux argents des consoles") images the desired object and again draws the reader's attention to the writing of the text.

Are these eyes made of jewels as Wallace Fowlie's translation, "my eyes of crystal and silver from the consoles," proposes (Rimbaud, 1966, 277)? Or are these eyes filled with the sight of jewels as suggested by Louise Varèse's terms, "eyes on the silver and crystal of the consoles" (Rimbaud, 1946, 133)? When read in the latter manner, "consoles" repeats the "baldaquin" supporting her jewels, that is, "her adored gems and her physical masterpieces." Moreover, a link with an obscured signifying chain, *consoler le chagrin*, overdetermines this association. The desired object, in sight yet out of reach, no doubt chagrins the subject by thwarting its desire. Not only do tears console, but their cathartic power also transforms chagrin altogether. The subject's "grief" becomes the desired object.

DESIRING SUBJECT, DESIRED OBJECT

The most incongruous image of *Bottom* ensues: "Tout se fit ombre et aquarium ardent." An earlier locution, "les ombres de la soirée," exteriorized a pervasive darkness. Here, however, obscurity is confined to an unusual aquarium, an ardent or burning aquarium. Recall from Freud that dreams, where opposites coexist, produce connections by simultaneity. What relation, then, links shadow and light curiously contained in the space of this aquarium customarily designed to hold water that is highly mutable and mobile?

At first glance, such incongruity chagrins the reader, though through the dreaming mind's eye we see differently. We could trace the signifier "aquarium ardent" to what Rimbaud might have seen or read.[52] Emptied, however, of this previous signifying content in the context of the zoological network (bird-bear-*fish*-ass) cast in *Bottom*, "aquarium ardent" gains a new significance. As in dreams, day residues and permanent memory become the material of creative mental activity. Rimbaud alludes to this pre-text in part four of *Jeunesse:* "Ta mémoire et tes sens ne seront que la nourriture de ton impulsion créatrice" (Rimbaud, 1972, 148).[53]

The subject's desire, "aquarium ardent," submerged and immobilized by overwhelming chagrin, nonetheless moves toward its subsequent transformation. For chagrin, released through tears, veils only temporarily the intense heat of passion. A symbolic site of passage from night ("tout se fit ombre") to day ("Au matin, —aube de juin batailleuse") metamorphoses something into its opposite. The desiring subject becomes the desired object: "Au matin . . . —je courus aux champs, âne, claironnant et brandissant mon grief, jusqu'à ce que les Sabines de la banlieue vinrent se jeter à mon poitrail." Released from constricting spaces associated with repressed desire and rising to a call to arms, masculine virility becomes at once the desired object and so the object of the subject's desire.

In the body of the text, a feminine subject, "les Sabines," appears to ravage the masculine "âne," the "poitrail" of which repeats the "poil chenu de chagrin" ascribed both to the desiring subject and to the desired object. These reversed roles displace the legendary rape of the Sabine women to stage the scene of the Other, where the subject fulfills his or her desire only by becoming its object. The signifying chains of dreamwork in *Bottom* demonstrate the role that desire and identification play in the ongoing formation of the subject's identity in and through its discourse.[54]

POIESIS AND DREAMWORK: *BARBARE*

The pathways of Rimbaud's imaginative writing in *Barbare* also reveal a structuring similar to that of dreams. Day residues and permanent memories become the signifying elements of associative metaphoric-metonymic networks along the syntagm. Unlike, however, the narrative structure in *Bottom* comprised of a series of metamorphoses, in *Barbare*, the absence of conjugated verbs disorients the reader. I examined earlier in this chapter the dialogic construction of the poetic subject in *Barbare* that calls to mind the mental alienation of the dreaming subject. A syntactic sense of dissociation renders the textual surface all the more dreamlike, that is, incoherent and puzzling. The discontinuous scene of this text embodies the amorphous energy of unconscious mental activity that gives rise to form through the impulse to create. *Barbare*, symbolically read as the Other, produces a sense of estrangement that suggests the voice of the unconscious speaking to the poetic subject:

> Bien après les jours et les saisons, et les êtres et les pays,
> Le pavillon en viande saignante sur la soie des mers et des fleurs arctiques; (elles n'existent pas.)
> Remis des vieilles fanfares d'héroïsme—qui nous attaquent encore le coeur et la tête, —loin des anciens assassins—
> Oh! Le pavillon en viande saignante sur la soie des mers et des fleurs arctiques; (elles n'existent pas.)
> Douceurs!
> Les brasiers, pleuvant aux rafales de givre, —Douceurs! —les feux à la pluie du vent de diamants jetée par le coeur terrestre éternellement carbonisé pour nous. —Ô monde! —
> (Loin des vieilles retraites et des vieilles flammes, qu'on entend, qu'on sent,)
> Les brasiers et les écumes. La musique, virement des gouffres et choc des glaçons aux astres.
> Ô Douceurs, ô monde, ô musique! Et là, les formes, les sueurs, les chevelures et les yeux, flottant. Et les larmes blanches, bouillantes, —ô douceurs! —et la voix féminine arrivée au fond des volcans et des grottes arctiques.
> Le pavillon . . . (1972, 144–45)

The title—*Barbare*—condenses the signifiers barbarian (*manque de civilisation*), barbaric (*cruel*), and foreign (*étrangère*) (Littré 1:294). In the broader context of the creative process discussed in the seer letters, where poetic discourse interweaves *forme* with *informe*, in the first sense of *barbare* (or primitive), we also understand the aesthetically formless. Following this signifying chain, the locution "Bien après les jours et les saisons, et les êtres et les pays" evokes a primal scene estranged from customary associations of time, human existence, and space. The real, marginalized on the border of the unreal, suggests the interpenetration of form and the unformed. The flag/banner on the sea presents a recognizable metonymy, flag for ship, whereas the attribution "en viande saignante" sets forth an unreal image informed by varying hidden associations.

The literal designation of a flag displaying "raw or red meat" gives rise to barbaric impulses, at once cruel, in the sense of violence, and primitive or irrational. Along with political connotations of bloody revolution (*drapeau de sang*), an erotic fantasy overdetermined by the occluded signifier *oriflamme* and the locution *montrer sa viande* (bare one's flesh) informs "Le pavillon en viande saignante." Viril force appears to triumph "over the silk of the seas," appropriating to itself the reproductive energy that "mers," by homophonic association with *mères* (mothers), embodies.[55] In yet another sense, *le pavillon*, meaning tent, and, by extension, a hyperbolic form of the womb, unwittingly projects onto procreation the impulse to create.

A hidden signifying chain links "le pavillon en viande saignante" to the triumph of the creative impulse. "Pavillon" as the sky ("Ciel, pavillon de l'homme" [Littré 3:1018]), read in conjunction with the attribution "en viande saignante" as a blood-red sunrise, draws textual attention to its grounding in poiesis.[56] Laid bare against the formlessness and inexhaustible profundity of the sea, which evokes "the abyss out of which forms arise to unfold their potentialities within existence" (Cirlot 242), "le pavillon . . . " becomes a sign of novel emergence. Moreover, the ceaseless movement of the sea—together with the interminable repetition of "le pavillon . . . "—suggests an unbounded energy. We read here the chaotic impulse informing creative insight that subverts customary associations and gives rise to what has yet to exist in external reality, that is, "des fleurs arctiques (elles n'existent pas)."[57]

Barbare casts forth a hallucinatory poietic "sequence" by recovering vague, fleeting memories of things seen or perhaps read by a creating subject: "Remis des vieilles fanfares d'héroïsme—qui nous attaquent encore le coeur et la tête, —loin des anciens assassins—." The apostrophe "Oh!" preceding the ensuing repetition of "Le pavillon" voices through its address a boundless impetus reinscribed in "Douceurs!," which recalls in turn the unspeakable pleasures embedded in the forever-undulating "mers." An ecstatic energy, literally without stasis in the etymological sense "to put out of place," brings about uncanny associations ("Les brasiers, pleuvant aux rafales de givre"), which elude the conscious control of the implicit creating subject. A connected, yet occluded, signifying chain, *son coeur/ sa tête est un brasier* (Littré 4:410), indeed connotes an impassioned, inspired state of creativity.

The ecstatic space of combustible chaos sparks the hallucinatory fusion of diametrically opposed elements of fire and water and of heat and cold. Condensed in "givre," we read *fleurs de givre*, which repeats the arctic flowers that do not exist. Through the poetic imagination, however, one sees what would not exist if one remained limited by a conscious outlook. The irrational mode of the creative impulse displaced in "Douceurs" again extends through the fusion of disparate elements its ecstatic energy. "Les brasiers pleuvant aux rafales de givre" overdetermine the ensuing series of signifiers ("brasiers"/"feux"; "à la pluie"/"pleuvant"; "aux rafles"/"du vent"; "de givre"/"de diamants").

Moreover, a dreamlike strategy syntactically dislocates and gives the customary signifying chain *ce diamant jette mille feux* a new form: "les feux à la pluie du vent de diamants jetée par le coeur terrestre éternellement carbonisé pour nous." Dreamwork also enables us to trace the displacement of the vital force of "le pavillon en viande saignante," from which the light of a new day emerges only to disappear back into the depths of the night, and "brasiers" ("feu de charbons ardents" [Littré 1:410]), in "le coeur terrestre éternellement carbonisé pour nous." My work of interpretation proceeds along semiotic lines to follow the circuitous signifying path of *Barbare*.

The next exclamatory apostrophe, "Ô monde!," like a deictic, draws our attention to the spatio-temporal site of enunciation underscored by an implicit first-person narrative voice. The space or world voiced in and through the creative impulse breaks with the real while recalling real forms to configure the formless. A parenthetical aside ostensibly in third-person voice, which implies the estrangement of the creating subject from his or her discourse, observes the autonomous influx of material from distant memory, at once familiar and foreign: "—Ô monde! — / (Loin des vieilles retraites et des vieilles flammes, qu'on entend, qu'on sent)."

Preceding signifying chains condensed in "les brasiers" and "les écumes" implicitly recirculate "Le pavillon en viande saignante sur la soie des mers." This condensation transposes the formed, yet unreal, banner of red meat against the silk of the seas into formlessness. "Brasiers" evokes the transforming energy of fire, "écumes" that of water. "Brasiers" also exhibits the text's underlying creative impulse (*sa tête est un brasier*), which, like dreamwork, traces mobile and evanescent insights while covering connections between them.[58] This dialectic of presence and absence perpetually re-covers, in the opposing and coexistent senses of retrieving and hiding, what it discovers.

Shifting forms frame obscure gaps. These abysses simulate the dynamic rhythm of divergence and convergence from which novel configurations emerge: "La musique, virement des gouffres et choc des glaçons aux astres." Infinite depth and height converge and collide only to diverge once again and explode in ecstacy. The surface of *Barbare* exhibits this perpetual movement, which prevents stasis, from "Ô Douceurs" to "ô monde" then to "ô musique." This textually repeated succession of both abstract and concrete entities re-presents their juxtaposition without, however, making explicit what binds them, apart from the *ô* that announces the emergence of each element. Form and formlessness flow unbounded in this mobile space, where signifying pathways of the writing overlap through repetition: "Et là, les formes, les sueurs, les chevelures, et les yeux, flottant. Et les larmes blanches, bouillantes, —ô douceurs! —."

Read in conjunction with "le pavillon en viande saignante sur la soie des mers," this series of images—"sueurs," "chevelures," "yeux," "larmes blanches," "bouillantes," "douceurs"—reinscribes, on the one hand, an erotic fantasy that culminates in white tearlike drops of passion. While releasing an ardent union, this liquid dissolution implies, on the other hand, a return to a primitive, chaotic state, from which remerges a persistent feminine presence or voice. Overdetermined by the play of signifiers ("chevelures," "larmes," "douceurs"), "la voix féminine arrivée au fond des volcans et des grottes arctiques" recovers the creative impulse of the text, writing again its beginning, "Le pavillon . . . "

"Au fond des volcans," the site of combustible, ecstatic passion and, by extension, inspiration, re-presents through the work of condensation the previous signifying chain beginning with "Les brasiers . . . —les feux à la pluie . . . jetée par le coeur terrestre éternellement carbonisé pour nous." In one sense, "des grottes arctiques" call forth other depths of the formless seas. In metonymic-metaphoric conjunction with the term *écumes* and the concealed signifier *mers*, the feminine voice coming from these depths recalls the myth of Aphrodite giving rise to emergent form (Davies 38). In another sense, however, the qualifier *arctiques* recalls the arctic flowers that do not exist. "La voix féminine arrivée au fond . . . des grottes arctiques," exceeding a conscious outlook, signifies the primitive site/sight of the creative impulse that recovers the path to poetic insight and voice.

Detailed staging of the scene of the unconscious Other in *Bottom* outlines, through an analysis of the dreamlike strategy in the poem, a plausible narrative scheme. The more fragmentary material of *Barbare* does not appear to yield such a reading. Although one may comprehend individual elements in this text, whether intra- or intertexually, they do not cohere in a sequence. The metaphoric-metonymic interplay of these signifying elements suggests dream formation, which serves as a paradigm for creation in my reading of the *Illuminations*. Moreover, the parenthetical asides coincide with the secondary revision that functions in the Freudian dreamwork to "fill up the gaps in the dream-structure" according to considerations of representability (5:490). In *Barbare*, such editing only partly succeeds, for the dominant mode of this writing imitates primary process ideation. *Barbare* lays bare the creative process that, like dreams, voices the impulse of the unconscious Other within the self, the modern poetic subject of Rimbaud's *voyance*.

REVISING *LE MYTHE DE RIMBAUD*

In Claudel's preface to Rimbaud's complete works (Rimbaud, 1947), he names Rimbaud "un mystique à l'état sauvage." According to Claudel's map of (mis-reading) Rimbaud, a spiritual quest for unity of self and world in *Une saison en enfer* reveals the *supernatural* voiced in the *Illuminations*. These religious terms revise the psychical ascesis that for me illuminates the discourse of the unconscious Other in Rimbaud. I have restaged Rimbaud's *voyance* as an exploration and expression of the creative impulse of the unconscious mind, whereas Claudel hears in Rimbaud the voice of God and an attendant poetic revelation of the supernatural. Subsequent discussion will show that Claudel misidentifies the autonomous, immanent impulse of unconscious mental activity at play in the later Rimbaud with his own return to a divine transcendent source that empowers a mystic's vision.

The surrealists viewed Rimbaud as a seer whose vision sprang from an unconscious realm of mental activity and vehemently rejected Claudel's Catholic reading of his *voyance*.[59] In one instance, Breton, who otherwise heralded Rimbaud as the "father of surrealism" (Bays, "Rimbaud," 46), denounced him for having *allowed* Claudel to usurp him for the Catholic renaissance:

> Inutile de discuter encore sur Rimbaud: Rimbaud s'est trompé. Rimbaud a voulu nous tromper. Il est coupable devant nous, d'avoir permis, de ne pas avoir rendu tout à fait impossibles certaines interprétations déshonorantes de sa pensée, genre Claudel. (Breton, 1963, 80)[60]

A group that organized itself on the edges of the original surrealist movement and collaborated in the publication of *Le Grand Jeu* also rejected Claudel's myth of Rimbaud:

> Le catholicisme est un compromis de mauvais goût. Nous ne nous attarderons pas à réfuter la thèse imbécile de M. Paul Claudel, ambassadeur de France. Rimbaud n'a pas discuté avec Verlaine, quand celui-ci lui chanta des psaumes à Stuttgart: il l'a abattu d'un coup de poing. (Printemps 2:24)[61]

Here the term *mystic* with reference to Rimbaud recalls the Gnostics, who claimed the existence of a *surnature* or *surréalité*, not to be confused with the transcendent God in Claudel's scheme.[62]

The following account of the ego-self of Rimbaud's creative artist supplanted, not from above but rather from below, uses terms different from the individual unconscious upon which my analysis is based.[63] Nonetheless, Friedrich captures the fundamental divergence of Claudel's *mythe de Rimbaud* from that of the surrealists, whose indebtedness to Rimbaud has a more plausible literary basis.

> The proper subject is not the empirical "I," the self. Other powers supplant it, powers from below and of a prepersonal nature, but whose authority is compelling. They alone constitute the suitable organ for viewing the "unknown." In such lines, one can sense the mystic schema: the sacrifice of the self, the ego overpowered by divine inspiration. But now this overpowering comes from below. The ego sinks downward, deprived of its powers by collective strata in the subconscious (*l'âme universelle*). This is the threshold of modern poetry which no longer takes experiences from a worn-out world of matter, but from the chaos of the unconscious. It is understandable that the twentieth-century surrealists claimed Rimbaud as one of their ancestors. (42)

Claudel's mystical lyricism, based on an opposing theory of the divinely inspired subject, contrasts sharply with Rimbaud's fragmented subject. For Claudel, metaphor as analogy recenters the relation of self and world in God's image. Coming to poetic writing in the shadow of Rimbaud, Claudel illuminates the turning of his own creative impulse to divine inspiration.

FIVE

Revising the Poetic Subject, Repeating the Creative Word

> L'objet de la poésie, ce n'est donc pas, comme on le dit souvent, les rêves, les illusions ou les idées. C'est cette sainte réalité, donnée une fois pour toutes, au centre de laquelle nous sommes placés. C'est l'univers des choses invisibles.... Tout cela est l'oeuvre de Dieu, qui fait la matière inépuisable des récits et des chants du plus grand poète comme du plus pauvre petit oiseau ... il y a une *poesis perennis* qui n'invente pas ses thèmes, mais qui reprend éternellement ceux que la Création lui fournit.... L'idée d'un infini matériel ... c'est-à-dire d'un Fini sans bornes, comme elle est un scandale pour la raison, est un désastre pour l'imagination qui se voit contrariée dans son ressort essentiel, c'est-à-dire ce pouvoir d'ordre, de mesure, et de disposition que Dieu a mis en elle à l'imitation de son Verbe créateur.[1]
> —Paul Claudel, "Introduction à un poème sur Dante"

Through a revisionist turning away from his skepticism prior to 1886 back to an orthodox Catholic worldview, Paul Claudel uniquely pairs poetry in the etymological sense of poiesis and religion to elaborate a mystical lyricism. His project, outlined in the epigraph, assumes a theological conception of creativity in which an authentic, coherent subject authors his or her works like God, the Father Creator. Claudel's poetic subject diametrically opposes the split subjectivity upon which we saw Rimbaud insist. It is not the voice of the unconscious that speaks to Claudel. Rather, the poet-as-mystic repeats the creative Divine Word and thus relates self and world to God through the play of his or her analogical imagination.

Classical theological language, grounded in analogy, provides a model for the totalizing power of Claudelian mystical lyricism. His poetic writing, like all properly analogical languages, aims to produce "some order, at the limit, some harmony to the several analogues, the similarities-in-difference, constituting the whole of reality" (Tracy 408). Claudel writes *against* the Rimbaldian subject divided in and through discourse to connect self and world to a divine center. Misreading *je est un autre*, Claudel situates the creative impulse outside the self to practice a mystical lyricism inspired by God.

Recall from Claudel's account of his conversion that reading Rimbaud in 1886 inspired his own return to the church. Just as Rimbaud had a purported conversion experience on his deathbed, so too, according to Claudel, Baudelaire discovered an ardent faith in the last years of his life. The creative "correction" of these prior symbolist poets evolves Claudel's own mystical lyricism while positioning him in the "Catholic renaissance" in the early decades of twentieth-century French literature.

Along with Maurice Barrès, Marie-René Perse, and Charles-Pierre Péguy, among others, Claudel launches a literary defense against the devastating loss of the church's status and authority following the separation of church and state in 1905 and the abrogation of the *Loi Falloux* of 1850. This law had advocated for the liberty of teaching, which in a Catholic country established priestly schools. Contrary to the belief made popular by Claudel's preface that Rimbaud had prophesied the revival of Catholicism, it is Claudel's poetry that expresses a conversion with a proselytizing aim, notably his own return to a belief in God.

I shall follow the evolving interplay of poiesis and theology in a group of Claudel's works, beginning with *Connaissance de l'Est*.[2] This poetic prose collection develops poetry as an *instrument de connaissance* that reveals God at the center of creation. A break with a positivistic account of empirical reality introduces a transcendent order. Claudel's return to a certain subject of knowledge notably deviates from Rimbaud's fragmented subject, which we now understand in Lacanian terms. Sensory observation and contemplation of external reality lead to poetic vision. Seeing like a mystic, Claudel's lyric subject apprehends the material world's meaning in the image of the Divine Creator.[3]

Subsequent linking of metaphysics and aesthetics in *Art poétique*, where emended traces of Aristotelean, Thomist, and Bonaventurean notions overlap, sets forth a theory of metaphor as analogy that orders the relations of God, self, and world. This mystical view of universal harmony informs the lyric *Cinq grandes odes*, which reaffirm God as the first cause and thus as the center from which everything emanates and to which everything refers: "Dieu est une sphère infinie dont le centre est partout et la circonférence nulle part" (qtd. in Poulet, 1961, iii).[4] Claudel aims to reveal through his inspired vision and voice the divine order of all of creation.

TOWARD ANALOGICAL IMAGINATION: FROM REALISM TO SYMBOLISM

When Claudel began to compose *Connaissance de l'Est* in 1895, neither his aesthetics nor his worldview was yet established. Searching for his *own* voice, Claudel experimented with style (see Claudel et Amrouche 120, 134–35). What Nina Hellerstein (1973, 36) views as prose poems, Roger Mallet calls "poetic prose" (see Claudel et Gide 268). Fowlie considers *Connaissance de l'Est* "a form of intimate journal accompanying the [*Vers d'exil*]," which describes the five-year period of solitude, silence, and meditation Claudel spent in China, 1896–1900 (12). In *Mémoires improvisés*, Jean Amrouche too observes a spiritual itinerary, yet, unlike Fowlie, he reads the texts as poems (see Claudel et Amrouche 120). Along with experimental writing that includes both realism and symbolism, this collection debates opposing worldviews: positivism versus idealism.[5]

Descriptions in *Connaissance de l'Est* bear out Jules Renard's realism. In short, Renard bases aesthetics on the observation and articulation of precise formal detail, as in the realist and naturalist novel: "Il ne faut pas confondre l'image vaguement belle avec l'image exacte, bien supérieure" (qtd. in Claudel, 1973, 19).[6] Moreover, for Renard "tout est beau. Il faut parler du cochon comme d'une fleur" (19).[7] Along with the topic, then, the descriptive technique in Claudel's prose poem *Le Porc* evokes the real à la Renard. The speaking subject asserts his or her knowledge by naming and carefully portraying the object in question:

> Je peindrai ici l'image du Porc. C'est une bête solide et tout d'une pièce; sans jointure et sans cou, ça fonce en avant comme un soc. Cahotant sur ses quatre jambons trapus, c'est une trompe en marche qui quête, et toute odeur qu'il sent, y appliquant son corps de pompe, il l'ingurgite. (Claudel, 1973, 181)[8]

The text details the physical form of the pig perceived by various sense organs of the observing subject. Thus, the subject knows the *porc* as he or she apprehends the animal. Moreover, distinct from the ambiguous relation of the subject to his or her perception in Rimbaud, Claudel's subject assumes his or her discernment to accurately represent knowledge. Precise description in this text exemplifies the meticulous consideration of phenomena throughout *Connaissance de l'Est*. Observation, linked with contemplation, opens up to the mind's eye the occluded structure of the material world.

At the Lycée Louis-le-Grand, Claudel assimilated the positivistic view prevalent in the 1880s, also upheld in literary circles by such realists as Gustave Flaubert and such naturalists as Emile Zola (see Rémond). Reading Mallarmé, however, challenged the idea that matter is the sole, or at least the ultimate, reality and consequently questioned realist aesthetics. Mallarmé is indeed an important source for Claudel's evolving poetics of the subject and of language. Hugo, too, presents a model for Claudel's poetic contemplation that reveals the divine order in external reality.

Yet it is with Rimbaud that Claudel repeatedly underscores a primordial identification and asserts both a spiritual and a literary affinity. Resemblances between them, however, do not cohere. Claudel posits a conscious, stable subject strikingly different from Rimbaud's split subjectivity. Moreover, metaphor as analogy at the level of the signified in Claudel indeed deviates from the psychopoetics of *metaphora* developed in Rimbaud. I shall show, then, that Claudel's projected similarity to Rimbaud unwittingly exposes what distinguishes them. Revising his avowed precursor's psychical conception of the boundary between the real and the unreal in his own religious terms, Claudel corroborates the signifying difference between them.

Realism in *Le Porc* differs significantly from idealist or symbolist aesthetics à la Mallarmé in other texts collected in *Connaissance de l'Est*. Rather than naming per se, symbolism evokes through suggestion.[9] Contemplation thus transfigures natural scenes and reveals a symbolic aspect of the visible world in *La Dérivation*:

> A l'heure où la sacrée lumière provoque à toute sa réponse l'ombre qu'elle décompose, la surface de ces eaux à mon immobile navigation ouvre le jardin sans fleurs. Entre ces gras replis violets, voici l'eau peinte comme du reflet des cierges, voici l'ambre, voici le vert le plus doux, voici la couleur de l'or. Mais taisons-nous: cela je sais est à moi, et alors que cette eau deviendra noire, je posséderai la nuit tout entière avec le nombre intégral des étoiles visibles et invisibles. (1973, 185–86)[10]

Such emblematic writing also harks back to Rimbaud. In striking contrast to his ostensible precursor, however, Claudel's subject blindly asserts his or her knowledge as master of the evoked poetic vision: "cela je sais est à moi." This identification of the *sujet de l'énonciation* and the *sujet de l'énoncé* in Claudel differs radically from Rimbaud, who does not uphold the illusion of the self as one or whole.

Moreover, antithetical to uncertainty of narrative authority in Rimbaud, Claudel's "I" claims to "possess" through contemplation a transcendent vision. The poet-as-seer, or *voyant*, thus mediates between humanity and God's creation—precisely the role that Hugo attributes to the poet. Claudel's projected identification with Rimbaud turns away from an apparent link to a predecessor widely recognized as a great French poet. Reckoning with Rimbaud and Mallarmé as his precursors enables Claudel to conceal his significant debt to Hugo and highlight instead his own *original* mystical lyricism.

Claudel assimilates a fundamental query from Mallarmé's idealism that guides the observation and comprehension of phenomena in *Connaissance de l'Est* while leading to the metaphysics advanced in *Art poétique* (compare Claudel, 1973, 28–29, and Claudel et Amrouche 97). Reason dominates in the materialist worldview that underlies positivism. What one perceives through the senses *is* solely what exists. An idealistic approach entails instead the domain of abstract or intuitive thought, which expands the perception of reality to a transcendent domain. Diverging from Mallarmé's subjective idealism, Claudel's treatment of *connaissance* identifies this realm with God.[11]

Connaissance signifies both a theory and a process of knowledge by which we describe, define, and situate phenomena in relation to ourselves and the world.[12] Retrospective statements elucidate *connaissance* as a mode of analysis largely derived from Aristotle and Saint Thomas Aquinas.

> Quand vous avez bien compris la raison d'être de quelque chose, vous comprenez mieux et les conséquences . . . et la place qu'elle occupe dans l'univers. C'est ce que m'a appris justement la fréquentation d'Aristote et de saint Thomas. Presque partout, dans *Connaissance de l'Est*, vous voyez que l'intelligence et la raison interviennent. Il ne s'agit pas de description pure et simple, il s'agit d'une connaissance, il s'agit d'une compréhension. (Claudel et Amrouche 128–29)[13]

Claudel's elaboration also profits from Mallarmé's idealism. Knowing from direct sensory observation shifts to another type of vision. We can also see, and apprehend, through the mind's eye. Claudel thus considers *Connaissance de l'Est* to be his "oeuvre la plus mallarméenne" (Claudel, 1973, 28) and explains this predecessor's lesson in *Mallarmé: La Catastrophe d'Igitur*: "Mallarmé est le premier qui se soit placé devant l'extérieur, non pas comme devant un spectacle, ou comme un thème à devoirs français, mais comme devant un texte, avec cette question: Qu'est-ce que ça veut dire?" (Claudel, 1965, 511).[14] An analogical mode of thinking about the world derived from Mallarmé prefigures the poetics of metaphor that Claudel elaborates in *Art poétique*.

POET-AS-MYSTIC: REVEALING DIVINE DESIGN

Mallarmé renounces the realism of Flaubert and the naturalism of Zola to read the visible world symbolically, that is, in terms of signs. Rephrased in semiotic terms, contrary to the ostensible production of meaning through signifiers that I analyzed in Rimbaud, Mallarmé restores the patent interplay of the signifier and the signified. Claudel appropriates Mallarmé's subjective symbolism in religious terms to read the visible as the sign of the invisible God:

> Nous savons que le monde est en effet un texte et qu'il nous parle, humblement et joyeusement de sa propre absence, mais aussi de la présence éternelle de quelqu'un d'autre, à savoir son Créateur. Non pas seulement l'écriture, mais le scripteur, non pas seulement la lettre morte, mais l'esprit vivant, et non pas un grimoire magique, mais le Verbe en qui toutes choses ont été proférées. (1965, 512)[15]

This worldview emerges in *Connaissance de l'Est*, where Claudel as poet-as-mystic joins poiesis and theology to articulate through the use of analogy an inchoate sense of universal harmony and order.

Connaissance de l'Est resembles a tapestry in which patterns emerge from various threads woven together. Recurrent notions form the developmental stages of Claudel's mystical lyricism. The texts selected for analysis here broadly outline his nascent vision of universal harmony. A narrator, identified with the poet, dons guises of *promeneur*, *nageur*, and *navigateur*. This stable poetic subject discerns through observation and contemplation the occluded significance of the empirical world. Poetic meditations culminate in the perception of a transcendent order that unifies through analogy the similar among the dissimilar. *Art poétique* develops more fully the particular notion of analogy that, used interchangeably with metaphor, structures Claudel's lyric voice and mystical word.

In *Connaissance de l'Est*, from the superior position in which the poet observes the phenomenal world, he strives to transcend the diversity stretching out before him (*Octobre, Novembre, Splendeur de la lune, La Mer supérieure*) or surrounding him (*Salutation, Ardeur*).[16] *Rêves* can be read as the emblem of the cohesive, lyric subject's central site throughout this collection. He observes and sees as if through the Divine Creator's eyes, since presumably nothing escapes the speaking subject's sight:

> —Et je me revois à la plus haute fourche du vieil arbre. . . . De là comme un dieu sur sa tige, spectateur du théâtre du monde, dans une profonde considération, j'étudie le relief et la conformation de la terre, la disposition des pentes et des plans; l'oeil fixe comme un corbeau, je dévisage la campagne déployée sous mon perchoir, je suis du regard cette route qui . . . se perd enfin dans la forêt. Rien n'est perdu pour moi. (1973, 67)[17]

From his consistently higher and central vantage point, the poet senses a mystical order joining disparate phenomena into universal accord. *Le Temple de la conscience* expresses this perceived harmony:

> De la hauteur vertigineuse où je chemine, la vaste rivière apparaît dessinée comme une carte. . . .
> Ne comparerai-je ce vaste paysage qui s'ouvre devant moi jusqu'à la double enceinte des monts et des nuages à une fleur dont ce siège est le coeur mystique? N'est-il point géométrique où le lieu, se composant dans son harmonie, prend, pour ainsi dire, existence et conscience de lui-même, et dont l'occupant unit dans la contemplation de son esprit une ligne et l'autre? (155–56)[18]

A perpetual movement aligns otherwise different phenomena, for this constant rhythm also permeates the poet's mind and body.

Sur la cervelle associates mental activity with the perpetually new rhythm that emanates from a divine center to which it constantly returns: "La cervelle est un organe. . . . L'appareil assure l'épanouissement, l'expansion à tout le corps de l'onde cérébrale, constante comme le pouls" (321–22).[19] A universal rhythm pervades the microcosm (humankind) and the macrocosm (the world). This vibration involves "ce mouvement double et un par lequel un corps part d'un point pour y revenir. Et c'est là l'*élément* même, le symbole radical qui constitue essentiellement toute vie" (322).[20] The use of analogical language enables Claudel to order phenomena by revealing their comparable structuring.[21] Just as sensation and perception originate in organs of the body, so too all movement derives from an original impetus since God is the first cause: "La vibration de notre cervelle est le bouillonnement de la source de la vie, l'émotion de la matière au contact de l'unité divine dont l'emprise constitue notre personnalité typifique. Tel est l'ombilic de notre dépendance" (324).[22] Humankind apprehends the world by the senses, the instrument of our knowledge, or *connaissance* (323).²³ We know the world both in relation to ourselves and *as* we know ourselves, created in God's image. This illusion of the completely known self and, by extension, of the authentic knowledge of reality that Claudel sustains could not withstand the Lacanian Other that dialogizes the subject in Rimbaud.

Universal harmony provides the cornerstone of Claudelian aesthetics and metaphysics. *La Marée de Midi* presents this notion through the agency of the inner rhythm of the mind and, by extension, the pulse of the human heart, both of which parallel the continual motion of the waves of the sea: "Moi de même, et comme une ville par ses secrets égouts, mon esprit, par la vertu vivante de ce liquide dont je suis compénétré, communique au mouvement des eaux" (97).²⁴ *Art poétique*, as subsequent discussion elucidates, develops the poet's inchoate notion of constant movement throughout the created world and humankind alike and elaborates a mystical worldview that unites similars without erasing their differences. *Ça et là* expresses the emergent analogical imagination in *Connaissance de l'Est* that voices the divine impulse at the origin of creation:

> Puisque chaque créature née de l'impression de l'unité divine sur la matière indéterminée est l'aveu même qu'elle fait à son créateur, et l'expression du Néant d'où il l'a tirée. Tel est le rythme respiratoire et vital de ce monde, dont l'homme doué de conscience et de parole a été institué le prêtre pour en faire la dédicace. (273)²⁵

The mystery of the visible universe is revealed to the mystic who *sees* the world as an image of eternal creation. The poet becomes a *voyant* in the religious sense, as in Hugo. This notion of *voyance*, as further analysis will show, clearly diverges from that of Rimbaud, whom Claudel nonetheless re-creates as his primary precursor.

CLAUDELIAN *VOYANCE:*
AU FOND DE L'INCONNU POUR TROUVER DIEU

Rimbaud explores the unknown within the individual psyche as a source of new poetic visions. Recall Claudel's opposing view that phenomenal reality provides an inexhaustible source of revelation. In citing Baudelaire's call to new poetic arms, "au fond de l'inconnu, pour trouver du nouveau," Claudel writes "Infini" (the hidden God) rather than "inconnu."²⁶ This revision against the unconscious in Rimbaud underscores Claudel's belief that God created the world in His image.²⁷ The world, at once ordered yet continuously renewed and thus the site of *poesis perennis*, reveals through its harmonious rhythm and consummate design His eternal presence. Empirical reality reveals its meaning, that is, makes sense, with relation to God. A 1927 essay, *Religion et poésie*, encapsulates well the emergent Catholic worldview we have followed up to now in *Connaissance de l'Est*:

> La Religion non seulement nous apporte le chant, elle nous apporte aussi la parole . . . non seulement la joie mais aussi le sens. Puisque nous savons que le monde n'est pas l'ouvrage du Hasard . . . nous savons qu'il a un sens. Il nous parle de son créateur, il nous donne les moyens de comprendre son oeuvre ou en tout cas de l'interroger. (1965, 64)[28]

For, "in the beginning was the Word, and the Word was with God, and the Word was God" (John 1.1). The Word of God signifies more than speech (*logos*). It *is* God revealed through *connaissance*, a knowing that, as we shall find in *Art poétique*, Claudelian metaphor analogically structures and embodies.

Divine inspiration authors the intuition and nascent articulation of universal harmony and order in *Le Promeneur*. This text, which interweaves various threads of *Connaissance de l'Est*, exemplifies Claudel's coming mystical lyricism. By observing the visible world and comprehending its invisible accord, the poet perceives the eternal source of all of creation. This contemplation of external reality, radically different from Rimbaud's *voyance* on the border of conscious and unconscious mental activity, again harks back to Hugo:

> Chaque arbre a sa personnalité, chaque bestiole son rôle, chaque voix sa place dans la symphonie; comme on dit que l'on comprend la musique, je comprends la nature, comme un récit bien détaillé qui ne serait fait que de noms propres; au fur de la marche et du jour, je m'avance parmi le développement de la doctrine. (Claudel, 1973, 262–63)[29]

Physical sight, like inner vision, centers comprehension. A focal eye/I supports for Claudel a centered relation of self to world modeled upon that of God to creation. Revealing an eternal pattern enables the poet to deny the unpredictable effects of unconscious processes prevalent in Rimbaud:

> Jadis, j'ai découvert avec délice que toutes les choses existent dans un certain accord, et maintenant cette secrète parenté par qui la noirceur de ce pin épouse là-bas la claire verdure de ces érables, c'est mon regard qui

> l'avère, et, restituant le dessein antérieur, ma visite, je la nomme une révision. Je suis l'Inspecteur de la Création, le Vérificateur de la chose présente; la solidité de ce monde est la matière de ma béatitude! (263)[30]

By virtue of his analogical imagination, Claudel the poet-as-mystic discovers that phenomena disclose divine design. Just as thinking by analogy allows one to perceive this occluded order, so metaphor as analogy expresses this poetic revelation.

Through analogous structuring, harmony unites visible and invisible realms of reality. Claudel's poetic subject discovers universal accord made manifest by similar outer and inner movement of all created forms. The Lacanian split subjectivity and uncertainty of narrative authority in Rimbaud contrasts sharply with the centered "I" in Claudel who is *blindly* certain of his or her knowledge:

> Et je marche, je marche, je marche! Chacun renferme en soi le principe autonome de son déplacement par quoi l'homme se rend vers sa nourriture et son travail. Pour moi, le mouvement égal de mes jambes me sert à mesurer la force de plus subtils appels. L'attrait de toutes choses, je le ressens dans le silence de mon âme. (262–63)[31]

Now that Claudel understands the harmony of the world, he seeks to grasp, or comprehend, its melody. In music, harmony connotes the congruent arrangement of parts, such as the combination of simultaneous musical notes in a chord. Melody entails the agreeable succession or arrangement of sounds. In linguistic terms, we would associate harmony with the paradigmatic axis (metaphor) and melody with the syntagm (metonymy). What orders the various relations (the combined parts) that form the coherent whole before the poetic subject? This is the fundamental question that sensory observation of phenomena poses and that theology ultimately answers. The harmony of the world becomes for Claudel a metaphor for divine design. Each element of creation embodies a melody in the image of the Eternal Creator.

SEEING, IMAGINING THE WHOLE: CLAUDELIAN *CONNAISSANCE*

Connaissance de l'Est alternately presents two paths to knowledge: sensory observation and contemplation. These varying modes of seeing and, by extension, of knowing suggest an affinity with Saint Bonaventura's theory of knowledge. In a note to *La Poésie est un art*,

Claudel cites Bonaventura more specifically as a source of his notion of analogy: "Saint Bonaventure a donné la formule de l'analogie: *A* est à *B* come [sic] *C* est à *D*" (1965, 54).³² Since Bonaventura's works were not readily available in the later 1890s, Gilbert Gadoffre argues that Claudel more likely assimilated his notion of analogy from Joris-Karl Huysmans's 1898 *La Cathédrale*.³³

Although Gadoffre correctly links Claudel's view of analogy with a theological worldview, more plausible sources exist in Aristotle and Saint Thomas Aquinas. In *The Metaphysics*, Aristotle writes that "things are not all said to exist actually in the same sense, but only by analogy—as *A* is in *B* or to *B*, so is *C* in or to *D*" (447). In *Summa Theologiae*, Thomas Aquinas defines multiple references to analogy in these terms: "whenever a word is used analogically of many things, it is used of them because of some order or relation they have to some central thing" (3:69). Whichever derivation we adopt for Claudelian analogy, the question of sources becomes an issue of appropriation in the Bloomian sense of mis-reading. Although my study focuses on the revisionist relation of Rimbaud and Claudel, a similar dynamic links Claudel with other prior voices, such as Bonaventura. In short, Claudel deviates from predecessors to write on his own terms. From my critical perspective of the anxiety of influence that shapes poetic history, there is nothing so extraordinary about this for great poets. What is striking, however, is that Claudel's moves toward discontinuity retain the precursors' terms, albeit in a novel context, or sense.

Connaissance through poetic revelation in Claudel derives from Bonaventura's view that sensory observation leads to mystic vision: "since . . . the world is itself a ladder for ascending to God, we find here certain traces [of His hand], certain images, some corporeal, some temporal, some aeviternal; consequently some outside us, some inside" (Bonaventura 8). *Le Promeneur* employs Bonaventura's notion that "the sensibles, which [human beings] see, may be carried forward to the intelligibles which they do not see, as if by signs to the signified" (20). In *La Lampe et la cloche*, however, Claudel situates the perception of harmony within the poet's soul and thus substitutes inner vision for physical sight:

> La nuit nous ôte notre preuve, nous ne savons plus où nous sommes. Lignes et teintes, cet arrangement . . . du monde tout autour de nous, dont nous portons avec nous le foyer selon l'angle dont notre oeil est à tout moment rapporteur, n'est plus là pour avérer notre position. Nous sommes réduits à nous-mêmes. (1973, 333)³⁴

Physical blindness, however, does not prevent insight. We apprehend by other senses, the acuity of which increases in inverse proportion to the descent of night: "Mais si la nuit occlut notre oeil, c'est afin que nous écoutions plus, non point avec les oreilles seulement, mais par les ouïes de notre âme respirante à la manière des poissons" (334).[35] Saint Bonaventura similarly observes that our sensory organs serve as doors through which the "whole sensible world enters into the human soul through apprehension" (16). These external sensibles, moreover, enter "not through their substance, but through their similitudes" (16). Claudel's coherent subject of knowledge analogically relates the world to the self, without questioning, as Rimbaud does, the identification of *je* with the poetic subject.

This idea of proportion in similitude perceived by a cohesive subject informs the theory of *connaissance* sketched in *La Lampe et la cloche*. Here, as in *Sur la cervelle*, respiration discloses the internal rhythm of the human being, which resonates with the perpetual movement of the external world, both of which constitute life. Claudel's subject created in the image of God willfully possesses the creative impulse: "Je contiens le pouls créateur" (1973, 335).[36] A retrospective comment confirms the assumption of a fixed, unified speaking subject in Claudel: "L'homme est indéchirable, somme toute, et c'est la leçon de *Connaissance de l'Est* que jamais il n'y a abandon des facultés, et en particulier de la volonté. Je ne perds jamais le sentiment de ma personnalité" (Claudel et Amrouche 132).[37] This is precisely the notion of the self that Rimbaud refuted, endorsing instead an autonomous voice speaking (to) and dividing the subject from itself in and through speech.

Read emblematically, the constant pulse that pervades all of creation in *Connaissance de l'Est* becomes a source of poiesis, in Claudel's idiosyncratic sense of the term, preparing the fundamental notion of *co-naissance* articulated in *Art poétique*. *Co-naissance* is a double birthing of self and world. It is the act through which the transcendent order of the universe is revealed to the subject. This knowing makes *sense*, in the classical terms of metaphor as analogy: "chaque chose ne subsiste pas sur elle seule, mais dans un rapport infini avec toutes les autres" (1957, 143).[38] Again, a Lacanian viewpoint would challenge the positioning of *conaissance* between self and world at the level of consciousness alone. As we saw in Rimbaud, the simultaneous origination of the unconscious and consciousness forever alienates the subject from the Other within the self.

THE WORLD IS (A) METAPHOR: *ART POÉTIQUE*

The fundamental query "qu'est-ce que cela veut dire" inferred from Mallarmé, as discussed above, informs *Art poétique*. As the title itself suggests, an aesthetics supports this metaphysical exposé, which presents a revisionist response to Aristotle and Saint Thomas. Claudel's reading of a theory of knowledge based on syllogistic reasoning in *The Metaphysics* purges the positivism he absorbed from Auguste Burdeau at the Lycée Louis-le-Grand. In Claudelian *connaissance*, metaphor supplants syllogism. Further still, *Summa Theologiae* Christianizes Aristotle by elaborating a rational explanation of the world in which all things are analogically interconnected through their relation to God.[39] Claudel thus unites poiesis and theology in a Catholic worldview recapitulated in *Mémoires improvisés*: "J'avais à introduire . . . le dogme catholique dans le monde rationnel et dans le monde sensible qui était le mien comme artiste" (Claudel et Amrouche 40).[40] *Art poétique*, then, articulates more fully the quest for understanding the relations among God, self, and world outlined in *Connaissance de l'Est*. Two essays, *Connaissance du temps* (1903) and *Connaissance du monde et de soi-même* (1904) comprise *Art poétique*. I shall respect the order of Claudel's exposition and yet treat interpenetrating notions as they evolve throughout the two essays.

Along with the repetition of the term *connaissance*, we notice an immediate continuity between the sensory observation of nature recounted in *Connaissance de l'Est* and a similar point of departure in *Connaissance du temps*:

> Nous ne chercherons point à comprendre le mécanisme des choses de par dessous, comme un chauffeur qui rampe sur le dos sous sa locomotive. Mais nous nous placerons devant l'ensemble des créatures, comme un critique devant le produit d'un poëte, goûtant pleinement la chose, examinant par quels moyens il a obtenu ses *effets*. (1957, 127)[41]

From the perspective of Aristotle's metaphysics, as Claudel explains, reading the world as a text situates elements in relation to the whole. Thus one reasons by syllogism that the general, taken as an immutable law, explains the particular: "Le syllogisme est le procédé par lequel nous reconnaissons les choses et nous reconnaissons nous-mêmes parmi elles" (130).[42] The general assertion, however, may have no bearing on the problem. Claudel advances instead that phenomena of the created world are defined by their differences: "Déjà l'enquête logique nous livre ce point, que nous ne pouvons *définir* une chose ... *que par les traits* en qui elle diffère de toutes les autres" (131).[43]

Consequently, Claudel shifts from syllogism to metaphor and to a theological view of analogy to set forth a new logic of the generative impulse that structures the relations of God, self, and world. Along with the presumed existence of God, the assumption of a cohesive subject plays a fundamental role in this scheme of apprehension. The lack of self-knowledge that we observed in Rimbaud would put asunder the Catholic worldview that Claudel's poetic project reconstitutes.

In *Art Poétique*, as in *Connaissance de l'Est*, the path to knowledge develops from sensory to intellectual comprehension. Humankind, through respiration and heartbeat, both senses and participates in the harmonious universal rhythm that links all matter through incessant, and thus productive, movement: "L'homme connaît le monde non point par ce qu'il y dérobe mais par ce qu'il y ajoute: lui-même. Il fait lui-même l'accord qui est l'objet de sa connaissance" (1957, 133). "Il sent en lui, il possède en lui le mouvement même dont les horizons successifs qui s'élargissent autour de lui sont les réporteurs circonférents" (142).[44] This paradigm of the sensible world in a state of perpetual flux reads in a new manner the organizing principle that unites its diverse surface. Metaphor becomes the fundamental key that opens, through analogy, the occluded structure that pervades the created world and mind. The primordial principle of Claudel's aesthetics and metaphysics deviates from the Aristotelean and Thomist use of syllogism. *Poesis perennis*, the *Art poétique* of the universe, has for Claudel the mimetic aim of revealing God.

Art poétique recalls the *promeneur* who perceives relations that unite disparate phenomena: "je vis, quoique grandement distants, juxtaposés par l'alignement de mon oeil, la verdure d'un érable combler l'accord proposé par un pin" (143).[45] Thus Claudel proposes to read "ce texte forestier, l'énonciation arborescente ... d'un nouvel Art poétique de l'Univers, d'une nouvelle Logique" (143).[46] This statement, combining aesthetics and metaphysics, prepares the inference of the divine creative impulse from the text that the empirical world sets forth. Whereas Aristotelean logic has syllogism as its basis, Claudel's new logic finds its source in metaphor, "le mot nouveau, l'opération qui résulte de la seule existence conjointe et simultanée de deux choses différentes" (143).[47]

Just as syntax combines various elements to form a *meaning*ful, coherent sequence, so too metaphor associates disparate phenomena:

> La seconde Logique en est comme la syntaxe qui enseigne *l'art de les rassembler, et celle-ci est pratiquée devant nos yeux par la nature même. ... La*

métaphore, l'iambe fondamental ou rapport d'une grave et d'une aiguë, ne se joue pas qu'aux feuilles de nos livres: *elle est l'art autochtone employé par tout ce qui naît.* (143; emphasis added)[48]

Claudel's reading of metaphor as "the art of gathering [various elements] together" obliquely implies the role played by metonymy. Here association by contiguity results in the perception of resemblance attributed to metaphor. Yet, differing from *metaphora* that resists mimetic discursivity in Rimbaud, for Claudel metaphor works mimetically to disclose to the perceiving subject the inherently divine order of the created world.

Claudel does not adhere to a strict classical view narrowly derived from Aristotle in which metaphor distinguishes a poetic discourse separate from quotidian language. Just as metaphor brings about fresh insight in Aristotle, so metaphor produces understanding in Claudel.[49] More precisely, this creative apprehension avows the divine. As Amrouche aptly remarks, with the view that "quand Dieu fit l'homme à son image, c'était à son image de Créateur," Claudel intends a *connaissance créatrice* (Claudel et Amrouche 199).[50] We recall a strikingly different sense of the aesthetic role played by the metaphoric in Rimbaud.

The emphasis in Claudel on the mimetic function of metaphor at the level of the signified is diametrically opposed to Rimbaud's *metaphora* grounded in metonymy at the level of the signifier. Moreover, mimesis supports Claudel's joining of poiesis and theology. This union positions the creative impulse outside the self in a transcendent realm, in the image of which both the microcosm and the macrocosm are conceived. Counteracting the disruptive effects of unconscious processes upon the subject and his or her knowledge in Rimbaud, divine order subsumes difference in Claudel's scheme.

POETIC METAPHYSICS: CLAUDELIAN METAPHOR

Metaphor serves as the basis of Claudel's metaphysics to connote the inherent design of the universe. Metaphor also structures our construal of this perpetual movement of divergence and convergence. For Claudel, we make sense of the world by intuiting and articulating the similarity between dissimilars to relate disparate elements: "Je comprends que chaque chose ne subsiste pas sur elle seule, mais dans un rapport infini avec toutes les autres" (1957, 143).[51] Fowlie implies the *poietic* role attributed to metaphor in *Connaissance du temps*:

Claudel characterizes this operation of metaphor as the poet's testimony to . . . the principle of modulation and change by which the world continues to exist. Two things which seemingly were moving in opposite directions, without any relationship between them, are suddenly and unexpectedly joined. (27)

At once creative construal and mimetic expression, metaphor re-produces connections between disparate phenomena that *exist* in a state of constant flux. Metaphor, inherent in both thought and language, thus mediates Claudelian *connaissance* while relating God, self, and world.[52] Diverging from Rimbaud, who identifies creation with the unconscious Other within the self, Claudel identifies poiesis with the original divine creative impulse.

Knowledge of the self, related to the world, increases through a continuous *co-naissance*.[53] Incongruous with the construction that splits the subject in Rimbaud, this co-birthing is inherently centered in the Divine Father. The movement that decenters in Rimbaud is precisely what joins in Claudel: "Toute chose donc est définie et définissante; elle est définie sur tous ses points, elle définit par un seul. Elle connaît par ce qu'elle exclut, de fait ou de nature. . . . La connaissance donc prise ici dans son sens *réel* de causation et d'action sur le dehors exercée, c'est l'effet de soi-même suivi chez les autres" (1957, 150).[54] All things exist in relation to each other. The space of the *écart* (difference or gap) that distinguishes phenomena—that is, *A is* to *B*—also connects them. This recalls to us the analogical basis of classical metaphor, in which *A* is to *B*, as *C* is to *D*. The copula, which signifies at once *is* and *is not*, associates by similitude without erasing differences: "Nous connaissons les choses en leur fournissant le moyen d'exercer une action sur notre 'mouvement.' Nous les *co-naissons*, nous les produisons dans leurs rapports avec nous" (176).[55] For Claudel, who believes in an inherently divine order, difference structures the perception of similarity at the level of the signified.

This positioning of meaning significantly deviates from the effect of meaning at the level of the signifier alone in Rimbaud. From the perspective of Claudel's analogical imagination, humankind comprehends the world *in terms of* the relations that constitute empirical reality. We make *sense* of these connections through language: "les mots sont les signes dont nous nous servons pour appeler les choses; nous les *appelons*, en effet, nous les évoquons en constituant en nous l'état de co-naissance qui répond à leur présence sensible" (178).[56] Language thus mediates our apperception and comprehension of reality with relation to ourselves. "Toute 'proposition' est premièrement l'énonciation des rapports, de la balance que nous établissons entre la chose et nous, entre le sujet et l'objet" (179).⁵⁷ As I have already suggested, Claudel's metaphor is poietic in bringing about construal and, by extension, insight or new meaning. This poiesis at the level of the signified diverges from Rimbaud's creative production, which gives voice to the unconscious Other within the self at the level of the signifier. Central to Claudel's theory of language, which enables the speaking subject to ascertain his or her place in the created world, is a specifically mimetic view of analogy based in Thomist aesthetics.

THEOLOGY AND *POESIS PERENNIS*

Saint Thomas, like Plato, does not attribute any truth value to poetry: "Poetry employs metaphors for the sake of representation, in which we are born to take delight" (1:35). His use of metaphor in theological language conveys our knowledge of God and His creation. This strictly mimetic aim has its basis in analogy of proper proportionality. Aristotelean reasoning by analogy, as Gerald Phelan asserts, "has nothing to do with analogical knowledge" (16). Thomist doctrine, however, insists on "the unequivocal possession of the characteristics upon which an analogy is predicated" (Phelan 16).

For Saint Thomas, "whatever perfection is analogically common to two or more beings is intrinsically (formally) possessed by each, not however, by any two in the same way or mode, but by each in proportion to its being" (Phelan 22). To illustrate Thomist analogy, Phelan gives this example:

> [K]nowledge is to the angel as knowledge is to man. . . . What is stated is that the proportion between knowledge and angel *holds*, i.e., angels know as angels are; and that the proportion between knowledge and man *holds*, i.e., men know as men are; and further . . . there is a proportion between the way the first proportion *holds* and the way the second proportion *holds*. (23–24)

Saint Thomas's poetics of analogy reasserts in theological terms Aristotle's notion of a final cause. God, then, is the first measure of things: "we must say, therefore, that words are used of God and creatures in an analogical way, that is in accordance with a certain order between them" (3:65). Although we may desire to know God, we can love Him perfectly and yet know Him only imperfectly (Fowlie 100–101). Theological language underscores for Saint Thomas humankind's indirect knowledge of God of whom we can speak only metaphorically or analogically (3:57, 71).

Claudel admits Saint Thomas as a formative source for *Art poétique* and, more generally, for his evolving metaphysics and aesthetics.[58] Yet, as Claudel states in 1947, his view of metaphor breaks with Saint Thomas's adherence to syllogism:

> Pendant que saint Thomas sur les bases de la révélation construit avec le syllogisme son immense édifice, son émule dans l'ordre fraternel et rival, saint Bonaventura, remet aux poètes et aux savants de l'avenir avec l'analogie l'inépuisable clef de la découverte. Quelle heure pour l'humanité que celle où la vérité appuyée sur la raison se tourne vers l'amour qui l'interroge avec un visage incontestable. (1965, 640)[59]

The linkage of poetry with cognition and the revelation of the divine order of the universe in *Art poétique* deviates from Thomist thought. Claudel's metaphysical treatise nonetheless retains the Thomist idea that the created world and beings resemble God analogically, for He created them in His image: "l'homme . . . se produit dans sa corrélation avec Dieu, il se connaît, engendré, dans sa corrélation avec le générateur. . . . Comme il connaît c'est ainsi qu'il se connaît . . . du fait de cet Auteur et de ce Maître dont il a reçu pouvoir" (1957, 190).[60] In Claudel's Catholic worldview, humankind differs from animals, which are limited to sensory *connaissance*. By virtue of its God-given conscience, humankind anchors to itself its understanding of the outside world: "Il constitue lui-même partout où il est, un centre, et ce centre, il jouit de la faculté de le transporter où il veut" (170).[61] In striking opposition to Rimbaud, who assumes a heterogeneous, decentered subject, Claudel upholds a unified, centered subject of knowledge.

Claudelian *connaissance* is anthropomorphic and thus *subjective*. Mallarmé's "qu'est-ce que cela veut dire" becomes for Claudel "qu'est-ce que cela veut *me* dire." With transcendent vision inspired by God, Claudel's poetic subject perceives divine order in nature.[62] All converges in God and diverges from Him. This continuous rhythm is the organizing principle of the universe and mirrors the metaphoric structure of thought and of language. *Art poétique* thus grounds a theory of *connaissance* in universal harmony: "au sens large, connaître, c'est exister en même temps. . . . Il y a une harmonie, à chaque temps entre toutes les parties de la création" (1957, 202).[63] This poetic metaphysics informs *Cinq grandes odes*, in which Claudel's poetic subject sublimates the personal self to voice the divine creative impulse. Claudel thus takes his stance of mystical lyricism against the postromantics, such as Rimbaud, and resurrects God in the Catholic world that his poetry celebrates.

SIX

Revealing Divine Order
Poesis Perennis

The *Cinq grandes odes* poeticize the metaphysics elaborated in *Art poétique* and develop through a debate on poetic voice Claudel's stance of mystical lyricism.[1] A fundamental conflict between the poet-as-willful-creator and the autonomy of the creative process surfaces in the first ode to *Les Muses*. This tension informs subsequent odes, most notably *La Muse qui est la Grâce*, and recalls the ambiguous source of creativity that I traced in Rimbaud. Claudel struggles throughout the first four odes against an autonomous impulse that decenters the cohesive poetic subject that he assumes. The turn to a fixed world order that begins and returns to the Divine Creator asserted in the final ode, *La Maison fermée*, subsumes desire and its unpredictable effects on poetic expression. Claudel thus rejects personal lyricism and ascertains the subject's role in poiesis by adopting a mystical lyric voice inspired by and centered in God.

Subjective idealism characteristic of romantic poets, such as Lamartine and Hugo, who express their individual sensibility, poses a fundamental problem for Claudel, who seeks to reconcile the aims of the poet-as-willful-creator and the poet-as-religious-mystic.[2] How can a subject-centered voice claim to speak for God? Can a creative artist overcome personal subjectivity and still speak as a poet? The harmonious union of poetic voice and mystical vision becomes the central project of the *Odes*, beginning with the ode to *Les Muses*, where Claudel seeks to comprehend the ineffable source of creativity. I have identified this nameless impulse in Rimbaud with the unconscious Other within the self that forever splits the speaking subject. Claudel, to the contrary, attempts to sublimate personal desire and unify the poetic subject by positioning the creative impulse outside the self in a realm associated with God the Creator.

Various themes and movements compose the ode to *Les Muses* in consonance with the musical paradigm underlying Claudel's theory of poetry. To elucidate the poetic subject in the *Odes*, I shall focus on the thematic interplay of an aesthetic problem concerning voice and a struggle involving vocation.[3] A retrospective statement captures this strife between poet and priest:

> J'avais, en somme, plus ou moins consciemment à refouler [les parties d'imagination, de sensibilité] . . . au profit de la formation rationnelle et spirituelle que je poursuivais. . . . Alors sous-jacent à tout mon travail artistique de cette époque-là, il y avait cette pensée lancinante: qu'est-ce qui m'attend . . . vais-je essayer la vie monastique? C'est le problème que j'ai essayé de résoudre à mon retour en 1900. (Claudel et Amrouche 146–47)[4]

Conscious repression of poetic sensibility, associated here with irrational desire, safeguards the unified speaking subject integral to Claudel's poetics of mystical lyricism.

The final ode, *La Maison fermée*, unequivocally asserts a transcendent divine order, at once an infinite source of poiesis and an invariable ontological point of origination. Claudel thus recenters the poetic subject and identifies the creative impulse with divine inspiration. Unifying self and other in God, Claudel mis-reads in religious terms Rimbaud's *autre*, the unconscious Other that we now understand dialogizes, or splits, the subject in and through discourse. Self-surrender overcomes alterity and enables Claudel's poet-as-mystic, like a priest who acts out of God's authority, to reveal truths that otherwise remain inaccessible to human understanding, or *connaissance*.

IDENTIFYING THE CREATIVE IMPULSE: THE POET'S MUSE

The ode to *Les Muses* (begun in 1900 and completed in 1904) details the nine Muses sculpted on a sarcophagus housed in the Louvre.[5] This observation, following the theory of *connaissance* practiced in *Connaissance de l'Est*, then develops a meditation on poetic inspiration. Broader questions about the nature of creativity, unconscious versus conscious, and the relation of the poet to his or her discourse frame this lyrical *ars poetica*. The poet, speaking in the first person, invokes the nine Muses, here identified with a mysterious voice at the genesis of the creative process:

> Je vous ai reconnu, ô conseil complet des neuf Nymphes intérieures!
> Phrase mère! engin profond du langage et peleton des

femmes vivantes!
  Présence créatrice! Rien ne naîtrait si vous n'étiez neuf! (1957, 222)[6]

This address ostensibly situates the Muses within the self and, moreover, within language ("dark instrument of language"). We shall discover, however, that this voice does not relate to the unconscious Other, as in Rimbaud, but rather inspires the subject who passively awaits the birth of poetry from the creative impulse of the nine Muses.

Creativity, here synonymous with inspiration, erupts spontaneously from silence. Subsequent *versets* symbolize this emergence as the white of a blank page upon which the black ink of the poet's pen inscribes a text:

> Voici soudain, quand le poëte nouveau comblé de
> l'explosion intelligible,
>   La clameur noire de toute la vie nouée par le nombril dans
> la commotion de la base,
>   S'ouvre, l'accès
>   Faisant sauter la clôture, le souffle de lui-même
>   Violentant les mâchoires coupantes,
>   Le frémissant Novénaire avec un cri!
>   Maintenant il ne peut plus se taire! L'interrogation sortie
> de lui-même il l'a confiée pour toujours . . .
>   Au savant choeur de l'inextinguible Echo! (222)[7]

Claudel's special spelling of *poëte* (instead of *poète*, writer of verse) derives from the Greek term *poiesis*, which means a creation or a making. This orthography implies the creative work of the divinely inspired poet who, by naming objects, gives them meaning. The ode to the Muses configures this inspiration as an unexpected, violent cry that escapes the poet's mouth.[8] In this sense, poetic voice does emerge physically from within the speaking subject. *Novénaire*, which alludes to the nine months of pregnancy and to the *nine* Muses, indeed associates the emergence of poetry with birth per se. However, the *source* of the creative impulse for Claudel's poetic subject comes from outside the self, more precisely from God. Although conscious of an indeterminate, obscure clamor within itself preceding the moment of inspiration and, by extension, creative expression, the poetic subject can neither ascertain the origins nor control the emergence of this internal impulse. In *Les Muses*, Claudel's "poëte pareil à un instrument où l'on souffle" becomes the instrument, literally speaking, the mouthpiece, that voices what is *in*spired (225).[9]

Inspiration escapes the poet's conscious control in Claudel, albeit in a manner unlike the autonomous creative impulse in Rimbaud. The seer letters set forth an immanent source of the creative urge that we have associated with unconscious mental activity. In the ode to *Les Muses*, the creative impulse, imaged by *souffle* (breath), implies instead a transcendent source. The verb *souffler* signifies to breathe out, whereas *inspirer* means to breathe in. Moreover, *souffler* also connotes what is suggested by someone outside the speaking subject, for example, *qui lui a soufflé cette idée* (who gave him that idea?). Claudel's poetic subject thus expresses, or voices, what God inspires.

The poetic act, then, emanates from the Divine Father who first insufflated His breath into all of creation.[10] An explicit identification of the Muse with God centers poetic voice by ordering the creative impulse and, moreover, defends the subject against the unpredictable effects of unconscious mental processes upon expression in Rimbaud. For Claudel, "il n'y a pas de poète, en effet, qui ne doive inspirer avant de respirer, qui ne reçoive d'ailleurs ce souffle mystérieux que les Anciens appelaient la Muse. . . . Cette inspiration n'est pas sans analogie avec l'esprit prophétique" (1965, 422).[11] *Poesis perennis*, thus enlivened, repeats the original divine order.

AESTHETICS AND METAPHYSICS: DIVINE RHYTHM

The ode to *Les Muses* links aesthetics with metaphysics to develop the creative process in a stance of mystical lyricism. In the light of the Catholic worldview that Claudel constructs, he equates *le blanc* (white) margin from which a poem arises through inscription with the silence out of which God created the world: "O mon âme! le poëme n'est point fait de ces lettres que je plante comme des clous, mais du blanc qui reste sur le papier" (1957, 224).[12] This statement, which also harks back to Mallarmé's aesthetics, implies the structure of the primordial creative impulse defined as metaphor in *Art poétique*. Metaphor, as the fundamental iamb constituted by a continuous movement of divergence and convergence, suggests the interaction of speech and silence.[13] Moreover, this interplay, like that of the inscribed text and the white of the page in the ode to *Les Muses*, has an iambic rhythm associated with respiration and inspiration that distinguishes Claudel's *lyric* voice.[14]

Réflexions et propositions sur le vers français elaborates Claudel's idea that poetic discourse imitates physiological rhythm: "Le vers composé d'une ligne et d'un blanc est cette action double, cette respiration par laquelle l'homme absorbe la vie et restitue une parole intelligible" (1965,

32).[15] Both our respiration and our pulse have iambic structure, that is, an unstressed syllable followed by a stressed one in accentual meter. This structuring recalls the basis of *connaissance/co-naissance* in *Connaissance de l'Est* and *Art poétique*. Just as Claudel finds iambic rhythm characteristic of corporeal and mental processes, so too this movement provides a model for his lyric *verset* in the *Odes*, a form that textually configures the divine rhythm of creativity.[16] Biblical verse, too, notably in the Psalms, informs Claudel's *verset*.

The *verset*, as Claudel explains in *Sur le vers français*, embodies *poesis perennis*:

> Le vers nouveau n'est plus seulement comme la ligne latine une énonciation solitaire. . . . Il n'existe plus seulement, il fonctionne. Il n'est plus seulement le résultat de l'élaboration poétique, il en est l'organe vivant, le battement régulier de la pompe qui puise dans l'inconnu le sentiment et l'idée. (1965, 7–8)[17]

Read with reference to the white page upon which the poet inscribes his or her text, *inconnu* refers to the silent margins out of which creative expression springs. Poetic speech thus imitates God, who drew (created) the world out of silence. The immaculate space from which Claudel's poetry emerges is not the unconscious source of creativity disclosed in Rimbaud. Rather, as in the ode to *Les Muses*, the creative artist awaits the onset of inspiration from outside the self.

> O mon âme! il ne faut concerter aucun plan! O mon âme sauvage, il faut nous tenir libres et prêts,
> Comme les immenses bandes fragiles d'hirondelles quand sans voix retentit l'appel automnal! . . .
> Que mon vers ne soit rien d'esclave! mais tel que l'aigle marin qui s'est jeté sur un grand poisson,
> Et que l'on ne voit rien qu'un éclatant tourbillon d'ailes et l'éclaboussement de l'écume! (1957, 224–25)[18]

Sublimation silences the personal self as the source of the creative impulse. The poet thus receives the impulse to create, the inception and expression of which escape his control.

Subsequent *versets* affirm spontaneous poetic expression that springs for Claudel from a dialogue with the Divine Other outside the self:

> Que le langage nouveau, comme un lac plein de sources,
> Déborde par toutes ses coupures! . . .

> L'activité de l'âme composée sur le son de sa propre parole!
> L'invention de la question merveilleuse, le clair dialogue avec le silence inépuisable. (226–27)[19]

Reference here to a "transparent dialogue with inexhaustible silence" is strikingly different from the dialogism at play in Rimbaud's poetic project. Put another way, the clarity of knowledge and, by extension, of poetic expression underscores the unified subject that Claudel presumes. The idea of "inexhaustible silence" implies an unbounded, limitless poiesis. This autonomous urge nevertheless deviates from the postromantic notion of the unconscious Other in Rimbaud that displaces the narrative authority and credibility traditionally associated with a cohesive poetic subject. Claudel the Catholic submits to divine inspiration as the source of poetic voice and so subjects his creative impulse to eternal order.

FROM SUBJECTIVE TO MYSTICAL LYRICISM

The elaboration of universal harmony in *Connaissance de l'Est* and *Art poétique* prepares and informs *Cinq grandes odes*. Why, then, does Claudel repeatedly focus on the unpredictable eruption of the creative impulse in the ode to *Les Muses*? In what terms can we understand this struggle with an autonomous impulse that overcomes the ordered view of visible and invisible reality espoused by his project? Henri Massis, one of Claudel's most vehement critics, "finds in the subjective lyricism of Claudel, an incommunicability and a disorderliness which are contrary to the spirit of order, discipline, and hierarchy inherent in the Revelation in which the poet believes" (qtd. in Fowlie 93). Although subject centered, this subjective lyricism is not strictly personal, as Massis asserts. For the poet in Claudel sublimates his desiring lyric self, that is, the poet-as-willful-creator, to take the stance of poet-as-mystic. In this sense, Claudel fulfills the subject's desire for knowledge of self and world by seeing all of creation, as if through the creator's eyes, as unified in God and therefore whole. From the Lacanian viewpoint developed in Rimbaud, such mystical lyricism blindly refuses the modern insight that the poetic subject inherently lacks self-knowledge and thus speaks in a fragmentary voice the desire of and for the Other (Lacan, 1966, 186). Claudel's project turns to a unified poetic subject: "O poëte, tu ne chanterais pas bien / Ton chant si tu ne chantais en mesure . . . O grammairien dans mes vers! Ne cherche point le / chemin, cherche le centre" (1957, 227).[20]

What organizes and synthesizes in harmony the interwoven and intersecting thematic threads or melodies of the *Odes*, like the various *movements* of a symphony, is their center. The poet-as-mystic affirms God as this center.

> Mais ton chant, ô Muse du poëte,
> Ce n'est point le bourdon de l'avette, la source qui jase,
> l'oiseau de paradis dans les girofliers!
> Mais comme le Dieu saint a inventé chaque chose, ta joie
> est dans la possession de son nom.
> Et comme il a dit dans le silence 'Qu'elle soit!' c'est ainsi
> que, pleine d'amour, tu répètes, selon qu'il l'a appelée,
> Comme un petit enfant qui épelle "Qu'elle est."
> O servante de Dieu, pleine de grâce! (229–30)[21]

Poiesis in Claudel becomes "a direct imitation of the silence in and out of which God himself spoke the words that became the things and beings of the universe" (Kalb 40). Thus conceived, Claudel, Catholic poet, recovers the genesis of humankind in the image of the Divine Creator. Just as Adam gave names to God's creatures in the Garden (Gen. 3.21), so too the *voyant*, speaking metaphorically, restores the divine order of the created world. This speech is poietic in its construal yet mimetic in the insight that metaphor brings about. For Claudel aims to reveal God in and through His creation.

Seen in this light, Claudel's analogical poetic word illuminates universal harmony centered in the Divine Creator. The poet-as-mystic, voicing the creative impulse configured here as the Muse, enacts *conaissance* and repeats the divine ordering at the *origin* of the created world. To reveal the mystery (the divine meaning) of empirical reality, the poet plays the role of a priest who mediates a believer's knowledge of God. Just as a priest reads the Word of God—the Bible—as the source of our knowledge of God, so too Claudel reads the empirical world as a text that tells universal truths. Poetic writing discloses the divine design at the origins of creation.

> Tu l'approuves substantiellement, tu contemples
> chaque chose dans ton coeur, de chaque chose tu cherches
> *comment la dire*!
> Quand Il composait l'Univers, quand Il disposait avec
> beauté le Jeu, quand Il déclenchait l'énorme cérémonie,

> Quelque chose de nous avec lui, voyant tout, se réjouissant dans son oeuvre,
> Sa vigilance dans son jour, son acte dans son sabbat!
> Ainsi quand tu parles, ô poëte, dans une énumération délectable
> Proférant de chaque chose le nom,
> Comme un père tu l'appelles mystérieusement dans son principe, et selon que jadis
> Tu participes à sa création, tu coopères à son existence!
> Toute parole une répétition
> Tel est le chant que tu chantes dans le silence, et telle est la bienheureuse harmonie
> Dont tu nourris en toi-même le rassemblement et la dissolution. (1957, 230)[22]

This poetic voice, linking aesthetics and metaphysics, re-creates universal harmony in a Catholic world. Moreover, we read between these lines the notion of *connaissance/co-naissance* elaborated in *Art poétique*. Not only does the poet *create* the relations among phenomena in the world by comprehending them, he also *knows* reality in relation to himself.[23]

The concluding *versets* to *Les Muses* generally affirm the anthropomorphic stance couched in lyric tones of the poet-as-mystic.[24] This ode appears to resolve the conflict concerning vocation, priest versus poet, discussed at the outset of this chapter, by ascribing the creative impulse to God:

> J'ai trouvé le secret; je sais parler; si je veux, je saurai vous dire
> Cela que chaque chose *veut dire*.
> Je suis initié au silence; il y a l'inexhaustible cérémonie vivante, il y a un monde à envahir, il y a un poëme insatiable à remplir. (231)[25]

Yet the poet-as-willful-creator reemerges through this affirmation of the unequivocal expression of knowledge inspired by God. Preceding allusions to "ivresse," "la Bacchante roidie," and "un oeil chargé de désirs" (231–33) challenge passive submission to inspiration informed by order. Whereas we followed the play of unbounded desire at the level of the signifier in Rimbaud, reference to desire configured as "ce feu secret qui me ronge" in Claudel advances a willful Promethean attempt to steal poetic fire from God. This personal urge breaks with divine

Revealing Divine Order

inspiration and threatens to supplant the poet-as-mystic's vision and voice. A similar tension between subjective and mystical lyricism surfaces in the fourth ode, *La Muse qui est la Grâce*, and restages the conflict between poet and priest. Intervening odes, however, prepare the marriage of poiesis and theology that will bind poetic voice to God.

CREATIVITY AND ITS DOUBLE: IMAGINATION AND REASON

The debate between the poet-as-willful-creator and the poet-as-mystic in the ode to *Les Muses*, which I have related to a struggle with vocation, also has its basis in Claudel's aesthetics. We saw that Rimbaud develops the dialogic play of unconscious and conscious mental processes in the creative process. To the contrary, as expressed in a *Lettre à l'Abbé Bremond sur l'inspiration poétique*, Claudel presupposes an order that subsumes the decentering effects of desire upon poetic expression:

> La poésie est l'effet d'un certain besoin de faire, de réaliser avec les mots l'idée qu'on a eue de quelque chose. Il faut donc que l'imagination ait eu une idée vive et forte, quoique d'abord et forcément imparfaite et confuse, de l'objet qu'elle se propose de réaliser. Il faut en plus que notre sensibilité ait été placée à l'égard de cet objet dans un état de désir. . . . L'oeuvre d'art est le résultat de la collaboration de l'imagination avec le désir. . . . Et peu à peu, sous cette impulsion régulière, entre les deux pôles de l'imagination et du désir, le flot des paroles et des idées commencent à jaillir. (1965, 45–46)[26]

For Claudel, poetic writing strives to fulfill the subject's desire. This scheme may suggest Lacan's view that language mediates the subject's relation to lack (1966, 159). Yet, as Claudel writes to Henri Bremond, desire does not subsist in his poetics of mystical lyricism as a strictly unconscious impulse but is concurrently informed by a sense of harmony: "De même qu'avant la voix, il y a le souffle, avant l'expression il y a le désir de s'exprimer et cette poussée de l'âme qui se traduit chez l'homme par des mots. . . . Mais dans ce souffle même, dans ce désir, il y a déjà l'ordre et l'intelligence y est intéressée" (1965, 47).[27] Poiesis in Claudel, as in all creation, strives for order and in this manner expresses divine design: "C'est en ce sens que la poésie rejoint la prière, parce qu'elle dégage des choses leur essence pure qui est de créatures de Dieu et de témoignages à Dieu" (48–49).[28]

Claudel the poet-as-mystic, a "prophet working under God's eye" (Raymond 205), resolves "élucider toutes choses, de leur restituer leur signification authentique. Un tel dessein interdit au poète d'attribuer comme fin à son travail une *catharsis* égoïste. . . . Tout dans l'oeuvre doit servir. . . . Tout en elle *veut dire* quelque chose, comme l'univers, en ses moindres parties" (Raymond 207–8).[29] In a striking revisionist turn from the widespread skepticism of both his French symbolist predecessors and his contemporaries to belief in a Christian God, Claudel asserts through mystical lyricism the unequivocal meaning of a Catholic world. Clearly different from the persistent uncertainty of narrative authority in Rimbaud, which implies the appropriation of voice by the unconscious Other within the self, Claudel's poetic subject knows both what to say and what the created world means to say. This knowledge, however, does not stem from the poet's willfulness but rather, as I have repeatedly remarked, from divine inspiration.

As demonstrated in the preceding discussion, the ode to *Les Muses* explores the role played by the poet and presents the creative impulse centered in and inspired by the Divine Father. The primary movement of the second ode, *L'Esprit et l'eau*, joins poiesis and theology through the affirmation of universal harmony. Thus the poet-as-mystic analogically reads the union of spirit and matter in God, who created humankind in His image. In a secondary movement in the ode, the poet-as-willful-creator again struggles against an unbounded creative impulse that threatens the expression of divine order. This resurgent chaotic impulse underscores the ongoing debate in Claudel about the source of poetic voice, at once a personal question of vocation and an aesthetic one. Moreover, this resurfacing controversy evolves a revisionist strategy. Recentering the fragmented poetic subject in Rimbaud enables Claudel to submit a Promethean impulse to create to the voice of God.

MYSTICAL VISION AND VOICE: *L'ESPRIT ET L'EAU*

The poet-as-mystic calls forth the second ode, *L'Esprit et l'eau*, as though from the silence out of which God called creation.

> Après le long silence fumant . . .
> Soudain l'Esprit de nouveau, soudain le souffle de nouveau . . .
> Voici l'Ode, voici que cette grande Ode nouvelle vous est présente. (1957, 234–35)[30]

Divine inspiration authors this poetic expression. A leap of the imagination frees the speaking subject from the physical boundaries that otherwise imprison him within the walls of Peking. Could the impulse to create also liberate the poet from God's authority? A subsequent Promethean stance incompatible with the more passive role ascribed to the poet-as-mystic in the first ode indeed alleges the poet's personal will to create and thus to free himself from the physical spaces ("vos cruels arrangements") that impede his vision.

> Puisque je suis libre! que m'importent vos cruels arrangements? puisque du moins je suis libre! puisque j'ai trouvé! puisque moi du moins je suis dehors!
> Puisque je n'ai plus ma place avec les choses créées, mais ma part avec ce qui les crée, l'esprit liquide et lascif! (235)[31]

Read metaphorically with reference to the title, *L'Esprit et l'eau*, "l'esprit liquide" implies the transcendent power of the poet's vision.[32] However, this resurgent poet-as-willful-creator does not attribute the power of his voice to God: "Je partage la liberté de la mer omniprésente" (236).[33] Poetic vision, compared here to water, penetrates all matter: "Je sens, je flaire, je débrouille, je dépiste, je respire avec un certain sens / La chose comment elle est faite!" (237–38).[34] Possessing an omniscient gaze, the poet-as-willful-creator sees himself as a stable speaking subject of knowledge. The identification of *je* and *moi* in Claudel counters the *méconnaissance* discerned in Rimbaud:

> Moi, l'homme,
> Je sais ce que je fais,
> De la poussée et de ce pouvoir même de naissance et de création,
> J'use, je suis maître,
> Je suis au monde, j'exerce de toutes parts ma connaissance.
> Je connais toutes choses et toutes choses se connaissent en moi.
> J'apporte à toute chose sa délivrance.
> Par moi
> Aucune chose ne reste plus seule mais je l'associe à une autre dans mon coeur. (Claudel, 1957, 238)[35]

This passage reiterates the notion of *co-naissance* in *Art poétique*. The poet-as-willful-creator (and, by extension, each person) knows him- or herself in relation to the world by perceiving and therefore creating this relation. Later *versets*, however, identify poetic vision and voice with

God. In Claudel's stance of mystical lyricism, humankind's ability to create emanates from the Divine Poet.

An ongoing process of *connaissance* advances the work of an analogical imagination. Claudel seeks to anchor limitless connections by *again* finding the divine key that unites spirit and matter:

> O mon Dieu, je la vois, la clef maintenant qui délivre,
> Ce n'est point celle qui ouvre, mais celle-là qui ferme! . . .
> Il est fermé par votre volonté comme par un mur et
> par votre puissance comme par une très forte enceinte! . . .
> Il est fermé et voici que toutes choses à mes yeux
> Ont acquis la proportion et la distance. (240)[36]

The poet-as-mystic, once recentered in God, reads empirical reality as a closed—yet mobile—space. Fixed relations among God, self, and world and the continuous movement that constitutes them inform the poet's text: "Je vois bien des manières de ne pas être, mais il n'y a qu'une manière seule / D'être, qui est d'être en vous, qui est vous-même!" (238).[37] Discovering the divine center affirms universal harmony:

> Salut donc, ô monde nouveau à mes yeux, ô monde
> maintenant total!
> O credo entier des choses visibles et invisibles, je vous
> accepte avec un coeur catholique! (240)[38]

By *coeur catholique*, Claudel means both the Catholic Church and a universality. *L'Esprit et l'eau* asserts a mystical truth from a Catholic viewpoint. The *voyant* embraces a perfectly centered universe.

The created world reflects, albeit imperfectly, the Divine Author. Thus the poet intuits His presence, although God is visibly absent from His creation. *L'Esprit et l'eau* reiterates this Catholicism:

> Tout être, comme il est un
> Ouvrage de l'Eternité, c'est ainsi qu'il en est l'expression.
> Elle est présente et toutes choses présentes se passent en
> elle.
> . . . On ne rend que ce que l'on a reçu
> Et comme toutes choses de vous
> Ont reçu l'être, dans le temps elles restituent l'éternel. (241–42)[39]

Claudel's *voyant* expressly rejects personal subjectivity. Created in God's image, he speaks in His eternal voice:

> J'ai une voix, et j'écoute, et j'entends le bruit qu'elle fait.
> ... Ainsi la voix avec qui de vous je fais des mots éternels!
> je ne puis rien nommer que d'éternel....
>   Et moi qui fais les choses éternelles avec ma voix,
> faites que je sois tout entier
>   Cette voix, une parole totalement intelligible. (242–43)[40]

Totally intelligible speech presumes an unequivocal speaking subject identified with poetic voice and the view that language communicates presupposed meaning.[41]

Claudel the Catholic poet repeats the *Verbe* at the origin of creation: "Dieu qui avez soufflé sur le chaos ... vous avez mis dans mes narines le même esprit de création et de figure" (243).[42]

> Le verbe intelligible et la parole *exprimée* et la voix qui est l'esprit et l'eau!
> ... elle n'est tout entière que mesure même,
>   La mesure sainte, libre, toute-puissante, créatrice....
>   C'est un aliment invisible, c'est la mesure qui est au-dessus de toute parole. (247–48)[43]

La mesure sainte is the primordial metaphoric structure of *connaissance*. Metaphor as analogy of mimetic proportionality joins invisible and visible reality. Poetic voice, both spiritual (*l'esprit*) and material (*l'eau*), transcends difference. Claudel's mystical lyricism, then, connects poiesis with the divine act at the origin of creation. Three remaining odes celebrate the revelation of God in His creation while also countering through sublimation intermittent eruptions of the poet's will to create. Submission to divine inspiration indeed endorses mystical lyricism over subjective idealism and makes God the master of the creative impulse.

VOICING MYSTICAL LYRICISM: *MAGNIFICAT*

The third ode, *Magnificat*, embraces the "poetic duty ... to discover God in all things and make them accessible to Love" (Claudel, 1957, 248):

> Mon âme magnifie le Seigneur.
> ... Et je fus devant vous comme un lutteur qui plie

> Non qu'il se croit faible, mais parce que l'autre est plus
> fort.
> Vous m'avez appelé par mon nom
> Comme quelqu'un qui le connaît, vous m'avez choisi
> entre tous ceux de mon âge. (248–49)[44]

To resolve the struggle between the self-willed creator and the Divine Author of all creation, the poet-as-mystic again represses his subjectivity. The assumption of a cohesive subject of knowledge counters the divisive effects of the Lacanian Other that we considered in Rimbaud. Voicing the creative impulse transcends the personal in Claudel:

> Et de cet esprit et bruit que vous avez mis en moi, ...
> Que le bruit se fasse voix et que la voix en moi se fasse
> parole!
> Parmi tout l'univers qui bégaie, laissez-moi préparer mon
> coeur comme quelqu'un qui sait ce qu'il a à dire ...
> que je trouve seulement la parole juste, que j'exhale
> seulement
> Cette parole de mon coeur, l'ayant trouvée, et que je
> meure ensuite ... comme le vieux prêtre qui meurt en
> consacrant! (250–51)[45]

The poetic subject speaks unequivocally, as Claudel writes, "like a man who knows what it is he has to say." This intelligible poetic speech, however, is not that of a self-willed creator. Insight through which the inspired artist sees and then transposes the invisible divine design of the empirical world into discourse does not stem from the individual psyche or, more precisely, does not arise from the unconscious Other within the self in Rimbaud. Rather, Claudel's *voyant* receives inspiration from God.

> A la tâche qui m'est départie l'éternité seule peut suffire.
> Et je sais que je suis responsable, et je crois en mon maître
> ainsi qu'il croit en moi.
> J'ai foi en votre parole et je n'ai pas besoin de papier.
> C'est pourquoi rompons les liens des rêves, et foulons aux
> pieds les idoles, et embrassons la croix avec la croix.
> Car l'image de la mort produit la mort, et l'imitation de la
> vie
> La vie, et la vision de Dieu engendre la vie éternelle. (253)[46]

Revealing Divine Order

In striking opposition to the implicit recourse to dreamlike strategies we traced in Rimbaud, Claudel "break[s] the bondage of dreams." Whereas we followed Rimbaud's opening up of poetic discourse to the unconscious Other within the self, Claudel links poetic discourse with unbounded inspiration outside the self, with the eternal God.

In the *Odes*, the new poetic language, which marries lyricism and mysticism, harks back to the poetic metaphysics outlined in *Art poétique*. *Magnificat* echoes the notion of *connaissance/co-naissance* that we now understand informs Claudel's theory of poetic voice and worldview. The lyric, which finds the basis of its rhythm in the body, generally ascribes personal expression to an individual speaking subject. Claudel refuses personal lyricism to see in God's light and to speak in the name of the Divine Father. His poetic vision transcends the individual body and, moreover, disparate bodies or elements and illuminates through the principle of mimetic analogy an occluded unity:

> ... ce n'est pas de ce corps seul qu'il me faut venir à bout,
> mais de ce monde brut tout entier, fournir
> De quoi comprendre et le dissoudre et l'assimiler
> En vous et ne plus voir rien
> Réfractaire à votre lumière en moi!
> Car il y en a par les yeux et par les oreilles qui voient et qui entendent,
> Mais pour moi c'est par l'esprit seul que je regarde et que j'écoute.
> Je verrai avec cette lumière ténébreuse! (255)[47]

Magnificat bears out the turn from sensory to intellectual apprehension developed in *Connaissance de l'Est* and repeated in *Art poétique*. Here the divinely enlightened poet sees in and through his contemplation of the visible world a realm synonymous with an invisible spiritual reality. Whereas we related Rimbaud's illuminations to the unconscious Other, Claudel's poetic sight, like that of a priest, derives from the soul in communion with God (261, 263).[48] The poet-as-mystic speaks the divine impulse of all creation and sees clearly God's shadow in the empirical world.

The first three odes, at once spiritual and aesthetic exercises directed at Claudel's calling, poet versus priest, advance an emergent poetic stance in a Catholic world. The evolving interplay of aesthetics and metaphysics in these texts presents an alternating emphasis. The ode to *Les Muses* focuses on the nature of inspiration and the poet's role; *L'Es-*

prit et l'eau and *Magnificat* give thematic precedence to theological questions. The fourth ode echoes the examination of the creative process in *Les Muses*. *La Muse qui est la Grâce* also highlights through explicit psychical ascesis the developing relation of lyric voice to mystic vision in the *Cinq grandes odes*. A wavering in the three preceding odes, where the poet alternately wrestles against and submits to the voice within himself, culminates in this fourth ode. In a revisionist sublimation of personal lyricism traditionally identified in literary history with the figure of the Muse, Claudel's scheme exalts the divine impulse of creation.

REVISITING THE MUSE: FINDING GOD WITHIN THE CREATIVE SELF

Having embraced the task of illuminating God in His creation, Claudel again confronts his own desire to create. The *argument* preceding *La Muse qui est la Grâce* makes explicit this struggle within the personal self: "Dialogue du poëte avec la Muse qui devient peu à peu la Grâce. Il essaye de la refouler, il lui demande de le laisser à son devoir humain, à la place de son âme il lui offre l'univers entier qu'il va recréer par l'intelligence et la parole" (1957, 263).[49] This dialogue between the poet and his Muse presents a defense against the decentering effects of unconscious mental activity that I traced in Rimbaud. By positioning this autonomous impulse outside the self and identifying this inner voice with divine inspiration, Claudel moves toward the Catholic worldview upon which his poetic project insists.

The dialogic form of *La Muse qui est la Grâce* simulates the poet in self-address, questioning his relation to an inner voice.

> Ah, je suis ivre! ah je suis livré au dieu! j'entends une voix en moi et la mesure qui s'accélère....
> Que m'importent tous les hommes à présent! Ce n'est pas pour eux que je suis fait, mais pour le
> Transport de cette mesure sacrée!
> O le cri de la trompette bouchée! ô le coup sourd sur la tonne orgiaque!
> Que m'importe aucun d'eux? Ce rythme seul! Qu'ils me suivent ou non? Que m'importe qu'ils m'entendent ou pas?
> Voici le déploiement de la grande Aile poétique! (264–65)[50]

Rimbaud assumes a split self to configure the relation of subject and discourse. The poet in Claudel, however, seeks to master his voice and thus overcome such division. In terms that later will be echoed by Jung, it is a matter of harmonizing the masculine principle of reason, the animus, and the feminine, creative impulse, the anima, associated with the imagination.[51] In *La Muse qui est la Grâce*, the poet withstands the eruption of a voice within that he cannot identify as his own:

> Et que je suis un peu ivre en sorte qu'un autre mot parfois
> Vient à la place du vrai, à la façon que tu aimes,
> Laisse-moi avoir explication avec toi,
> Laisse-moi te refouler dans cette strophe, avant que tu ne
> reviennes sur moi comme une vague avec un cri félin!
> Va-t'en de moi un peu! laisse-moi faire ce que je veux un
> peu!
> . . . Du moins laisse-moi faire de ce papier ce que je veux et
> le remplir avec un art studieux,
> Ma tâche, comme ceux-là qui en ont une. (265–66)[52]

This dialogic struggle with the voice that the poet does not yet recognize as the Muse of Divine Inspiration (*la Grâce*) implies a refusal to open up poetic discourse to the Other that disrupts the structure of poetic expression. Moreover, contrary to the passive role played by the speaking subject in previous odes, here the poet attempts consciously to control his role in creativity.

> Et moi je dis qu'il n'est rien dans la nature qui soit fait sans
> dessein et propos à l'homme adressé,
> Et comme lumière pour l'oeil et le son pour l'oreille,
> ainsi toute chose pour l'analyse de l'intelligence,
> Continuée avec l'intelligence qui la
> Refait de l'élément qu'elle récupère . . .
> Et je puis parler, continue avec toute chose muette,
> Parole qui est à sa place intelligence et volonté.
> Je chanterai le grand poëme de l'homme soustrait au
> hasard! (267)[53]

Indeed the poet intends to master his voice: "I shall sing the great song of man set free from chance." Yet, as in preceding odes, inspiration, by virtue of its nature, escapes conscious control. Here in the fourth ode, the Muse repeats this point: "Je ne suis pas accessible à la raison, tu ne feras point, tu ne feras point de moi ce que tu veux, mais je chante et danse!" (268).⁵⁴ Like "the heart that has its reasons that reason cannot know," the Muse—the voice that the poet hears within himself—mocks his effort to *reason* with her: "O sot, au lieu de raisonner, profite de cette heure d'or! . . . apprends le grand rire divin!" (268).⁵⁵ This inner voice notably differs from the unconscious Other that alienates the speaking subject from itself in Rimbaud. The voice that Claudel's poetic subject hears within himself is the creative word that God inspires.

The Muse then identifies herself as a sign of *Grâce (fureur divine)*, a revelation prepared metaphorically by the title. The identification of the Muse with grace or divine inspiration ("Tu m'appelles la Muse et mon autre nom est la Grâce" [275]) presents the essential synthesis of poiesis and theology in Claudel's mystical lyricism.⁵⁶ The poet, however, does not yet see clearly and thus initially beseeches God to free him from the "temptress's words": "Alors ne permettez point à celle-ci qu'elle vienne me tenter comme un jeune homme / Non point avec un chant et avec la beauté de son visage" (271).⁵⁷ This unpredictable voice does not intend to incite the poet's desire per se but rather demands, through the sublimation of the poet's personal subjectivity, the death of the self. The poet recognizes the sacrifice ("O mort de moi-même et de tout, en qui il me faut souffrir création" [273]), without yet understanding the source of the voice that demands this self-surrender.⁵⁸ In Christian terms, one must lose oneself to gain God. The inspired voice of the poet-as-mystic, which transcends difference inside and outside the speaking subject, so emerges from the death of personal lyricism:

> Car c'est toi-même que je demande.
> O libérateur des hommes! ô réunisseur d'images et de cités!
> Libère-toi toi-même! Réunisseur de tous les hommes, réunis-toi toi-même!
> Sois un seul esprit! sois une seule intention! (275)⁵⁹

Claudel's poet must oppose the inherently divided self in Rimbaud. Speaking from the divine center at the origin of creation, the poet-as-mystic voices the relations that unite different aspects of creation and thus silences the alienating impulses of the unconscious Other within the self.

TRANSCENDING THE PERSONAL, VOICING THE DIVINE

The various movements underscored in the first four odes—priest versus poet, poet-as-mystic versus poet-as-willful-creator, the autonomous nature of poetic inspiration, and the relation of the subject to discourse—converge in the final ode, *La Maison fermée*. The title suggests closure and, moreover, the resolution of conflicting vocations, voices, and visions. This completion alluded to in the *argument* preceding the ode is at once personal and universal: "Pour être capable de contenir, il faut que le poëte lui-même soit fermé, à l'imitation de l'Univers que Dieu a créé inépuisable et fini" (1957, 277).[60] In other words, only a cohesive subject can express the fixed unity of the created world: "Mon devoir premier est Dieu et cette tâche qu'il m'a donnée à faire qui est de réunir tout en lui" (277).[61]

The poet's self, reiterating the sublimation of desire in *La Muse qui est la Grâce*, dies to become the voice, the *porte-parole*, of God.

> Jadis j'ai connu la passion, mais maintenant je n'ai plus que celle de la patience et du désir
>   De connaître Dieu dans sa fixité et d'acquérir la vérité par l'attention et chaque chose qui est toutes les autres en la recréant avec son nom intelligible dans ma pensée. (280)[62]

The poet-as-mystic sublimates the unbounded desire of the poet-as-willful-creator and thus, as previous odes have already suggested, submits his will to God. Desire in Claudel unites rather than, as in Rimbaud, dividing.

> Mon désir est d'être le rassembleur de la terre de Dieu!
>   ... Le Verbe de Dieu est Celui en qui Dieu s'est fait à l'homme donnable.
>   La parole créée est cela en qui toutes choses créées sont faites à l'homme donnables. (280–81)[63]

By *le Verbe*, Claudel understands at once the Word at the source of all poetic creation, "le Verbe par excellence, le Verbe transcendant, le Verbe qui est Dieu, le Verbe qui est chez Dieu, le Verbe Etre" (*Oeuvres complètes* 29:223).[64] The metonymic principle of juxtaposition underlying metaphoric expression in Rimbaud pulls elements apart. In Claudel, the metaphoric copula joins disparate elements by surpassing their differences. Poiesis thus incorporates theology. As Raymond Jouve affirms, Claudel intends "remettre Dieu dans sa Création et sa Création en Dieu à l'aide de ce Verbe qui a été si généreusement départi au poète" (58). "C'est par ... son Verbe que le poète restitue le Monde à Dieu" (60).[65]

In a Catholic world, everything comes from and returns to the Divine Father.

God created humanity in His image. So too the finite universe reflects the divine impulse, fixed in design yet ever evolving through the movement that constitutes it. This iambic rhythm, central to both *connaissance* and metaphor, analogically structures Claudel's mystical lyricism:

> O point de toutes parts autour de moi où s'ajustent les fins indivisibles! univers indéchirable! ô monde inépuisable et fermé! . . .
> O Dieu, rien n'existe que par une image de votre perfection! (1957, 281)[66]

The created world, albeit an imperfect reflection of the divine, is the sight/site of *poesis perennis* for the poet. In short, visible reality mirrors God. The poet-as-mystic voices the eternal measure, which relates through *connaissance* the many and varied phenomena of the empirical world:

> Soyez béni, mon Dieu, qui ne laissez pas vos oeuvres inachevées
> Et qui avez fait de moi un être *fini* à l'image de votre perfection.
> Par là je suis capable de comprendre étant capable de tenir et de mesurer.
> Vous avez placé en moi le rapport et la proportion
> Une fois pour toutes; . . .
> Poète, j'ai trouvé le mètre. Je mesure l'univers avec son image que je constitue. (284–85)

"[C']est moi qui lui confère son sens; toute chose en moi devient / Eternelle en la notion que j'en ai" (288).[67] The metaphoric work of the poetic subject's word, inspired by the Divine Father, analogically joins self to world and self to God. As Claudel declares, "notre imagination ne peut pas ajouter un seul chiffre à ce Nombre en extase devant Votre Unité" (289).[68] In striking opposition to the production of meaning at the level of the signifier in Rimbaud, Claudel's analogical imagination reproduces the Word at the origins of creation.

The vast poetic project that I have traced from *Connaissance de l'Est* to *Art poétique* and then to *Cinq grandes odes* constitutes, in short, a metaphysics. Claudel's mystical lyricism connects through analogy of mimetic proportionality self, world, and God. Metaphor, at once poietic principle of construal and mimetic expression, transposes universal harmony into discourse and thus reveals the hidden meaning of the visible world. Claiming to have been deeply *inspired* by Rimbaud, Claudel reads his avowed precursor's poetic word as an instrument of divine revelation. This religious mis-reading of the unconscious Other within the self in Rimbaud projects in turn Claudel's own divine source of poetry.[69] The stark contrast between the immanent source of the Other in Rimbaud and the transcendent source of the Other in Claudel directs us to read their relation as a compelling case of projected literary paternity. What Claudel finds in Rimbaud reflects his own desire, vision, and voice.

TWISTS AND TURNS OF POETIC HISTORY

Claudel encloses Rimbaud's abandoned quest to illuminate the unknown within the circle of mimesis and hears in this *fils du Soleil* the voice of the Eternal Father.[70] His mystical lyricism, consonant with his own turning back to Catholicism, joins poiesis and the original *Verbe* to recover *le lieu et la formule* of the supernatural. This transcendent center grounds poetic re-creation of universal harmony in the structuring principle of metaphor as analogy. Rimbaud's ambiguous allusions to Christianity, which repeatedly refute God, hardly support Claudel's myth. Rather, the religious twists and turns that Claudel transfers onto Rimbaud, like the critical turns of *metaphor/a* that we followed in their respective poetics, fundamentally distinguish them. This poetic revisionism enables us to see more clearly how their discontinuity constructs a significant chapter of French poetic history.

Poetic sensibility informs the linguistic means adopted by a poet to relate self and world. Rimbaud rejects the view of language as self-centered and denotative and demystifies the analogical unity of God, self, and world. He discloses, through an examination of creativity, the signifying relations that form the poetic self in terms of the unconscious Other. His postmodern poetics assumes the decentering effects of the primordial *écart* constitutive of the speaking subject and discourse alike. Claudel, to the contrary, aiming to express a transcendent divine hierarchy to which the created world attests, returns to unequivocal meaning. This union of poiesis and religion restores metaphor as mimetic proportionality to apprehend the relation of self and world centered in God.

As the expression of an eventual conversion, Claudel's correction of

Rimbaud projects his own spiritual crisis and debate with creativity. This revisionist scheme works against influence to map out different creative impulses. What escapes from Claudel's blindly enclosing stance is the unconscious Other that speaks by not saying what it means and by meaning what it cannot say. Reading this postmodern voice *dans tous les sens* illuminates the unspeakable impulse to create in Rimbaud and in artists, such as Claudel, writing in his shadow. Poetic history indeed repeats itself—more precisely, creatively corrects itself—yet does not tell us the whole story, a story that we see even more darkly without the light of mis-reading.

APPENDIX
NOTES
WORKS CONSULTED
INDEX

APPENDIX

Critical Turns of Metaphor

NEOCLASSICAL TURNS OF *METAPHORA*: DUMARSAIS VERSUS FONTANIER

The terms *neoclassical* and *romantic* intend the principles and sensibility associated with contrasting aesthetic movements that evolved in literature and art chiefly in the seventeenth and eighteenth and in the late eighteenth and early nineteenth centuries, respectively. Generally speaking, whereas neoclassicism involves rigid adherence to canons of form derived mainly from classical antiquity, romantic aesthetics encourages freedom of treatment with an emphasis on imaginative writing.

French neoclassical rhetoricians César Chesneau Dumarsais and Pierre Fontanier debate a tropological approach to rhetorical figures as stylistic and/or semantic deviation from quotidian language. Dumarsais, writing in 1730, blurs the line between mimesis and poiesis, whereas Fontanier upholds a strict classical approach. The romantic view that evolves concurrently takes the metaphoric split a step further. With the premise that all language has its genesis in metaphor, the critical romantic turn implies paradoxically that ordinary language is in fact a deviation from an original figurative or metaphoric discourse.

Dumarsais begins *Les tropes* by refuting the skewed Aristotelean legacy that "figure" or metaphor separates poetic discourse from ordinary speech (1–3). For Dumarsais, figurative expression pervades all language. He then questions whether the poetic derives from the quotidian or vice versa. Although ostensibly situating the prosaic first, Dumarsais asserts in turn that language without figures is inconceivable. He thus supports the metaphoric genesis of all language asserted in what will be the romantic view:

> En éfet, je suis persuadé qu'il se fait plus de Figures un jour de marché à la Halle, qu'il ne s'en fait en plusieurs jours d'assemblées académiques. Ainsi, bien loin que les Figures s'éloignent du langage ordinaire des hommes, ce seroient au contraire les façons de parler sans figures qui s'en éloigneroient, s'il étoit possible de faire un discours où il n'y eût que des expressions non figurées. (1–3)

Dumarsais retains an Aristotelean notion of deviation in his view of the figurative manner of speaking in *all* language. Yet, unlike his predecessor, he conceives of rhetorical intentionality as pertaining to a change in style rather than in meaning (13–14). Semantic deviation enters into Dumarsais's account not to differentiate poetic language as a separate and distinct category but to distinguish trope as a particular type of figure or manner of speaking found in all language.

Tropes for Dumarsais involve semantics, whereby the figurative (metaphoric) meaning of a word supplants the literal one (18). Contrary to Aristotle, Dumarsais rejects common usage to distinguish "le sens propre" from "le sens figuré." He adopts instead a diachronic, or historical, approach and makes the first use of a term its true (literal) meaning. Although this approach to figurative meaning ("un mot pris dans un sens métaphorique perd sa signification propre et en prend une nouvèle" [155]) selectively adheres to Aristotelean rhetoric by joining the syntagmatic and the paradigmatic axes to formulate various figures of the poetic mode, Dumarsais unwittingly makes a modern move.

A Jakobsonian before his time, Dumarsais suggests the intermingling of the metonymic and the metaphoric axes and, by extension, prose and poetry and thus hints at the poietic work of metaphor grounded in metonymy. Metonymy for Dumarsais stands as the structural exemplar of all trope figures construed in semantic terms:

> Le mot de *Métonymie* signifie transposition, ou changement de nom, un nom pour un autre. En ce sens cette figure comprend tous les autres tropes; car dans tous les tropes, un mot n'étant pas pris dans le sens qui lui est propre, il réveille une idée qui pourroit être exprimée par un autre mot. (76–77)

In this scheme, metaphor is a trope figure: *trope* because it modifies proper or literal meaning; *figure*, because it involves a manner of speaking different from ordinary usage or style found in all language. Whereas the rhetoric of metaphor stemming from an *uncommon* combination of terms presents a semantic anomaly, its poietic functioning overcomes this incompatibility by evoking a novel association. This double nature of metaphor in Dumarsais recalls its ambivalent status in Aristotle, at once mimetic and poietic.

NEOCLASSICAL RETURN TO METAPHOR: FONTANIER

Both Aristotle and Dumarsais conflate the decorative-constitutive opposition and, by extension, the role of deviation by aligning metaphor with mimesis and poiesis. To the contrary, in the definitive version of *Traité général des figures du discours*, Fontanier in 1830 again draws a strict line between the figurative expression and the literal one. However, his return to a mimetic view of metaphor unwittingly crosses with a poietic role.

Fontanier collapses Dumarsais's distinction between *figure*, based on stylistic deviation, and *trope*, grounded in semantic deviation. *Figure*, in Fontanier's view, *also* involves tropic meaning since "one could find thousands of examples where the most bold figures in the beginning cease to be regarded as such once they become common and usual" (59). He strictly separates the literal/proper from the figurative/metaphoric. This *écart* embodies the structural principle of figure that deviates *both* in form (Dumarsais's *figure*) and in meaning (Dumarsais's *trope*) from ordinary expression. By "sens littéral," Fontanier understands "the sense stemming from words taken literally, words understood according to their ordinary usage: it is consequently the one that comes immediately to mind for those who understand the language" (59).

Notwithstanding the line drawn between figurative and proper meaning, and thus a strict metaphoric split, Fontanier's definition of the *figurative* recalls the poietic aspect of metaphor in Aristotle that brings about fresh insight:

> Le sens spirituel, sens détourné ou figuré d'un assemblage de mots, est celui que le sens littéral fait naître dans l'esprit par les circonstances du discours, par le ton de la voix, ou par la liaison des idées exprimées avec celles qui ne le sont pas. Il s'appelle *spirituel*, parce qu'il est tout de l'esprit . . . c'est l'esprit qui le forme ou le trouve à l'aide du *sens littéral*. Il n'existe pas pour celui qui ne sait pas que *la lettre tue* et que *l'esprit vivifie*. (59)

Echoing also Dumarsais's observation that "ce n'est que par une nouvelle union des termes, que les mots se donnent le sens métaphorique" (161), Fontanier seems to advance that novel associations thus produced have no literal substitute.

The production of figurative expression, that is, of metaphoric form, may indeed be poietic. Fontanier nonetheless has recourse to a mimetic principle to decode its meaning. For him, figure has a substitutable literal equivalent, the simple expression from which it deviates (64). Fontanier insists on the paraphrasable (literal) meaning of figure. Dumarsais exposes instead the self-regulated functioning of figure in Aristotelean rhetoric and thus prefigures the modern debate concerning the poeticity of all discourse.

Modern literary theorists continue the neoclassical debate about the structure of figure. Todorov challenges the rhetoric of Gérard Genette, "where the figure exists only by opposition to a literal expression" (*Poetics* 36–37), as in Fontanier, and of Jean Cohen, who with similar presuppositions defines figure in terms of the transgression of a linguistic rule. Todorov upholds instead Dumarsais's definition as the right one, noting how a figure draws attention to itself as an effect of discourse: "A figure is what gives discourse a character of its own, what renders it perceptible; figurative discourse is an opaque discourse, discourse without figures is transparent" (38). Blocking the immediate transmission of information assumed in a communicative model of language, figurative discourse forefronts through a complex structuring the mode of the

Appendix

utterance itself rather than the message. This view situates the work of metaphor in discourse, a critical turn that endorses its poietic functioning over mimesis in what will be the romantic view.

PROTOROMANTIC METAPHOR IN CONDILLAC

In *Essai sur l'origine des connaissances humaines* (written in 1746), Vico's French contemporary Etienne Bonnet de Condillac adopts the precedence of figurative language. Although Condillac assumes a broader materialist premise, he analyzes the development of language in more specific terms of "le principe de la liaison des idées" (246–47). His theory of language strikes us as largely romantic rather than as neoclassical, since he connects the original metaphoric character of language with the work of the imagination.

Lacking the power to reason, to think analytically, argues Condillac, humankind first communicated through gestures and unintelligible sounds to express emotions and physical needs (8–9). The rudimentary language that followed functioned metaphorically to convey relations perceived between observable entities (91–92). Like Vico, Condillac asserts that primitive language consisted of sensible images and was necessarily figurative. Conventional signs to designate what would be called literal or proper meaning had not yet emerged: "Le style, dans son origine a été poétique, puisqu'il a commencé par peindre les idées avec les images les plus sensibles" (93). *Poétique* here connotes both the imagistic mode and the evocative capacity of nascent linguistic activity.

For Vico, the first humans anthropomorphically apprehended the unknown in terms of the known. Condillac underscores a similar associative process through which humankind's comprehension increased (170). Language used metaphorically ("et les mêmes noms servirent à désigner les uns et les autres") enables comprehension, that is, mentally grasping one thing *in terms of* another. The structure of the mind and language thus overlap in the *poietic* work of metaphor.

Condillac distinguishes a creative role played by the imagination in the metaphoric transposition through which language first emerged and developed:

> L'imagination travailla pour trouver dans les objets qui frappent les sens des images de ce qui se passoit dans l'intérieur de l'âme. . . . Enfin on se contenta d'avoir trouvé un rapport quelconque entre une action de l'âme et une action du corps, pour donner le même nom à l'une et à l'autre. . . . On voit évidemment comment tous ces noms ont été figurés dans leur origine. (126–27)

Condillac assumes, as does Vico, the precedence of figurative language from which ordinary discourse deviates while retaining the trace of its original metaphoric mode. Moreover, they similarly observe the shift from imagination to reason as the dominant capacity of the mind and the subsequent emergence of prosaic discourse. In their view, this development both obscures and supersedes the figurative origins that the romantic theory of the putative genesis of language recovers:

> On oublia l'origine de ces signes, aussitôt que l'usage en fut familier, et on tomba dans l'erreur de croire qu'ils étaient les noms les plus naturels des choses spirituelles. On s'imagina même qu'ils en expliquoient parfaitement l'essence et la nature, quoiqu'ils n'exprimassent que des analogies fort imparfaites. (Condillac 130–31)

The idea that language in its nascent state was imagistic in form and metaphoric in function evolves in Jean Jacques Rousseau.

ROMANTIC TURN TO METAPHORIC ORIGINS OF LANGUAGE IN ROUSSEAU

In *Essai sur l'origine des langues* (written in or before 1750, published in 1781), Rousseau retains the view espoused by Vico and Condillac that "the first language must have been figurative" (424). In his account of the genesis of language that reaffirms the gestural language of the first peoples (417) and its imagistic mode (419), he states that language evolved naturally because of a "faculté propre à l'homme" (421), an assertion echoing Vico's *sapienza poetica*. Humankind, Rousseau argues, sensed or felt before it could begin to reason. Thus, internal passions first motivated speech (423). Language originally emerged as an expression of pathos. This transposition from psychical into oral and later written trace rendered a figurative mode:

> Comme les premiers motifs qui firent parler l'homme furent les passions, ses premières expressions furent des tropes. Le langage figuré fut le premier à naître; le sens propre fut trouvé le dernier. On n'appela les choses de leur vrai nom que quand on les vit sous leur véritable forme. D'abord on ne parla qu'en poésie; on ne s'avisa de raisonner que long-temps après. (424)

By *figuré*, Rousseau, like Vico and Condillac, means that, on the one hand, the first peoples lacked the power to abstract and therefore used concrete or sensible images to convey their feelings and thoughts. On the other hand, he also intends figurative expression, which *deviates* from the literal. We shall see that in Rousseau's scheme language emerges through three stages: first, the figurative (in the imagistic sense); second, the proper; and third, the metaphoric (in the tropic sense).

Appendix

To discuss how language evolved from its original expression, Rousseau introduces at once the idea of transposition and the notion of deviation, shifting from *figuré* (synonymous with imagistic form) to a semantic opposition between *figuré* and *propre*:

> L'image illusoire offerte par la passion se montrant la première, le langage qui lui répondait fut aussi le premier inventé; il devint ensuite métaphorique, quand l'esprit éclairé, reconnaissant sa première erreur, n'en employa les expressions que dans les mêmes passions qui l'avaient produite. (425)

Language for Rousseau originates in and as figure. He posits the genesis of language in metaphoric transposition from psychological content to imagistic expression. Literal discourse, which advances in a second stage, thus departs from an original figurative language. A third stage then shifts from quotidian to metaphoric expression in the classical sense of semantic deviation.

In Jacques Derrida's view, by grounding the developmental stages of language in semantic deviation, Rousseau unwittingly adopts a primarily logocentric theory:

> Ainsi, tout en affirmant en apparence que le premier langage fut figuré, Rousseau maintient le propre. . . . A l'origine, puisque l'idée première de la passion, son premier représentant, est proprement exprimée. A la fin, parce que l'esprit éclairé fixe le sens propre. (1967, 392)

However, the introduction of a gap between literal and figurative language in Rousseau's treatment of the emergent stages of language does not necessarily deconstruct his formulation of an original figurative language. By connecting the elaboration of common language to that of reason, Rousseau does not abandon his premise that all language originates in metaphor. Rather, like Vico and Condillac, he relates the obfuscation of the initial metaphoric nature of language in ordinary speech to the advent of the analytical functioning of reason, which in turn supersedes the *primitive* faculty of creative association. The competition between imagination and reason in the neoclassical and romantic views that develop from Aristotle informs current debate on the relation of metaphor to language.

NOTES

1. POETIC SUBJECTS AND THEIR DOUBLE: CLAUDEL'S MAP OF MIS-READING RIMBAUD

1. "Rarely, in fact, does one read without preoccupation, in a state of perfect receptiveness; most often every person asks of the text before him or her an answer to his or her own anguish; the meaning of one's spiritual adventure, the solution to one's drama: but the truth that one finds was already within oneself. . . . Why is it strange then that Claudel discovered in Rimbaud what he himself had put there?" In a similar vein, André Suarès remarks that "Claudel n'y voit rien que ce qu'il veut y voir" (qtd. in Pinquet 100; "Claudel sees [in Rimbaud] only what he wants to see"). Translations are my own unless otherwise indicated.

2. "*the illuminator* of all the paths of art, religion, and life." Claudel's letter to Paterne Berrichon is dated juin 1911.

3. "It seems to me that Claudel was not subjected to an influence as much as he tried to respond to questions that Rimbaud's work raised. . . . Claudel interprets Rimbaud in terms of his own development [as a poet]."

4. In contradistinction to my revisionist reading of Rimbaud and Claudel, John MacCombie presupposes a mystical union and an attendant literary affinity between them (xii). He highlights the themes in Claudel's poetic and dramatic works that support connections with Rimbaud and concludes that "when considered in the aggregate these thematic similarities present formidable and all but irrefutable evidence that Rimbaud's influence was indeed all that Claudel said it was" (186). MacCombie, however, unwittingly suggests Claudel's mis-reading of Rimbaud: "Rimbaud's works are really a questioning to which the answer is suggested but never totally offered, and which Claudel brought to what was for him its logical conclusion" (185–86).

5. Bloom identifies a creative conflict at the psychic core of English and American poetry, for example, the voice of Milton in Wordsworth, Keats in Tennyson. For an insightful discussion questioning this model for the history of the French epic in particular, where the anxiety of influence or imitation often involves looking at once backward at precursors and forward to successors, see Godfrey.

6. " . . . I cannot speak about Rimbaud objectively. He had such an influence on me in every way that I feel tied to him both in mind and in poetic instinct by such secret and intimate communications that he seems to be a part of me."

7. Restricting signs of influence to the surface of the text, Frédéric Lefèvre

apparently recognizes a coherent religious symbolism linking the disparate images in Rimbaud's texts that he does not, however, elaborate. In Lefèvre's view, the quest for "truth in one soul and body" in Rimbaud symbolizes a search for God, for the supernatural thought to exist coterminously with the phenomenal world (45). Moses Nagy also supports a unity between Rimbaud and Claudel based on imitation rather than on revisionism: "Upon reading *Les Illuminations* and *Une Saison en Enfer*, [Claudel] finds not only the master to imitate but he also sees the failure of the poet to whom the transcendent refused to yield the secret of the universe" (1978, 10).

8. "I propose to write to you one day about certain subjects close to my heart such as: Catholicism and Arthur Rimbaud (toward whom you seem unjust). Since the initial love at first sight with which the first issue of *La Vogue* struck me where I read the *Illuminations* for the first time, I can say that I owe Rimbaud all that I am intellectually and morally, and I believe that there are few examples of such kindred spirits."

9. In a more recent reexamination of Rimbaud's influence on Claudel, Whitaker restates this "idea of the symbolic" where Rimbaud and Claudel converge in terms of the *sacré* (1987, 13–24).

10. "Rimbaud exerted a major influence on me. Others, and principally Shakespeare, Aeschylus, Dante, and Dostoevsky were my masters and showed me the secrets of my art. But Rimbaud alone exerted an influence that I will call *seminal* and *paternal* and that made me really believe that the act of generation is integral to the nature of the mind and body alike."

11. "I will always remember that morning in June 1886 when I bought the issue of *La Vogue* containing the first part of the *Illuminations*. It was really an illumination for me. I finally left the loathsome world of [Hippolyte] Taine, of [Ernest] Renan, ... this prison, this frightening mechanism governed entirely by immutable laws, to crown it all, both knowable and teachable. ... I discovered the supernatural." Claudel is referring to the May–June issue of *La Vogue*.

12. Petralia similarly observes the equivocal sense of the supernatural in Claudel's early writing about Rimbaud, meaning most likely a worldview based on idealism rather than on positivism (219).

13. For Claudel, who attributed the "revelation of the supernatural" to his reading of the *Illuminations*, which brought him out of the "loathsome world of a Taine or a Renan," as Hugo Friedrich writes, "Rimbaud's chaos of unreality spelled salvation from the confines of reality. It was the impulse leading to Claudel's conversion, although this act itself was entirely Claudel's responsibility. Rimbaud, even more than Baudelaire, should not be interpreted as a Christian, although his poetry contains powers akin to those of religious ecstasy. These powers, however, vanish into the nothingness of an empty supernaturalism" (40–41).

14. "Genius appears there in its most sublime and pure form, like inspiration from an unknown source."

15. "There is no man ... whose memory is dearer to me, to whom I owe

Notes to Pages 6–7

more and to whom I devoted a cult more religious than Arthur Rimbaud. Other writers instructed me, but Rimbaud alone formed me; he was for me the enlightener in a moment of profound darkness, the illuminator of all the paths of art, of religion, of life; such that it is impossible for me to imagine what I would have been without the encounter with this angelic spirit, certainly illumined with the light from above. I feel ties with him that link us to a spiritual ancestor." Paterne Berrichon emphasizes Rimbaud's spiritual influence in his reading of Claudel's statement: "J'y lis . . . qu'il se reconnaît *le fils spirituel* de l'auteur des *Illuminations*" (445; emphasis added; "I understand that Claudel sees himself as the *spiritual* son of the author of the *Illuminations*").

16. Lefèvre cites this letter to Berrichon to pair Claudel with Rimbaud on the basis of spiritual influence: "Arthur Rimbaud fut avant tout une âme religieuse et il n'y a pas lieu de s'étonner que la méditation de son oeuvre et de sa vie ait déterminé la conversion au catholicisme de Paul Claudel" (62; "Arthur Rimbaud was above all a religious soul and thus it is not at all surprising that the meditation of his work and life caused Paul Claudel's conversion to Catholicism").

17. "On a human level, I owe my return to faith to Rimbaud. I was floundering in the swamps of rationalism and thought that the entire world could be explained as easily as a thresher, when the small issue of *Vogue* arrived to break the walls of the loathsome prison where I was suffocating and to bring me the prodigious revelation of the supernatural present everywhere around us. No book helped me more than *Une saison en enfer* in this terrible agony of recovering lost truth."

18. Catharine Savage Brosman so remarks, "Claudel's greatest focus of interest in Rimbaud's work was on *Une saison en enfer*, which he took to be the expression of the poet's most daring attempts at prometheism [sic] and satanism and his consequent hellish suffering and recognition of error (which he compared to his own) and in which he saw 'the trace of God,' the light of the supernatural" (32).

19. A retrospective comment by Claudel on the reign of materialism underscores the primordial role played by Rimbaud in his conversion: "C'est à ce moment-là que l'auteur de ma conversion a paru, que j'ai découvert Rimbaud. Je vois encore ce mois de mai 86, où j'ai ouvert la première livraison de *La Vogue* où les *Illuminations* commençaient à paraître" (Claudel et Amrouche 23; "It was at that moment that the author of my conversion appeared, that I discovered Rimbaud. I still recall that month of May in 1886, when I opened the first issue of *La Vogue* in which the *Illuminations* began to appear").

20. "Arthur Rimbaud was an untamed mystic, a spring arising without direction from saturated soil. His life, a misunderstanding, the vain attempt to flee from the voice that solicits him and harasses him, and that he does not want to recognize; until finally, reduced, his leg amputated, lying on this hospital bed in Marseilles he would believe!"

21. " 'We are not in the world!' — 'Through the spirit, humankind goes to God! . . . This moment of awakening gave me the vision of purity . . . ' "

22. "Everything suggests that in evoking Rimbaud, Claudel was obsessed by his own case." See also Morisot (609–10).

23. "In a moment my heart was touched and I believed. . . . In trying . . . to reconstruct the moments that followed this extraordinary instant, I found that the ensuing elements formed a single flash . . . that divine providence used to reach and to open the heart of a poor desperate child."

24. Yves Bonnefoy questions a Christian portrayal of Rimbaud: "It is not true, as some Catholic authors have been pleased to state, that Rimbaud's life was the flight of a conscience before a divinity it had tried to deny—up to the final moment when, vanquished and ravished, it yielded to that inexorable love. Such a conception has the virtue of turning this exemplary destiny into indirect evidence of the existence of God . . . and if Rimbaud's work has any value as a testimony, it is clearly and only as a witness to that *death* of the divine that Nietzsche also described" (1973, 143). Bonnefoy's statement recalls Petralia's remark that "s'il y a une analogie entre les poètes, c'est seulement dans la lutte, non dans sa conclusion" (222; "if there is an analogy between [these] poets, it is only in the struggle, [and not] in its conclusion").

25. "The Arthur Rimbaud of the 1912 [preface] is a double of Claudel himself working towards conversion."

26. "But it is not speech that he heard. Is it a voice?"

27. "Is it then foolhardy to think that a superior will inspires him?"

28. "Is it common to see a sixteen-year-old child gifted with the faculties of expression of a man of genius?"

29. "He contemplates with ardent and profound curiosity, with a mysterious understanding that can no longer be expressed in 'pagan words' the things that surround us and that he knows we see only through reflections and enigmas. . . . All of life is not too much for the spiritual conquest of this universe opened up by the explorers of this end of the century, to exhaust creation, to know something about what it means, to endow with words this crucifying voice within him."

30. Etiemble vehemently denounces Claudel's canonization of Rimbaud and writes of Claudel's 1912 preface to Rimbaud's works, "le texte fameux sur le 'mystique à l'état sauvage,' un des textes les plus faux, les plus malfaisants jamais écrits sur Rimbaud, car il le fut par un écrivain de génie, secondé par une Eglise; de plus, il orne tous les exemplaires de l'édition qui, pendant plus de trente ans, sera de beaucoup la plus lue" (114; "the famous text about the 'untamed mystic' [is] one of the most false and damaging texts ever written about Rimbaud because it was written by an author of genius, backed by [the] church; moreover, [this text] embellishes the edition of [Rimbaud's works] that will be read the most for over thirty years").

31. "that of violence, of the strictly male, of blind genius that emerges like

a gush of blood, like a cry that one cannot restrain, in verse of unheard force and abruptness."

32. "[The] *Illuminations* awakened, that is, revealed, the supernatural that continuously accompanies the natural."

33. "In the morning, when [one] and [one's] memories are not awake at the same time, or throughout a long day's walk, a continuity develops between the soul and the body subjected to its rhythmic mode. A sort of open hypnosis establishes itself, a unique state of pure receptivity."

34. See Claudel's discussion of Rimbaud *le voyant* in *Présence et prophétie* (*Oeuvres complètes* 20:411).

35. "For us, language takes on less value as expression and more as sign; fortuitous words that come to mind . . . form a type of incantation that blocks consciousness, while our intimate mirror is left in relation to things outside of us in a state of almost material sensibility."

36. Fowlie's observation supports my reading, albeit in different terms: "Claudel learned from the example of Baudelaire and Rimbaud the lesson of 'pure receptivity,' a state in which language will be far less an expression through words than a revelation of meaning through symbols. Words, rising up almost fortuitously from the subconscious or from the secret depths of the poet's consciousness, will, on their own accord, produce the particular medium of communication that is, in fact, poetry" (38). Yet, as Fowlie adds, "Claudel transformed into his own religious symbolism the symbolist practice of Baudelaire, Rimbaud and Mallarmé" (39).

37. "The poet no longer finds expression by searching for words, but by silencing himself and making nature pass over him the sensible species that 'take hold and pull.' He and the world discover each other."

38. "Disordered images that substitute for grammatical elaboration and logic alike [are] a type of direct and metaphoric joining."

39. "With this powerful creative artist, the term 'like' disappearing, hallucination takes root and the two terms of metaphor seem equally real to him."

40. "An extreme practice, a kind of 'materialist' mysticism that could have confused this mind, [which] otherwise [is] solid and reasonable. But it was a question of going to the *spirit*, of pulling off the mask of this 'absent' nature, of finally possessing the text accessible to all of the senses, 'the truth in one body and soul,' a world adapted to our personal soul." Balakian also opposes Claudel to the surrealists by observing that a radically different mystical motivation underlies their respective texts (9, 10, 32, 65).

41. In *La poésie au XIXe siècle*, originally published in 1937 (*Oeuvres complètes* 29:222), Claudel attributes the *failure* of some nineteenth-century poetry to the expulsion of religion. He restores the truth value of poetry anchored by Catholicism.

42. "His mission accomplished, Rimbaud exiles himself, imprisoning himself in silence."

43. "Thought also no longer develops according to logic, but, like with a musician, by melodic designs and the relation of juxtaposed notes."

44. "I am one who took his word for it, someone who had faith in him."

45. Claudel, prefacing the account of his conversion, recalls the reign of scientific positivism that shaped him intellectually and morally prior to his reading of Rimbaud: "Que l'on se rappelle ces tristes années quatre-vingts, l'époque du plein épanouissement de la littérature naturaliste.... Tous les (soi-disant) grands hommes de ce siècle finissant s'étaient distingués par leur hostilité à l'Église. Renan régnait.... J'acceptais l'hypothèse moniste et mécaniste dans toute sa rigueur, je croyais ... que ce monde était un enchaînement dur d'effets et de causes que la science allait arriver ... à débrouiller parfaitement" (1965, 1009; "Let us not forget the sad [18]80s, the apogee of naturalist literature.... All the so-called great men in the final decades of [the nineteenth] century were distinguished by their hostility to the church. Renan reigned.... I accepted the monist and mechanistic hypothesis in all of its rigor, I believed ... that the world was a chain of effects and causes that science would succeed in explaining perfectly").

46. "The first glimmer of truth was given to me by the encounter with the books of a great poet to whom I owe eternal gratitude and who played a preponderant role in forming my thought, Arthur Rimbaud. Reading the *Illuminations*, then a few months later *Une saison en enfer*, was a major event for me. For the first time, these books cracked open my materialist prison and gave me the living and almost physical impression of the supernatural. But my state of asphyxia and despair remained the same." *Ma conversion*, written in 1909, was first published in *Revue des Jeunes*, 10 oct. 1913.

47. "All of a sudden I had the heartrending feeling of innocence, the eternal childhood of God, an ineffable revelation."

48. "This resistance lasted for four years.... This was the great crisis of my life, this agony of thought about which Arthur Rimbaud had written: 'Spiritual combat is as brutal as battle among men....' It's true, I vowed ... that Jesus Christ was the Son of God. It was to me, Paul, among all others that Christ spoke and promised me His love. But at the same time, if I did not follow Him, he gave me no alternative besides damnation. Ah, I didn't need for anyone to explain what Hell was, and I had had my Season [in Hell]."

49. Isabelle Rimbaud's essay on her brother's mysticism exemplifies the religious recovery of Rimbaud that we find in Claudel.

50. In contrast to Isabelle Rimbaud's insistence on her brother's Catholicism, Rolland de Renéville asserts, "on peut dire qu'il n'est point dans la *Saison* une réminiscence du catholicisme qui ne soit immédiatement suivie d'un violent refus" (170; "one can say that there is not a single recollection of Catholicism in the *Saison* which is not immediately followed by a vehement rejection [of Catholicism]"). Etiemble similarly repudiates the myth of the "Rimbaud mystique," underscoring the role that Claudel played in promulgating this "lie" (143). Etiemble, like Renéville, asks whether a reinterpretation of Rim-

baud in light of a secondhand account of his final surrender to God can disregard the fact that "il ait blasphémé, bafoué le nom de Dieu . . . que des jeunes gens par milliers lisent dans la *Saison* un cantique d'irréligion" (148; "that he desecrated, ridiculed God . . . that thousands of young people read the *Saison* as an irreligious canticle").

51. "The awakening of the soul and of poetic faculties occurred for me at the same time." "The idea that art and poetry are also divine things emerged little by little, slowly and painfully, in my heart."

52. Franco Petralia highlights the spiritual nature of Claudel's myth of Rimbaud (235).

53. "All is not well with the couple Animus and Anima, the mind and the soul." Critics, such as Antoine Adam, read the "Drôle de ménage" ("What an odd couple") in *Délires I* as the story of Rimbaud's liaison with Verlaine (Rimbaud, 1972, 963). See Morisot for a detailed analysis of the connection between Claudel's parable and Rimbaud's *Délires* along these lines (247–68).

54. "It's been a long time since, with the honeymoon over, that Anima could speak freely and Animus listened to her with rapture. After all, wasn't it Anima who brought her dowry and sustains the couple? But Animus did not allow himself to be reduced to this inferior position and soon he revealed his true nature, vain, pedantic, and tyrannical."

55. "Now Anima no longer has the right to say a word, [Animus] takes, as one says, the words right out of her mouth, he knows better what she wishes to say, and by means of his theories and recollections, he turns her words over in his mind, he arranges them so well that poor simple [Anima] does not recognize her own words. Animus is not faithful [to her words], but that does not prevent him from being jealous, because deep down he knows indeed that Anima has all the wealth, he is a beggar and lives only on what she gives him."

56. "The Lord created me at the beginning of his work, the first of his acts of old" (Prov. 8.22). For an insightful analysis of this biblical intertextual source, among others for Claudel's parable, see Millet-Gérard.

57. "But I who have lost wisdom . . . I can no longer speak."

58. "One day when Animus came home unexpectedly . . . he heard Anima singing alone behind a closed door: a strange song, something he did not know, and had no way to find the notes or the lyrics or the key, a strange and marvelous song. Since that time, he tried in an underhanded manner to make her repeat it, but Anima acts like she doesn't understand. She becomes silent as soon as he looks at her. The soul becomes silent when the mind looks at it."

59. "Well Animus finds a trick, he will make [Anima] believe that he is not there. He goes outside, he chats noisily with his friends, he whistles, he plays the lute, he saws wood, he sings silly refrains. Little by little, Anima feels at ease, she looks, she listens, she breathes, she thinks herself alone, and without a sound she will open the door for her divine lover."

60. Fowlie's reading of Claudel's parable to elucidate Rimbaud's text unwittingly suggests the struggle with the creative process that we find in Claudel,

that is, poet-as-willful-creator versus poet-as-mystic: "In this parable of the two selves, or the two parts of the soul, it is obvious that harmony is not easily achieved between *animus* and *anima*. The temptation of animus is the love of self, which may weaken the love of God; and the temptation of anima is, in the romantic sense, the excessive emancipation of the deep self and the resulting contempt of reason. Only in their ideal marriage is true humanity realized" (97–98).

61. " . . . I will not say, like Rimbaud, that *Je est un autre*; what is terrible and sometimes cruel, is precisely that 'I' is not an other, that it is itself, that it is . . . 'more myself than me' and that it is to this 'myself' that the superficial 'I' addresses its calling, the commandment of God that needs it, and often demands of it an unexpected effort for which it is not prepared. 'I' is not an other, it is itself, but an itself not yet complete, not yet having attained the adult state."

62. Gerald Antoine discerns the Jungian process of individuation in Claudel's parable (717–18).

63. "Arthur Rimbaud is not a poet, he is not a man of letters. He is a prophet upon whom the spirit fell . . . as upon Saul. . . . It pleased Providence to give to this 'sixteen-year-old' the faculties of expression of a man of genius. Here is the phenomenon of this monstrous innocent, suddenly charged with a message that he does not at all understand, how surprising then that he could not wrench it from himself without all sorts of spasms, gulps, contortions, and cries!"

64. "I would like to explain this word *prophet*. It is a question of something entirely different from saintliness or virtue. . . . This spirit of prophecy, that is, Inspiration, has never at any moment ceased to prompt humanity. It is this spirit that has inspired so many artists, poets, so many initiators of all sorts. . . . Its accent cannot be imitated, no type of talent or artifice could take its place, we recognize it in the depths of our heart." Littré so underscores the biblical roots of the term *voyant*, notably from prophet (4:2548).

65. "the message of Edenic Purity in the midst of a deadened world, wallowing in materialism."

66. "To *Christ comes*! It is this word . . . that links the *Illuminations* and *Une saison en enfer*." A previous mention of the *Illuminations* in *Un dernier salut à Rimbaud* exemplifies Claudel's hagiographic treatment of his avowed precursor's *Complete Works*, which move toward the the discovery of eternity in the *Saison* (1965, 523–24).

2. PRINCIPLES OF MIS-READING, STRATEGIES OF METAPHOR

1. My analysis profits from Patricia Parker's discussion of the metaphoric plot in these terms: "The copular 'is' of metaphor is less an apocalyptic joining than a playful evasion of all fixities" and thus opens up the multiple metaphoric roles (deviation and copulation, identity and transgression [46, 155]). These

Notes to Pages 20–21

various *plots* position the play of metaphor in its principle, that is, in the seeing of the similar in dissimilars. The metaphorical plot, or strategy, *is* its transport of mental and verbal displacements. Reading poetic discourse in a postmodern way, we re-cover the plot of metaphor without ever filling the gap that its movement or displacement opens. (See also Derrida, 1972, 247–324).

2. On the debate about whether metaphor poses a linguistic question or a cognitive one, see, for example, Tourangeau.

3. Eco articulates well the modern debate about the relation of metaphor to language: "Either a) language is by nature, and originally, metaphorical, and the mechanism of metaphor establishes linguistic activity, every rule or convention arising thereafter in order to discipline, to reduce (and impoverish) the metaphorizing potential that defines [the human being] as a symbolic animal; or b) language (and every other semiotic system) is a rule-governed mechanism, a predictive machine that says which phrases can be generated and which not, and which from those able to be generated are 'good' or 'correct,' or endowed with sense; a machine with regard to which the metaphor constitutes a breakdown, a malfunction, an unaccountable outcome, but at the same time the drive toward linguistic renewal" (1984, 88).

4. To avoid confusion with the field of psycholinguistics, I use the term *psychopoetic* to signify the imbrication of the structure of the mind (in the sense of mental activity, at once conscious and unconscious) and the structure of discourse.

5. See *Oxford English Dictionary* 11:1123. Lakoff and Johnson comment that "although Aristotle's theory of how metaphor works is the classic view, his praise of metaphor's ability to induce insight was never carried over into modern philosophical thought. With the rise of empirical science as a model for truth, the suspicion of poetry and rhetoric became dominant in Western thought, with metaphor and other figurative devices becoming objects of scorn once again" (192).

6. I shall develop in Claudel the expanded plot of metaphor that Eva Feder Kittay proposes: "The conception of thought and language necessary to move beyond a restricted view of metaphor requires an understanding of mind as active and creatively engaged in the forming of percepts and concepts and in unifying the diversity of the given" (5–6). Her formulation of the cognitive import of *metaphora* does not account, however, for metaphoric practice in Rimbaud unbounded from a unifying system or worldview.

7. The ambivalent positioning of metaphor by Aristotle in both poetry and prose informs subsequent neoclassical and romantic elaborations of metaphor. See appendix.

8. Liselotte Gumpel takes issue with a mistaken ontological category in Aristotle. She states that "what language 'says' or 'calls' and what 'is' or 'exists' in empirical reality are two different 'things'" and questions the "neat correspondence between *analogies* that *exist* in the *world* and four extant *words* or terms that *express* them as perfect stand-ins" suggested in Aristotle (218–19).

From Gumpel's critical view, metaphor and the transfer that it performs exist only in discourse. Irène Tamba takes a similar position that *locates* metaphor strictly in discourse. Tamba's treatment of metaphor as a discursive construction reveals the syntagmatic contexture that a strictly paradigmatic view of rhetorical figures conceals (176–77). This syntagmatic or metonymic structure develops the poietic aspect of metaphor at play in Aristotle.

9. Poststructuralist psychoanalysis makes rhetorical figures "homologous to the mechanisms of the unconscious" (Felman, 1985, 29).

10. Robert Haskell suggests the relation of metaphoric cognition to primary process ideation that my analysis elaborates (67–80, esp. 70–71).

11. Michelet, claiming Vico as an important precursor, included a translation of *The New Science* in his *Oeuvres complètes* (1:171). Thus, Rimbaud, who was familiar with Michelet's works, may very well have found a source for his poetics in the Vichian model of *sapienza poetica*.

12. See also Todorov, *Théories du symbole* (339–52, esp. 340–43); and Rice and Schofer (esp. 3–15).

13. Linda Waugh rightly elucidates this ambivalence: "Of course, the other side of equivalence is difference and the other side of similarity is dissimilarity. By projecting equivalence (and perforce difference) onto the axis of combination, the *contrast* between or within parallelistic elements comes to the fore and indeed contrast, as much as equivalence, becomes an important part of the structuration of the poem" (151).

14. Association by both contiguity and similarity forms the metonymic structuration of *metaphora* (compare Todorov, *Théories du symbole*, 317). In a recent essay on the work of the imagination in semantic innovation through metaphor, Ricoeur similarly notes the displacement or metonymic structuring that underlies metaphoric transposition or transfer (1982, 1883).

15. In "The Real, the True, and the Figurative in the Human Sciences," Hayden White takes a narrow view of the Freudian dreamwork "as a paradigm of ... analysis by defiguration that the human and social sciences practice in their efforts to discriminate between reality and those misrepresentations of reality found in deluded, mythical, ideological, and fictional discourse.... The interpretation thus consists of a literalist paraphrase of the latent thoughts figuratively represented in the manifest forms of the discourse" (16). With Meredith Skura, we understand instead that "the one rule, for Freud, is to distrust a literal or even a symbolic reading" (134).

16. In "La rhétorique de Freud," Todorov correctly distinguishes symbolic and associative techniques in Freud's innovative method of dream interpretation (*Théories du symbole*, 317). Yet Todorov skews the Freudian view of a universal dream symbolism by isolating the statement "[I]ncidentally, many of the symbols are habitually or almost habitually employed to express the same thing" (Freud 5:352), from Freud's overall scheme in *The Interpretation of Dreams*. Samuel Weber's analysis of the same material rightly underscores the idea omitted from Todorov's account: that "all elements of the dream—whether images, words, utterances, or their syntactical arrangement—only be-

Notes to Pages 27–30

come significant . . . through their contextual relations" (74). For a recent review of the "methodological rift" in Freud, see Rand and Torok.

17. Stanley Palombo similarly observes, "[W]e find that the meaning of each dream derives less from a single identifiable repressed impulse than from the network of associations in which it becomes embedded during the interpretative process" (1983, 303). See also Palombo's creative view of dream discourse (1980) and Moller (ix–xii).

18. Dreams, for Freud, "show us one of the paths leading to an understanding of [the] structure of [our mental apparatus]" (5:607–8). Here by *structure*, Freud understands unconscious mental activity. Compare Todorov, *Théories du symbole*, 316.

19. Weber, in citing this passage, superimposes the term *semiotic relations* onto Freud's *symbolic relation* and illustrates, as the title of his study suggests, Lacan's dislocation of psychoanalysis (73).

20. At the time he wrote *The Interpretation of Dreams*, Freud had yet to theorize transference in the clinical sense elaborated in the Dora case. Lacan reads the Freudian transference in semiotic terms, asserting that the unconscious has the structure of a discourse (1966, 281–82).

21. Compare Lacan's reading in Derridian terms of the psychic writing of dreams (1966, 310, 311).

22. The assimilation of metaphor to displacement coincides with the metonymization of metaphor in both linguistic and psychoanalytic accounts. See Genette (1972, 42) and Lacan (1981, 259).

23. In a footnote added to *The Interpretation of Dreams* in 1925, Freud states that "[many analysts] seek to find the essence of dreams in their latent content and in so doing they overlook the distinction between the latent dream-thoughts and the dream-work. At bottom, dreams are nothing more than a particular *form* of thinking, made possible by the conditions of the state of sleep. It is the *dream-work* which creates that form, and it alone is the essence of dreaming—the explanation of its peculiar nature" (5:506).

24. Structural linguistics, in its Saussurean derivation, views language as a system of signs that signify only in opposition to each other. This bipolar model opposes metaphoric to metonymic modes of association by basing the selection and substitution of signs on relations of similarity and the combination of signs on contiguity and contextuality. Critics often expand equivalences from these pairs, associating the terms condensation, metaphor, and paradigm on the basis of the perception of similarity; displacement, metonymy, and syntagm on the basis of contiguity (Archard 79; Thom 5; White 15). Such symmetry, however, is misleading, if not completely erroneous. For the competition between these devices, whether in linguistic or psychoanalytic terms, exceeds the binary oppositions that structural linguistics upholds. For an insightful analysis of how the primary processes interact, see Schofer and Rice.

25. Silverman rightly underscores the wavering principles according to which condensation and displacement operate (99–100).

26. I owe this formulation to discussions with Renée Kingcaid.

Notes to Pages 30–32

27. In *Revolution in Poetic Language*, Kristeva writes concerning the "vital role played by the processes of displacement and condensation in the organization of the semiotic" that "theory can 'situate' such processes and relations diachronically within the process of the constitution of the subject precisely because *they function synchronically within the signifying process of the subject himself*, i.e., the subject of *cogitatio*. Only in *dream* logic, however, have they attracted attention, and only in certain signifying practices, such as the *text*, do they dominate the signifying process" (29).

28. "in *The Interpretation of Dreams* every page deals with what I call the letter of the discourse, in its texture, its usage, its immanence in the matter in question. For it is with this work that the work of Freud begins to open the royal road to the unconscious" (trans. in Lacan, 1977, 159).

29. Ragland-Sullivan rightly argues that for Lacan "the dream's ambiguous and contradictory effects are not caused by censorship in any sense of the superego's agency" (241).

30. Weber elucidates the bracketing of the signified in the Lacanian scheme: "By redefining [the Jakobsonian poles of language] as a movement of signifiers, the contextuality of metonymy and the similarity of metaphor become a function of differential opposition and cease to depend upon the signified. The only contiguity that metonymy can therefore count on, is that of the signifying chain itself. And the sole 'similarity' presupposed by metaphorical substitution is the purely formal similarity among signifiers" (60). Thom similarly explains that, by rejecting "the Saussurean illustration of the relation existing between signifier and signified" to suggest that "the signifier answers to the function of representing the signified," Lacan "would hold, rather, that meaning springs from (metonymic and metaphoric) relations between signifiers" (12). On this point, see also Bär.

31. "The creative spark of the metaphor does not spring from the presentation of two images, that is, of two signifiers equally actualized" (trans. in Lacan, 1977, 157).

32. "One word for another"; "His sheaf was neither miserly nor spiteful" (trans. in Lacan, 1977, 157, 156).

33. "it is in the substitution of signifier for signifier that an effect of signification is produced that is creative or po[i]etic, in other words, which is the advent of the signification in question" (trans. in Lacan, 1977, 164). In an essay "On the History of the Psychoanalytic Movement," Freud states that his investigation of dreams, stemming from an initial study of neuroses, also led "to the analysis of works of imagination . . . the concept of unconscious mental activity ma[king] it possible to form a preliminary idea of the nature of imaginative creative writing" (14:36–37).

34. Frank Heynick similarly states that "Freud's own description of the dreamwork mechanism involves what some consider to be a typical variety of creative work: fragmentation, rearrangement, and a new synthesis of elements" (32).

35. As Freud explains, the work of displacement, which "strips the elements which have a high psychical value of their intensity, and . . . by means of *over-determination*, creates from elements of low psychical value new values which find their way into the dream-content," governs the selection of elements condensed into the manifest dream (4:307–8). *Over-determination* connotes multiple connections with other elements of the latent dream thoughts. Dream elements are overdetermined since "selections or substitutions always maintain a connection (or combination) with the rest of a signifying chain" (Ragland-Sullivan 248).

36. Bert States advances the cognitive work underlying poetry and psychology along lines followed in this study ("the true common denominator of art-making and dreaming is the production of images") and asserts that "the image of the poet is the high refinement of the dream's capacity to conceive the impossible" (78, 79).

37. In *The Interpretation of Dreams*, Freud infers unconscious psychical processes from conscious effects (5:612) and then derives the conscious from the unconscious (5:612–13). To simultaneously derive the unconscious from the conscious and vice versa plays upon the equivalence that the metaphoric copula projects along these lines: if *A* [unknown] *is* (like) *B* [known], then *B is* (like) *A*. In other words, for Freud the unconscious and the conscious systems are mutually illuminating. Although Freud's reasoning thus contradicts scientific explanations, it moves from an evolutionary (replacement) model of the relationship between conscious and unconscious to give us a sense of our *limited* knowledge of the innermost nature of our psychic systems: "The unconscious is the true psychical reality; in its innermost nature it is as much unknown to us as the reality of the external world, and it is as incompletely presented by the data of consciousness as is the external world by the communications of our sense organs" (5:651).

38. In Freud's view, poets discovered the unconscious, whereas he developed "the scientific method by which the unconscious can be studied" (Trilling 34).

39. "the aim of poetry is not, as Baudelaire says, to plunge 'into the depths of the Infinite to find the new,' but rather into the depths of the definite to find the inexhaustible."

3. REVISIONING THE SELF, CREATING THE SUBJECT

1. Lacan asserts the paradoxical relation of *langage* and *parole* in these terms: "c'est donc toujours dans le rapport du *moi* du sujet au *je* de son discours, qu'il vous faut comprendre le sens du discours pour désaliéner le sujet. Mais vous ne sauriez y parvenir si vous vous en tenez à l'idée que le *moi* du sujet est identique à la présence qui vous parle" (1966, 186; "It is therefore always in the relation between the subject's ego [*moi*] and the 'I' [*je*] of his discourse that you must understand the meaning of the discourse if you are to achieve the deal-

ienation of the subject. But you cannot possibly achieve this if you cling to the idea that the ego of the subject is identical with the presence that is speaking to you" [trans. in Lacan, 1977, 90]).

2. Raybaud hints at such dialogicity in a chapter on Rimbaud's "Moi expérimental" (31–45). Compare Guyaux, 1984, 41.

3. See the *Princeton Encyclopedia of Poetry and Poetics* (717) for a complete discussion.

4. In one instance, Freud rejects creativity as a question for psychology (13:187). But, as stated in an earlier note, in his essay "On the History of the Psychoanalytic Movement," he asserts that his investigation of dreams stemming from an initial study of neuroses also led him "to the analysis of works of imagination and ultimately to their creators.... The conception of unconscious mental activity made it possible to form a preliminary idea of the nature of imaginative creative writing" (14:36–37). On Freud's inconsistent positions, see Spector (esp. 77–80).

5. "If the old fools had not hit upon the false significance of the Ego only, we should not now have to sweep away these millions of skeletons who, since time immemorial, have been accumulating the products of those one-eyed intellects" (trans. in Rimbaud, 1946, xxv).

6. "If I send you some of these verses ... it is because I love all poets, all good Parnassians—since the poet is a Parnassian—in love with ideal beauty. It is because I esteem in you, quite simply, a descendant of Ronsard, a brother of our masters of 1830, a real romantic, a real poet.... I, too, gentlemen of the press, I will be a Parnassian!" (trans. in Rimbaud, 1966, 297).

7. "All ancient poetry ended in Greek poetry ... From Greece to the romantic movement" (trans. in Rimbaud, 1966, 350).

8. "the first romantics were *seers* without wholly realizing it: the cultivation of their souls began accidentally" (trans. in Rimbaud, 1966, 309).

9. "the second romantics are very much seers, but inspecting the invisible and hearing the unheard of is different from recovering the spirit of dead things" (trans. in Rimbaud, 1966, 311).

10. "the first seer, king of poets, a real god!"

11. "and yet he lived in too artistic a world, and the form so highly praised in him is trivial."

12. For a comprehensive history of the term *voyant* and Rimbaud's sources, see Eigeldinger (1975). To review this development in Eigeldinger, the biblical meaning of prophet divining the future and possessing a vision of the supernatural was similarly applied to esoteric sects like the Gnostics and Illuminists. In the nineteenth century, *voyant* gained the connotation of a medium with prophetic and visionary powers and was also extended to the poet who sees the unknown (11–12).

13. I make a philosophical distinction between *transcendent* and *immanent* to qualify the *psychical source* of the creative impulse, which exists in the mind rather than in an extramental world. The creative *process* which produces an

Notes to Pages 41–43

external effect (i.e., a work of art) is not therefore exclusively immanent but in fact transcendent in the sense that it exists outside the psyche of the artist. For an excellent discusssion of these distinctions, see essays on *immanence* and *transcendance* in Lalande (468–72, 1143–45).

14. Adam, connecting Rimbaldian *voyance* and transcendence, designates the Other in Rimbaud as the objective or impersonal (the personal assimilated by the universal). Adam offers Baudelaire's "Poème du haschisch" as a source for the Rimbaldian dictum, "Je est un autre." Yet we infer a different sense of the objective or impersonal from a subsequent comment that "le *je* qui parle en lui n'est pas son être conscient" (Rimbaud, 1972, 1076; "the 'I' that speaks in [Rimbaud] is not his conscious self"). This second statement implies that the objective in Rimbaud no longer signifies a transcendent but rather an immanent Other, that is, the speaking unconscious, that disrupts the primacy of the "I."

15. "As a matter of fact all you see in your principle is subjective poetry: your obstinancy in going back to the pedagogic trough—pardon me—proves it. But you'll just end up self-satisfied without having done anything, not having wanted to do anything. Not to mention that your subjective poetry will always be horribly wishy-washy. Some day I hope—many others hope so too—I'll see objective poetry in your principle. I shall see it more sincerely than you will do it!" (trans. in Rimbaud, 1946, xxii).

16. For a different view of this relation, see Steinmetz (1991, 82–84).

17. In "Le message automatique," Breton views Rimbaud as an auditor rather than as a *visionnaire* who listens to the voice of the Other within himself (1967, 85). Rimbaud's poetic project, predicated on inner sight (i.e., *voyance*), indeed has a homophonetic connection with *voix* (voice).

18. "The Romantics . . . prove so clearly that the song is very seldom the work, that is, the idea sung and understood by the singer" (trans. in Rimbaud, 1946, xxv).

19. "If brass wakes up a trumpet, it isn't to blame. To me this is evident: I am present at the birth of my thought: I watch it and listen to it" (trans. in Rimbaud, 1946, xxv). Alluding to this same passage, Rivière implicitly connects Rimbaldian *voyance* with giving voice to the autonomous creative impulse that produces insight through its expression (210–11).

20. "I think, therefore I am."

21. "I speak, therefore I am." For Benveniste, we affirm ourselves as subjects, as "I," through discourse (1966, 259). Benveniste postulates a unified subject: "la subjectivité . . . se définit, non par le sentiment que chacun éprouve d'être lui-même . . . mais comme l'unité psychique qui transcende la totalité des expériences vécues qu'elle assemble, et qui assure la permanence de la conscience. Or nous tenons que cette 'subjectivité', qu'on la pose en phénoménologie ou en psychologie . . . n'est que l'émergence dans l'être d'une propriété fondamentale du langage. Est 'ego' qui *dit* 'ego'" (259–60; "subjectivity . . . is defined, not by the feeling which everyone experiences of being him[/her]self . . . but as the psychic entity that transcends the totality of the actual experi-

ences it assembles, and that makes the permanence of the consciousness. Now we hold that 'subjectivity,' whether it is placed in phenomenology or in psychology . . . is only the emergence in the being of a fundamental property of language. 'Ego' is he[/she] who says 'ego' " [trans. in Benveniste, 1971, 224]).

22. Lacan takes issue with the Cartesian cogito (1966, 186, 276, 277, 283).

23. Compare Kittang (45) and Blanchot (*L'Espace* 17) on the decentered speaking subject, which has no identity.

24. As Ragland-Sullivan concludes, "[I]n conscious life two subjects appear: the subject of individuality and the subject of speech. . . . But the Real subject is that of the unconscious, and it is beyond both *moi* and *je*. There will never be only one subject. . . . Nor is the subject of identifications and objectifications—the *moi*—an ego or identity in the psychological sense. The subject is, instead, an unbridgeable gap between a person's perceptions and alienation in relation to an external Gestalt, an internal discourse, and Desire. . . . Rimbaud once said, 'Je est un autre' (I is an other). Lacan explained the poet's intuition" (66–67).

25. "I think where I am not, therefore I am where I do not think."

26. "What one should say is: I am not wherever I am the plaything of my thought; I think of what I am where I do not think."

27. "I want to be a poet, and I am working to make myself a *Seer*. . . . It is a question of reaching the unknown by the derangement of *all the senses*" (trans. in Rimbaud, 1966, 303).

28. "But this other self, a stranger to me and yet which springs from my creative thought, can I not recognize it as myself, as identical to me?"

29. "In this manner Rimbaud affirms the general principle of the otherness of self in relation to itself. This means: I can think myself other than what I am or was . . . I can create (or recreate) myself other than I was not."

30. "The first study for [one wishing] to be a poet is the knowledge of him[/her]self, entire. [One] looks for [one's] soul, inspects it, learns it. As soon as [one] knows it, [one] cultivates it; it seems simple: in every brain a natural development is accomplished: so many *egoists* proclaim themselves authors; others attribute their intellectual progress to themselves!" (trans. in Rimbaud, 1946, xxvi).

31. The ambivalence between the poet-as-willful-creator and the autonomy of the creative impulse in Rimbaldian poetics elaborated in my analysis has received some critical notice, albeit obliquely. Poulet upholds the idea of a self-willed creator and thus an identification with the Promethean legend of the poet while also highlighting an immanent source of creativity in Rimbaud's aesthetics (1980, 96–97).

32. The original trope is the unconscious constituted by a primal repression, which lies, as Freud explains, in "Repression," "in the psychical (ideational) representative of the instinct being denied entrance into the conscious. With this a *fixation* is established; the representative in question persists unaltered from then onwards and the instinct remains attached to it" (14:148). Freud's

account of an original repression suggests the genesis of language's metaphoric (i.e., transferential) functioning. An instinctual impulse turned away from, or refused access to, consciousness inscribes itself in unconscious psychical contents with which other "trains of thought" come into associative connection and thereby pass into a state of repression (14:148). The initial transposition of instinct into representative psychical contents structures the psyche metaphorically, that is, not topographically but transferentially. As Bloom puts it, "the creation of an unconscious implicitly models itself on poetic origins" (1982, 111). By "po[i]etic origins," we understand in Freud the formation of the unconscious system through a split, or *écart*, that stems from a primal repression and an insistence on the tropic functioning of psychic contents inferred from gaps in conscious discourse.

33. Freud writes that we proceed "by inference from the conscious effect to the unconscious psychical process" (5:612).

34. In *The Orphic Vision*, Bays contends that for a brief period of two years "Rimbaud had made the error of identifying the vision of the unconscious, the *Orphic* vision, with that of the mystic" (207). My analysis positions this ambivalence at the *center* of Rimbaud's poetics.

35. "So then, the poet is truly a thief of fire. Humanity is his[/her] responsibility; . . . [the poet] must see to it that his[/her] inventions can be smelled, felt, heard. If what he[/she] brings back has form, he[/she] gives form, if it is formless, he[/she] gives it formlessness. A language must be found" (trans. in Rimbaud, 1946, xxvii–xxvviii).

36. "Universal Mind has always thrown out its ideas naturally; [hu]man[kind] would pick up part of these fruits of the brain; they acted through, wrote books with them: and so things went along, since [humankind] did not work on [it]self, not being yet awake, or not yet in the fullness of [its] dream. Writers, functionaries. Author, creator, poet, that person has never existed!" (trans. in Rimbaud, 1946, xxvi). "The poet will define the amount of unknown arising in his[/her] time in the universal soul; he[/she] will give more than the formula of his[/her] thought, more than the annotation of *his[/her] march toward Progress!*" (xxviii).

37. Renéville argues that Rimbaud's poet awakens through psychical ascesis to a higher consciousness related to an Eastern notion of the universal soul (86). Eigeldinger associates Rimbaldian *voyance* "au travail sur soi," that is, Jungian individuation or a process of self-discovery ("Notes," 26). These inherently similar approaches may account for the autonomy of the creative process perceived by Rimbaud. Yet they do not offer a model for reading his nondiscursive poetic discourse, which suggests the effects of the unconscious on conscious discourse.

38. Although Baudelaire's *Correspondances* seems to support the notion of universal correspondences and thus the totalizing power of poetic language, his later sonnet *Obsession* implies instead the heterogeneity of poetic discourse. On this point, see de Man (1984, 239–62).

39. For opposing arguments see, for example, Eigeldinger (1975, 106) and Bays (*Orphic Vision* 198–200), who advance that Rimbaud aspired to achieve a coincidence between thought and discourse in his poetic language.

40. "form that one cannot define," "incomplete or semiconscious form," or "there where nothing is yet manifest."

41. In his early verse poem *Soleil et chair* (Rimbaud, 1972, 6–11), Rimbaud echoes the repudiation of rationalism by romantic Illuminists while presaging his poetics of *voyance* where the creative process voices the unconscious Other. Querying whether "the voice of thought [is] more than a dream," Rimbaud responds that "we cannot know" for "our pale reason hides the infinite from us" (9). He writes *l'infini*, not *l'Infini*, and thus invokes a notion of the unknown, what is not conscious, instead of a divine eternity. His response so admits the limitations of a conscious outlook according to which we cannot "know" unconscious activity of the psyche (la *Pensée*). *Pensée*, comprising more than conscious reflection, here connotes the "principe de la vie psychique," "l'essence même de l'âme" (Imbs 11; "principle of psychic life," "the essence itself of the soul").

42. "The poet makes him[/her]self a *seer* through a long prodigious and rational *disordering* of *all the senses*. . . . He[/she] searches him[/her]self, consuming all the poisons within, keeping only their quintessences. . . . For he[/she] arrives at the *unknown*. Since he[/she] has cultivated his[/her] soul—richer to begin with than any other! He[/she] arrives at the unknown, and even if, half crazed, in the end, he[/she] loses the understanding of his[/her] visions, he[/she] has seen them!" (trans. in Rimbaud, 1946, xxvi–xxvii). In a different context related to the elaboration of dream as a paradigm for poiesis, Meredith Skura writes that "dreams, if told, are always retold; we know about them only after we have lost them" (137).

43. "every word being an idea, the time of a universal language will come. . . . This language will be of the psyche for the psyche, summing up everything, perfumes, sounds, colors, thought [taking hold of] thought and pulling" (trans. in Rimbaud, 1946, xxviii). Concerning the assertion "toute parole étant idée," Renéville notes the role played by unconscious ideation in this immanent poiesis and differentiates what a psychoanalyst would call *primary* from *secondary* processes (47, 48).

44. In discussing the allusion to a theory of correspondences in Rimbaud's concept of a new poetic language, Plessen also observes the extent to which Rimbaud liberates the metaphoric functioning of language from the constraints of formal syntax and logic associated with secondary process ideation (1983, 206).

45. My elaboration profits from Felman's insightful analysis (1973).

46. On the equivocal identity of *tu* in *Une saison en enfer*, see Bandelier (189–99).

47. In this study, as mentioned earlier, I assume the widely accepted chronology for Rimbaud's works based on Verlaine's preface to the 1886 edition of

Notes to Pages 50–52

the *Illuminations* that dates them 1873–75 (see Verlaine, 1972, 631) and evidence given by Henri Bouillane de Lacoste concerning Rimbaud's evolving handwriting. For a recent comprehensive review of "La question chronologique," see Guyaux (1985, 13–74).

48. "I am no longer in the world"; "There is no one here and there is someone"; "Decidedly we are out of the world"; "Real life is absent. We are not in the world" (Compare Freud's view that "the unconscious is the true psychical reality" [5:613]); "I am in the lowest depths, and I have forgotten how to pray."

49. "The metaphor of the 'descent into hell' is an archetype deeply anchored in the human psyche; widespread in the alchemical tradition, it was recovered by psychoanalysis and continues to inform literature. For [this archetype] translates a psychical experience leading to the discovery of self; it represents a being's desire to find itself, to comprehend itself as a unified entity."

50. "Long ago, *if my memory serves me*, my life was a banquet. . . . This was the time of my eternal life, both unwritten and unsung, —something like the Providence . . . in which one believes . . . and that does not sing." Other statements express a similar nostalgia, for example, in *Matin*: "n'eus-je pas *une* fois une jeunesse aimable, héroïque, fabuleuse, à écrire sur les feuilles d'or, —trop de chance!" ("Had I not *once* a lovely youth, heroic, fabulous, to be written on sheets of gold, too much luck!" [trans. in Rimbaud, 1945, 81]).

51. "the nostalgia for a state [of unconsciousness] prior to speech . . . the state of an *infans*, of one who does not speak."

52. "From my Gallic ancestors, I inherit . . . idolatry and love of sacrilege. . . . I remember the history of France, eldest daughter of the Church. . . . I cannot see myself at the councils of Christ, nor at the councils of Lords—representatives of Christ" (trans. in Rimbaud, 1945, 9, 11).

53. "We are going toward the *Spirit*. There's no doubt about it, an oracle, I tell you. I understand, and not knowing how to express myself without pagan words, I'd rather remain silent" (trans. in Rimbaud, 1945, 11). Opposing readings include both the Christian view, such as Claudel's, which equates *L'Esprit* with God, and the identification of *L'Esprit* with the universal soul in Eastern mysticism by Renéville.

54. For Lacan the constitution of the unconscious and the subject's accession to the structure of language (if not actual speech) concur. In his scheme, the first act of symbolization occurs when an *infans* (one that does not speak) assumes an identification with its specular image, which enables the discovery of its otherness, of its separate *self*. The internalized, unified body image does not come from within itself but rather from its identification with the other perceived in the mirrored image. This other, which represents the *infans* to itself, plays the role of a signifier and thus brings the *infans*-subject into being. This symbolization illustrates the transferential (metaphoric) functioning of language that constructs the Lacanian subject: "This jubilant assumption of his specular image by the child at the *infans* stage . . . would seem to exhibit in an exemplary situation the symbolic matrix in which the *I* is precipitated in a pri-

mordial form, before it is objectified in the dialectic of identification with the other, and before language restores to it . . . its function as subject" (trans. in Lacan, 1977, 2).

55. "Pagan blood returns. The Spirit is near. Why doesn't Christ help me by granting my soul nobility and liberty? Alas! the gospel has gone by!" (trans. in Rimbaud, 1945, 11). "Greedily I await God" (13). "Yes, my eyes are closed to your light. . . . But I can be saved" (17). "My heart has known the *stroke of grace*" (19).

56. "*I don't fancy myself embarked on a wedding with Jesus Christ as father-in-law*" (trans. in Rimbaud, 1945, 21). "I am not a prisoner of my reason. I said: God I want freedom in salvation: how am I to seek it . . . ? *No more need of devotion or divine love. No more regrets for the age of tender hearts.* . . . I reserve my place at the top of the angelic ladder of common sense" (23). Starkie also refutes Western religious myths of Rimbaud (385). For other critics opposed to a Christian reading of Rimbaud, see Houston (1986, 23–49) and Renéville (147–70).

57. "I can no more explain myself than the beggar with his endless *Paters* and *Ave Marias. I can no longer speak*!"

58. Wing observes that, for Rimbaud, "the only language available to the narrator is one in which each articulation of *I* produces the mark of non-coincidence which deconstructs the search for meaning and presence"; this realization results in "the explosive recognition that attaining the coincidence of self and language is merely the deluded repetition of an origin which never existed" (1984, 50).

59. "Having recovered two cents worth of reason—it is soon gone! —I see that my disquietudes come from having understood too late that we are in the Occident" (trans. in Rimbaud, 1945, 71).

60. For a similar view that discursive relations construct the speaking subject, see Bandelier (10).

61. "You will always be a hyena . . . etc., shrieks the demon who crowned me with such pleasant poppies. . . . —But, dear Satan, a less fiery eye I beg you . . . ! you who love the absence of the instructive or descriptive faculty in a writer, for you let me tear out these few, hideous pages from my notebook of one of the damned" (trans. in Rimbaud, 1945, 5).

62. "We're not going. —Back over the old roads again, laden with my vice" (trans. in Rimbaud, 1945, 13).

63. "See how the fire flares up again! How nicely I burn. Go to it, demon!" (trans. in Rimbaud, 1945, 27). "Be quiet! do be quiet . . . ! Satan who says that the fire is contemptible . . . —Enough! . . . Fallacies they whisper to me, sorceries, false perfumes, childish music" (29).

64. "The hero of the Season [in Hell] is not addressing anyone, is wrestling only against himself, having become for the self the other of the story" (compare Rimbaud, 1972, 961).

65. "What tricks in observation in the country . . . Satan, Old Nick, runs

with the wild grain . . . Jesus walks on the purple briars and they do not bend . . . Jesus walked on the troubled waters. The lantern showed him to us, erect, white, with long brown hair . . . on the flank of an emerald wave . . . I am going to unveil all the mysteries . . . Listen! . . . I have all the talents! —There is no one here and there is someone: I would not squander my treasures. —Do you want Negro songs, the dances of houris?" (trans. in Rimbaud, 1945, 31).

66. "Have faith in me then, faith assuages, guides, restores" (trans. in Rimbaud, 1945, 17).

67. On the ambiguous status of *nous* and *on*, which further problematizes the identity of the speaking subject, see Bandelier (201–13).

68. "In the cities, suddenly the mud seemed red and black, like a mirror when the lamp moves about in the adjoining room, like a treasure in the forest" (trans. in Rimbaud, 1945, 17).

69. "Can I describe the vision? . . . Hallucinations are without number. At present, I am at the bottom of the world! O my friends! . . . no, not my friends . . . Never delirium and torture like these . . . I can no longer even speak" (trans. in Rimbaud, 1945, 27, 37).

70. For psychophysiological studies diagnosing Rimbaud's mental health with reference to schizophrenia, paranoia, and mental alienation, see, for example, Aubin; Auvinet; and Delattre, respectively. For an opposing view, see Wolff.

71. "an other speaks to them, *an other thinks them*."

72. "Do I know nature yet? Do I know myself? —*No more words*" (trans. in Rimbaud, 1966, 181).

73. "[Old poetics] played a large part in my alchemy of the word" (trans. in Rimbaud, 1945, 55). "I created all possible festivities, all triumphs, all dramas. I tried to invent new flowers, new stars, new flesh, new tongues. I thought I was acquiring supernatural powers. Well! I must bury my imagination and my memories! An artist's and a storyteller's precious fame flung away" (87).

74. "I invented the color of the vowels . . . I regulated the form and movement of every consonant, and with instinctive rhythms, I prided myself on inventing a poetic language accessible someday to all the senses. I reserved all rights of translation" (trans. in Rimbaud, 1945, 51).

75. "At first it was an experiment. I wrote silences and the night. I recorded the inexpressible. I fixed frenzies in their flight" (trans. in Rimbaud, 1945, 51).

76. "Finally I came to regard the disorder of my mind as sacred" (trans. in Rimbaud, 1945, 55).

77. By *cultivation*, we understand psychical ascesis. In a figurative sense, *cultiver* connotes "soumettre les composantes de la personnalité à un exercice en vue de les développer, de les faire s'épanouir et acquérir leur plein pouvoir" (Imbs 6:614; "to subject the aspects of the personality to analysis in order to develop them, to make them blossom and achieve their full potential").

78. "I became an adept at simple hallucination: in place of a factory, I really saw a mosque, a school of drummers composed of angels, carriages on the

highways of the sky, a drawing-room at the bottom of a lake. . . . Then I would explain my magic sophisms with the hallucination of words!" (trans. in Rimbaud, 1945, 55).

79. Frohock draws upon presuppositions that I share to assert, regarding Rimbaud's practice of *metaphor*, that "hallucination is, after all, the ultimate step in the formation of metaphor" (84). Whereas Frohock understands the actual joining of two disparate elements (i.e., signifiers [84–85]), my reading of the *Illuminations* demonstrates through connections retained with occluded signifiers the unconscious economy of *metaphora* in Rimbaud.

80. "Now for me. The story of one of my follies" (trans. in Rimbaud, 1945, 49). "Not a single sophistry of madness—madness to confine—was forgotten. I could recite them all again. I know the system" (65).

81. "Automatic writing . . . leads directly to visual hallucination . . . one needs only to refer to 'Alchimie du verbe' to see that Rimbaud practiced it long before me." We recall here Lacan's critique of the premise underlying the surrealist metaphor or poetic image based on the juxtaposition of two or more disparate elements along the syntagm. Lacan counters that the metaphoric spark occurs paradigmatically between two signifiers, one of which occludes the other.

82. Abastado carefully distinguishes the *zone* of the unconscious in Breton from unconscious mental *activity* in Freud (69).

83. Compare Bandelier who asserts that "le sujet d'*Une Saison en enfer* est l'écriture d'*Une Saison en enfer*" (12; "the subject of *A Season in Hell* is the writing of *A Season in Hell*").

4. ILLUMINATING THE DISCOURSE OF THE OTHER

1. See Bandelier; Yuasa; and Wing 1984.

2. "One calls [the] *subject*, the conscious mind, the self; [one calls the] *object*, the thing, whatever the mind is conscious of. One understands by *subjective*, what belongs to the thinking subject, to the self, and by *objective*, what belongs to the object of thought, to the nonself." On the nineteenth-century sense of the terms *subjectif* and *objectif*, see Eigeldinger (1975, 118–21).

3. Dialogism for Bakhtin means that "no living word relates to its object in a *singular* way: between the word and its object, between the word and the speaking subject, there exists an elastic environment of other, alien words about the same object . . . and this is an environment that is often difficult to penetrate" (276). This dialogic orientation involves the internal dialogism of the word, that is, all the alien words encountered in the object or referent. Moreover, along with this interaction between meanings, "every word," Bakhtin continues, "is directed toward an answer and cannot escape the profound influence of the answer word that it anticipates" (280). The subject thus speaks in and through a dialogized voice. Compare Lacan, "ce que je cherche dans la

Notes to Pages 63–67

parole, c'est la réponse de l'autre" (1966, 181; "what I seek in speech is the response of the Other").

4. "Consciousness of self is only possible if it is experienced by contrast. I use *I* only when I am speaking to someone who will be a *you* in my address. It is this condition of dialogue that is constitutive of *person*, for it implies that reciprocally *I* becomes *you* in the address of the one who in his [or her] turn designates him[/her]self as *I*" (trans. in Benveniste, 1971, 224–25).

5. The grammatical forms *je* (speaker) and *tu* (addressee) that are generally inextricably linked in Benveniste's scheme imply personal subjects (1966, 228). The third-person grammatical subject (*il*, or the one who is absent) does not designate a specific speaking subject and thus characterizes impersonal expression versus the personal one attributed to grammatical subjects "I" and "you." For Benveniste, *il* becomes a sign of objectivity that functions to express the nonperson(al), the "non-I" (228). Contrasting *je/tu* with *il* on this basis, Benveniste sets forth a strict opposition between subjective and objective discourse. The *Illuminations* examined here blur this dichotomy by dialogically structuring voice on its boundary.

6. Wing implicitly supports an aspect of the dialogic nature of the "I" in the *Illuminations*: "The literary self then ceases to function in relation to a real biographical entity and becomes a principle of organisation within the text itself. These various 'voices' are often discontinuous from text to text and even within the same poem" (1974, 15–16).

7. For Benveniste, "*je* ne peut être identifié que par l'instance de discours qui le contient et par là seulement" (1966, 252; " 'I' cannot be identified except in what we have called elsewhere an instance of discourse and that has only a momentary reference" [trans. in Benveniste, 1971, 226]). As a textual sign that produces subjectivity, however, *je* marks a speaking subject rather than a particular personal self per se (1966, 261–62).

8. Bertrand Mathieu observes that Varèse's and Fowlie's translations are "culpably timid in dealing with Rimbaud's special brand of coarseness" (Rimbaud, 1991, 173). In Mathieu's translation of *Parade*, for example, he makes explicit the pederastic thrust of the text. My analysis, focused instead on the positioning of the poetic subject in the text, does not delve into semantic aspects of the piece. I have nonetheless chosen Mathieu's modern translation for the nonspecialist reader to capture the semantic play of *Parade* that Varèse and Fowlie avoid. The title, *Side Show*, also has the sense of a conspicuous procession that at once invites attention and maintains distance; so too we situate the speaking subject both inside and outside the narrated scene. "Tough customers. Many of them exploited your worlds. Needing nothing, and in no hurry to make use of their brilliant faculties and their experience of your tender consciences. Pretty virile men! Eyes listless like a summer night, reddened and blackish, three-shaded, steel studded with yellow stars. Features twisted, leaden, bloodless, gutted. Moronic hoarsenesses! The merciless posturings of tinsel! —Some are young guys, —what would they think of Cherubino? —

with bloodcurdling voices and some pretty dangerous equipment. They send these studs to town to bugger, decked out in disgusting clothes. O the more violent Kingdom Come of the raging smirk! No comparison with your Fakirs and other stage antics. In costumes improvised with the taste of bad dreams, they act out sad songs and tragedies of thieves and demigods, more [witty] than history or religion have ever managed to be! Chinese, Hottentots, gypsies, nitwits, hyenas, Molochs, old lunacies, sinister demons, they mix much-loved oldtime ditties meant for Mom with bestial winks and caresses. They're authorities on new pieces for the stage and tunes about 'fair lassies.' Master stuntsmen, they can transform both the scene and the characters; they use magnetic tricks. Eyes glisten, blood sings, bones grow bigger, tears and little red lines glow. Their horseplay or their panic terror may last a minute, or whole months. I alone have the key to this [barbarous parade]" (89). Here *magnetic*, referring to animal magnetism, connotes the exerting of a psychokinetic influence.

9. On *la personne non-je*, see Benveniste (1966, 252).

10. See Freud's discussion of day residues (impressions of daytime life) 4:169 ff; 5:593 ff.

11. *Imagined* signifies "forming a mental image of something not present." The adjectival form of the term *image* means, more specifically, "to describe or portray in language especially in a vivid manner" (*Oxford English Dictionary* 7:667).

12. Most recently, James Lawler echoes the idea of fictive selves, aiming to "illustrate the project of self-dramatization" that demonstrates "the exceptional energy of a poet who invests himself with strange identities" (5).

13. "I have embraced the summer dawn. Nothing yet stirred in front of the palaces. The water was dead. The shadows still camped in the woodland road. I walked, waking quick warm breaths; and gems looked on, and wings rose without a sound. The first venture was, in a path already filled with fresh, pale glints, a flower who told me her name. I laughed at the waterfall that tousled through the pines: on the silver summit I recognized the goddess. Then, one by one, I lifted up her veils. In the lane, waving my arms. Across the plain, where I denounced her to the cock. To the city she fled among the steeples and the domes; running like a beggar on the marble quays, I chased her. Far up the road near a laurel wood, I wrapped her round with her gathered veils, and I felt a little her immense form. Dawn and the child sank down at the border of the wood. Waking, it was noon" (trans. in Rimbaud, 1946, 39, 41).

14. Benveniste (1966) distinguishes *histoire*/story ("le récit des événements passés" [239]; "the narrative of past events") marked by the verb tenses *passé simple* or *passé défini*, *l'imparfait*, and *le plus-que-parfait* from *discours*/discourse ("toute énonciation supposant un locuteur et un auditeur" [242]; "all speech presupposing a speaker and an interlocutor") indicated by the present, future, and perfect, all three of which *histoire* excludes; the imperfect, however, is common to both *histoire* and *discours* (243).

15. "The Dream is a second life . . . ; an obscure blurring seizes our thought, and we cannot determine the precise moment when the *self*, in a different form, goes on existing."

16. Jean-Pierre Richard unwittingly underscores this idea in his reading of *Je est un autre:* "Car si JE est un AUTRE, c'est bien je qui a produit cet autre" (193; "Because if I is an OTHER, it is indeed I that produced this OTHER").

17. " . . . 'I' and 'you' are reversible: the one whom 'I' defines by 'you' thinks of [it]self as 'I' and can be inverted into 'I,' and 'I' becomes a 'you' " (trans. in Benveniste, 1971, 199).

18. "As soon as the idea of the Deluge [had settled back down], a hare stopped in the clover and swaying flowerbells, and said a prayer to the rainbow, through the spider's web. Oh! the precious stones that were hiding, —and the flowers that already looked around. In the dirty main street, stalls were set up and boats were hauled toward the sea, high-tiered as in old prints. Blood flowed at Blue-Beard's, —through slaughter houses, in circuses, where windows were blanched by God's seal. Blood and milk flowed. Beavers built. 'Mazagrans' smoked in the little bars. In the big house with window panes still dripping, children in mourning looked at the marvelous pictures. A door banged; and in the village square the little boy waved his arms, understood by weather-vanes and cocks on steeples everywhere, in the bursting shower. Madame*** set up a piano in the Alps. Mass and first communions were celebrated at the hundred thousand altars of the cathedral. Caravans set out. And Hotel Splendid was built in the chaos of ice and of polar night. Ever afterward the moon heard jackals puling across the deserts of thyme, and eclogues in wooden shoes growling in the orchard. Then, in the violet and budding forest, Eucharis told *me* it was Spring. Gush, pond—[foam, curl over] the bridge and [above] the woods; black palls and organs, lightnings and thunder, rise and roll; waters and sorrows rise and launch the floods again. For since they have been dissipated— oh, the precious stones being buried and the opened flowers! —it is a shame! —and the Queen, the Witch who lights her embers in the earthen pot, will never tell *us* what she knows, the thing *we* do not" (trans. in Rimbaud, 1946, 3, 5; emphasis added). *Mazagran,* the name of a city in Algeria, here refers to weak coffee served in a tall glass rather than in a mug.

19. On the anonymous narrative voice that dialogism constructs, see, for example, Morace.

20. Benveniste defines *nous* as "une jonction entre 'je' et 'non-je,' quel que soit le contenu de ce 'non-je' " (1966, 233; "a junction of 'I' and 'non-I,' whatever the content of this 'non-I' ").

21. Benveniste insists on *je*'s primacy in the first-person plural (1966, 233). The orientation toward the other/Other informing his notion of *discours* undermines this *unicité*.

22. My introductory sections to this chapter work from the affinities between hallucinating, dreaming, and creating that were advanced in nineteenth-century French psychiatry. For example, French alienist Baillarger compares

the psychical state of the artist who seems to hear an alien voice within him- or herself and the mentally alienated addressed in the second person by an Other (283). See also Paliyenko.

23. "This is obvious to me. I witness the birth of my thought: I watch it and listen to it."

24. "Long after the days, seasons, beings, and countries, The banner of raw meat against the silk of seas and arctic flowers; (they do not exist). Recovered from the old fanfares of heroism, —which still attack the heart and head, —far from the [former] assassins, —Oh! the banner of raw meat against the silk of seas and arctic flowers; (they do not exist). —Bliss! [Glowing coals] raining in gusts of hoarfrost. —Bliss! —Those fires in the rain of diamond wind flung out by the earth's heart eternally carbonized for us. —O world! (Far from the old haunts and the old flames that one hears, that one feels.) Embers and foam. Music, [clashing] of chasms and shock of icicles against the stars. O bliss, O world, O music! And forms, sweat, eyes and long hair floating there. And white tears boiling, —Bliss! —and the feminine voice reaching to the bottom of volcanoes and grottos of the arctic seas. The banner . . . " (trans. in Rimbaud, 1946, 11, 13).

25. For a different approach to the problem of voice in *Barbare*, see Nakaji.

26. I acknowledge with appreciation discussions with Randa Duvick concerning these textual features that mark the dialogicity of poetic voice that my study underscores in the *Illuminations*.

27. "To objectify the subjective, to examine as an object of study our own self and each of its impressions or its processes." To analyze what Rimbaud intends by *poésie subjective/objective*, Eigeldinger ("Notes" 119) cites only the first part of Littré's elaboration of the couple *objectif/subjectif* in conjunction with the investigation of the self articulated by Rimbaud in the seer letter to Demeny. Littré adds that "objectiver le subjectif signifie aussi prendre pour objectif ce qui est subjectif, confondre le subjectif avec l'objectif" (3:775; "to objectify the subjective also means to take as objective what is subjective, to 'mix up' the subjective with the objective"). Reread in psychocritical terms, the idea of *confondre* (to merge or intermingle) supports a dialogic view of Rimbaud's poetic voice.

28. "In effect, one characteristic of the persons 'I' and 'you' is their specific 'oneness': the 'I' who states, the 'you' to whom 'I' addresses him[or her]self are unique each time. But '[s]he' can be an infinite number of subjects—or none. That is why Rimbaud's 'je est un autre [I is another]' represents the typical expression of what is properly mental 'alienation,' in which the 'I' is dispossessed of its constitutive identity" (trans. in Benveniste, 1971, 199).

29. "It is wrong to say: I think. One ought to say: Others think me."

30. Philippe Bonnefis suggests a supplanting of the paradigmatic or metaphoric axis by the syntagmatic or metonymic one in Rimbaud, where meaning becomes the effect of the production of signs (51, 57). Echoing Bonnefis, Anne

Freadman remarks in her reading of *Mystique* that indeterminacy characterizes metaphor in Rimbaud "by the ellipsis of the first term of the metaphors, and the suppression of the very notion of analogy in favor of that transformation" (71).

31. Bivort distinguishes dashes that serve to enumerate various elements from those marking the writer's distance from his or her creation, or text.

32. Other texts in which dashes mark shifts from the unreal to the real while presenting the unreal as real include *Marine, Angoisse, Jeunesse: Dimanche, Sonnet, Vingt ans, Métropolitain,* and *Scènes*.

33. Jean-Louis Baudry similarly remarks a process of displacement in the Rimbaldian text as an effect of writing, where the production of signs along the syntagm overcomes the reproduction or representation of meaning (1968, 49). In a more recent analysis of "Rimbaud's resistance to metaphor" in its social space (the commune's anarchistic culture), Kristin Ross implies the metonymic grounding of Rimbaud's poetic discourse that I elaborate in my study. Although Ross argues against a tropological reading of Rimbaud, she retains such a reading, albeit obliquely, by advancing that "Rimbaud's tropology (or antitropology, as the case may be) is historically conditioned" (129). Her inherently semantic approach cannot avoid this impasse. Nevertheless, the notion that Rimbaud's metaphor "goes beyond metaphor," exploding and scattering in all directions, invites a semiotic reading of its overlap with metonymic play at the level of the signifier. Ross's observation of a scattering of the metaphoric in Rimbaud echoes Kittang's view of a "réduction métaphorique" in Rimbaud's poetic text (see 197–98). Like Ross, Kittang hints at the interpenetration of metaphoric and metonymic modes at the core of my analysis of Rimbaud's *metaphora*.

34. "In the woods there is a bird; his song stops you and makes you blush. There is a clock that never strikes. There is a swamp with a nest of white beasts. There is a cathedral that goes down and a lake that comes up. There is a little carriage abandoned in the copse or that goes running down the road be-ribboned. There is a troupe of strolling players in costume, glimpsed on the road through the border of the woods. And then, when you are hungry and thirsty there is someone who chases you away" (trans. in Rimbaud, 1946, 63, 65).

35. "The dream is no longer for Rimbaud, as it was for Baudelaire, for example, a thematic element, but rather a reading device, an indication as to how one is to interpret the text one has before one's eyes" (trans. in Todorov, *Theories of the Symbol*, 227).

36. In "Rêve, réveil, éveil," revised from a 1978 essay, "L'autre et le rêve," Guyaux contends that the prose poems of the *Illuminations* oppose the structure of dreams (1991, 62–63). He concedes, however, that dreamwork is present in the margins of the text and cites *Bottom* in particular (64). The heterogeneity that Guyaux marginalizes is what characterizes Rimbaud's modernity and fundamentally structures the poetic subject in Rimbaud.

37. "to want to find out what they signify is to strip them of their essential message, which is precisely the impossibility of identifying the referent and understanding the meaning, which is manner and not matter" (trans. in Todorov, *Theories of the Symbol*, 237).

38. "Rimbaud had discovered language in its autonomous functioning—or disfunctioning—freed from its expressive and representative obligations, where the initiative has been given to the words themselves; he has . . . following [Friedrich] Hölderlin . . . bequeathed the discourse of schizophrenia as a model to twentieth-century poetry" (trans. in Todorov, *Theories of the Symbol*, 237).

39. Critics have consistently noted that metaphor in Rimbaud becomes less communicative (Trilling 38). Its autonomous nature (Kentner 298) not only resists the act of interpretation but, in many cases, becomes unreadable (Todorov, 1978, 215). Additional references to Rimbaud's nonmimetic metaphors are found in Lapeyre (409–12), Wing (1974, 77), and Plessen (1983, 211). We find an early reference to Rimbaud's nonmimetic discourse in Renéville, who relates the structure of images in the *Illuminations* to dreamwork that is fundamentally a metonymic mode of discourse (120, 128).

40. While I infer the dream paradigm from Rimbaud's poetic practice, the syntagmatic mode of dreams provides an explicit source for the surrealists, who claimed to follow Rimbaud's example. Compare Reich.

41. I agree with Baudry, who describes the *Illuminations* as writerly texts that produce rather than represent meaning with external or internal reference (1969, 51, 52).

42. For instance, a metaphoric-metonymic mode distinguished from the one-word tropes structures the dream landscapes in the two *Villes* (compare Todorov, 1983, 70, 71).

43. "I have had a dream—past the wit of man to say what dream it was. —Man is but an ass if he go about to expound this dream. . . . The eye of man hath not heard, the ear of man hath not seen; man's hand is not able to taste, his tongue to conceive, nor his heart to report what my dream was" (*A Midsummer Night's Dream* 4.1.204–6, 209–12).

44. Critics commonly use the terms *oneiric* and *dreamlike* to describe certain texts of *Une saison en enfer* and the *Illuminations*. Thus, it is surprising that, to the best of my knowledge, no one has considered this collection in terms of Freudian dreamwork. For an excellent analysis of *Mémoire* along similar lines, see Collier.

45. "Reality being too thorny for my great personality, —I found myself, nevertheless, at my lady's, an enormous gray-blue bird, soaring near the cornices of the ceiling and trailing my wings through the shadows of the evening. I was at the foot of the canopy supporting her adored gems and her physical masterpieces, a great bear with violet gums, fur hoary with sorrow, eyes on the silver and crystal of the consoles. Everything became shadow and ardent

aquarium. In the morning, —[combative] dawn of June—a donkey, I rushed into the fields, braying and brandishing my grievance, until the Sabine women of the suburbs came and threw themselves at my breast" (trans. in Rimbaud, 1946, 133).

46. Whereas bird, bear, and ass are explicit identifications in *Bottom*, my italics and question mark indicate that fish is an implicit one. Adam reviews three metamorphoses in *Bottom* (see Rimbaud, 1972, 1014); Hubert discusses four, inferring from the signifier *aquarium* an identification with fish (13–14).

47. Critics generally agree that *Bottom* alludes to a love affair with an unidentified woman, although they locate this affair in different places (see, for example, Rimbaud, 1989, 176). Jeancolas links *Bottom* to a town ten kilometers from London (55). In their critical edition of Rimbaud's *Oeuvres*, Bernard and Guyaux locate this purported liaison either in London or in Milan on the basis of Verlaine's testimony (Rimbaud, 1983, 532–33).

48. Reading *Bottom* solely on the basis of intertextual echoes oversimplifies its narrative complexity. After summarizing the three metamorphoses, Adam asserts that "[le narrateur] est maintenant un âne . . . et voilà pourquoi le poème s'intitule 'Bottom' comme dans 'Le Songe d'une nuit d'été' où Bottom est métamorphosé en âne" (Rimbaud, 1972, 1013–14; "[the narrator] is now an ass . . . and this is why the poem is entitled 'Bottom' like in 'A Midsummer Night's Dream' where Bottom is transformed into an ass"). Contrary to Adam, Kott's brief but provocative sketch of Rimbaud's *Bottom* as "the most succinct and astonishing 'writerly text' of *A Midsummer Night's Dream*" admits a dense semiotic network in the poem (52).

49. "*that* means literally and in all senses."

50. My reading of *gencives violettes* brings to mind *vagina dentata*, derived from the myth of Kronos who hid in his mother's vagina to castrate his father using a sharp-toothed sickle. In the context of *Bottom*, the rejection by the desired female object castrates the desiring male subject.

51. For instance, Houston writes that the metaphoric character of *Fleurs* is its point: "This pseudo-description is structured metonymically rather than referentially, establishing the fact of language as an experience in itself, beyond all concern for mimesis" (1986, 68).

52. For example, Vernon Underwood hypothesizes that the "burning aquarium" in *Bottom* alludes to a lighted aquarium Rimbaud had seen at the Crystal Palace in London (qtd. in Rimbaud, 1972, 1014).

53. "Your memory and your senses will merely serve to feed your creative impulses."

54. Jeancolas calls *Bottom* "un poème érotique où l'oiseau, les bijoux adorés, et le grief brandi prennent des sens obscènes" (55; "an erotic poem where the bird, the adored jewels, and the brandished grievance acquire obscene meanings"). Symbolic equations indeed support the discourse of desire in *Bottom* that my semiotic reading discloses. *Bird*, like *fish*, has in certain contexts the

meaning of a phallic symbol and thus signifies amorous yearning or the metamorphosis of a lover. This connotation of bird overdetermines through displacement the abrupt shift to an identification with the bear, symbolizing instincts and perilous aspects of the unconscious, namely, unbridled desire. An abrupt move then to *aquarium* interjects in the stream of associations cast forth in *Bottom* an implicit identification with *fish*. Symbolically speaking, *fish* signifies at once psychic being and extends through its penetrating motion to a phallic one, which maintains the speaking subject's desire in the body of Rimbaud's text. *Fish* then dissolves into an *âne*. This final transformation displaces the speaking subject's desire onto the display of its *grief*.

55. Bruno Claisse presents excerpts from Jules Michelet (*La Mer* and *La Montagne*) as an intertextual source for "Le pavillon en viande saignante" and "le coeur terrestre" (110, 112). And Michelet, in a chapter on "La femme, le mariage" in *Origines du droit français cherchées dans les symboles et formules du droit universel*, also makes reference to the *Nibelungen* where "la femme charme son barbare amant par sa force autant que par sa beauté" (3:660; "woman charms her barbarous lover as much by her force as by her beauty").

56. As a meditation on the creative process through the agency of a maritime voyage, *Barbare* echoes *Le Bateau ivre*.

57. See Ahearn for an insightful analysis of *Barbare* as an "ecstatic prose poem" (esp. 74–78). Ahearn's reading opens various paths of the text without, however, specifically configuring the creative impulse.

58. Todorov states that the "principal message of the *Illuminations* lies in the way that the sense appears, or perhaps, disappears" (1988, 15). His comment implicitly targets the dreamwork of these texts where a concentration of images produces only an illusory illumination, as also remarked by Gleize (1983, 84) and Lapeyre (409).

59. Baudry, implicitly countering Claudel's reading, underscores in Rimbaud the subversion of representation, of ultimate meaning as exemplified by God (1968, 55).

60. "It is useless to discuss Rimbaud any longer: he was mistaken. He wanted to deceive us. In our view, he is guilty of not having rendered impossible certain dishonorable interpretations of his thought, like [those of] Claudel's."

61. "Catholicism is a compromise in poor taste. We will not delay in refuting the ridiculous thesis of Paul Claudel, ambassador of France. Rimbaud did not discuss with Verlaine who sang psalms to him in Stuttgart: he belted him with his fist."

62. For a Gnostic treatment of Rimbaud, see Printemps 2:9.

63. Etiemble records various assertions associating Rimbaldian *voyance* with unconscious mental activity (133). For an opposing argument, see Lawler, who refutes the idea of Rimbaud's language as "approaching spontaneous and uncensored utterance" (100).

5. REVISING THE POETIC SUBJECT, REPEATING THE CREATIVE WORD

1. (Claudel, 1965, 423–24). "The object of poetry thus is not, as one often says, dreams, illusions or ideas. It is instead this holy reality given once and for all, in the center of which we are placed. It is the universe of invisible things. . . . All that is the work of God who makes the inexhaustible material of stories and songs of the greatest poet and the poorest little bird alike . . . there is a *poesis perennis* that does not invent its themes, but rather eternally repeats those that Creation furnishes. . . . The idea of infinite material, that is, of finite matter without limits, scandalous for reason, is disastrous for the imagination that sees itself thwarted in its essential mechanism, that is, the power of order, measure, and disposition instilled in it by God in the image of his creative Word."

2. Fowlie supports a continuous development in Claudel's three major works: "In purely spiritual terms, his entire work is a progression towards the consciousness of the 'Real Presence' in the world. All the parts of Claudel's vast work are interrelated. *Connaissance de l'Est* was a kind of sketchbook for the *Art poétique*. The *Odes*, written after the *Art poétique*, repeat and orchestrate themes of the treatises" (33). The dates of composition given for Claudel's poetic opus vary, although both the Gallimard edition (Claudel, 1957) and Gadoffre's critical edition (Claudel, 1973) give the same divisions for *Connaissance de l'Est*: first part, 1895–1900; second part, 1900–1905; *Art poétique*: *Connaissance du temps*, 1903; *Traité de la co-naissance au monde et de soi-même*, 1900; definitive edition, Mercure de France 1907, completed with "notice bibliographique" by Claudel in 1913; *Cinq grandes odes*, 1900–1908; definitive edition, 1910.

3. Fowlie similarly argues that, for Claudel, "since visible reality is the image of invisible reality, the poet is able to establish a relationship between the Creator and the created world. The meaning of each thing is the image it gives of God" (36).

4. This famous definition of God first appeared in a pseudohermetic manuscript in the twelfth century, entitled *Le livre des vingt-quatre philosophes*.

5. On the ideological debate in this collection, see Claudel (1973, 17–34) for Gadoffre's "Jules Renard ou Mallarmé?"

6. "One must not confuse the vaguely beautiful with the precise image which is far superior."

7. "All things are beautiful. One must speak of a pig in the same manner as one would speak of a flower."

8. "I shall paint here the pig's portrait. [It] is a solid beast, made all in one piece; without joints and without a neck; and [it shoves forward like a ploughshare], jolting along on four squat hams. [It is a questing] trumpet; and to

every odor that [it] scents [it] applies [its] pump-like body. [It] sucks it in" (trans. in Claudel, 1914, 68).

9. "*Nommer* un objet, c'est supprimer les trois quarts de la jouissance du poëme qui est faite de deviner peu à peu: le *suggérer*, voilà le rêve. C'est le parfait usage de ce mystère qui constitue le symbole: évoquer petit à petit un objet pour montrer un état d'âme, ou, inversement, choisir un objet et en dégager un état d'âme, par une série de déchiffrements" (Mallarmé, 1945, 869; "*Naming* an object suppresses three-quarters of the pleasure of the poem which comes from guessing little by little: *suggesting* [the object], that would be ideal. It is the perfect use of this mystery that constitutes the symbol: to evoke gradually an object to display a state of mind, or, conversely, to choose an object and draw from it a state of mind, through a series of readings"). I appreciate Moses M. Nagy's calling my attention to this reference.

10. "At the hour when the holy light evokes to complete response the shadow that she dissipates, the surface of these waters opens a flowerless garden to my motionless navigation. Between these [rich], violet ripples the water is painted like the reflection of tapers, [here is the] amber, [here is the most tender green], [here is] the color of gold. But silence! What I have discovered is mine, and now, as the water darkens, I will possess the night alone with [the integral number] of its visible and invisible stars" (trans. in Claudel, 1914, 71–72).

11. Subjective idealism is the view that "the object of external perception consists whether in itself or as known to us in ideas of the perceiving mind" (*Oxford English Dictionary* 7:616).

12. For other texts in *Connaissance de l'Est* (Claudel, 1973) that present such description, see *Le Banyan, Vers la montagne, Novembre, Peinture, Décembre, Tempête, Portes, Fleuve, Considération de la cité, La Cloche, La Tombe, Halte sur le canal, Le Pin, L'Arche d'or dans la forêt, La Source, Visite, Le Riz, Le Point,* and *Le Jour dans la fête-de-tous-les-fleuves.*

13. "When you have understood well the *raison d'être* of something, you understand better its effects . . . and its place in the universe. This is what I learned from reading Aristotle and Saint Thomas. Almost everywhere in *Connaissance de l'Est* you see that intelligence and reason intervene. It is not a question of pure and simple description, it is a question of a knowing, of an understanding."

14. "Mallarmé was the first to put himself in front of the external world, not like in front of a spectacle or a topic for a writing assignment, but rather as though before a text asking: What does it mean?" Compare Claudel et Amrouche (64–65). The double meaning of the expression *vouloir dire*, "what does that mean" and "what does one wish/mean to say," bears out the different poetics of language in Claudel and Rimbaud. In Claudel's mimetic view, it is a question of discerning presupposed meaning. Rimbaud's poietic approach to the production of meaning through signifiers, to the contrary, resists codifiable signification.

15. "We know that the world is in effect a text, and that it speaks to us hum-

bly and joyously of its own absence, but also of the eternal presence of someone else, namely its Creator. Not only writing, but also the writer, not only the letter, but also the spirit, and not an unreadable magic, but the Word in which all things were proffered."

16. In *Introduction à un poème sur Dante*, Claudel comments on the poet's superior position in relation to what he observes and his attendant vision of transcendent harmony (1965, 422).

17. "—And again I see myself at the highest fork of an old tree.... From there like a god on his pinnacle, observer of the theater of the world, I study with deep consideration the relief and the conformation of the earth, its disposition of slopes and planes; with the piercing eye of a crow, I inspect the landscape spread out under my perch, I follow this road that ... finally disappears into the forest. Nothing escapes my sight." See also *L'Entrée de la terre* (Claudel, 1973, 131–32), where the poet feels communion with nature, which he observes with increased comprehension; this communion prefigures the notion of *co-naissance* in *Art poétique*.

18. "From the giddy height where I climb, the wide rice-fields seem designed like a chart.... Let me compare this vast landscape which opens out before me as far as the double wall of mountains and clouds to a flower of which this seat is the mystic heart. Is it not the geometric center where the scene, united into an [sic] harmonious whole, virtually takes on existence and consciousness of itself, and where, to the studious contemplation of the occupant, all lines converge?" (trans. in Claudel, 1914, 54–55).

19. "The brain is an organ.... This apparatus assures the opening of a cerebral wave, constant as a pulse, to the entire body."

20. "this double movement and one by which a body proceeds from a point [of origin] to return to it. Here is the *element*, the symbol which constitutes essentially all life." *Le Fleuve* illustrates the centering role played by God in creation with the metaphor of a center from which a circle alternately emanates and returns (Claudel, 1973, 62).

21. "Toute vibration implique un foyer, comme tout cercle un centre" (Claudel, 1973, 322; "Every vibration, like every circle, implies a center").

22. "The vibration of our brain is the agitation of the source of life, the emotion of matter in contact with that divine unity whose possession constitutes our typical personality. This is the umbilical cord of our dependence."

23. Claudel cites *Sur la cervelle* in its entirety in *Art poétique* to explain his principle of *co-naissance* (1957, 160–61).

24. "I do likewise, and, by the living virtue of the sea in my blood, my mind communicates with the movement of the waters as does a city by its secret drains" (trans. in Claudel, 1914, 153).

25. "For every creature, born of the impression of Divine unity upon indeterminate matter *is* the very acknowledgment that [it] makes to [its] Creator, and the expression of the nothingness from which [it] has been drawn. This is the living, breathing rhythm of the world, where [humankind], [endowed]

Notes to Pages 100–103

with consciousness and language, has been instituted their priest to make dedication and offering of them" (trans. in Claudel, 1914, 136). *Splendeur de la lune* reiterates the idea of the poet's mystical vision (Claudel, 1973, 204–5).

26. Claudel, however, cites Baudelaire's verse accurately in his essay on Francis Jammes (1965, 554).

27. In keeping with his revision of Baudelaire, in *Art poétique* Claudel reads the world as the site of the unknown or infinite source of all that can be known (1957, 133). We find an explicit identification of the unknown with God in *La Ville* (154).

28. "Not only does Religion bring us song, but also speech . . . not only joy but also meaning. Because we know that the world is not haphazard . . . we know that it has meaning. It speaks to us of its Creator, it gives us the means to understand its structure, or in any event, to investigate it."

29. "Each tree has its personality, each little [creature its] role, each voice its place in the symphony. As they say music is comprehended, so I comprehend Nature. It is like a story of many details, where only the proper names are given. As my walk and the day proceeds, I advance in the development of a philosophy" (trans. in Claudel, 1914, 125).

30. "Already I have discovered with delight that all things exist in a certain accord; and though believing this secret relationship, by which the blackness of this pine below espouses the clear green of these maple trees, it is my purified sight only which establishes it; so, because of this restoration of the original design, I call my visit a Revision. I am the Inspector of Creation, the Verifier of all present things. The reality of this world is the cause of my beatitude[!]" (trans. in Claudel, 1914, 125). See also *La Terre vue de la mer*, on Claudel's idea that the poet perceives the infinite in the finite, and in this manner he unites himself with the universe (1973, 284–85).

31. "And I go on and on! Each one of us contains [within us] the autonomous power of motion by which [we] move toward [our] food and [our] work. As for me, the even motion of my legs serves to measure for me the intensity of more subtle appeals. [All things draw me toward them!] I feel it in the silence of my soul" (trans. in Claudel, 1914, 126).

32. "Saint Bonaventura provided the formula for analogy: A is to B as C is to D."

33. Claudel emphasizes the rationalism that he gleaned from *The Metaphysics* to articulate his theory of *connaissance*. He does not mention either Aristotle or Saint Thomas as a source of his notion of metaphor nor the attendant idea of analogy, which he attributes solely to Saint Bonaventura.

34. "The night takes away our proof, we no longer know where we are. Lines and hues, this order . . . of the world around us, the center of which we carry with us according to the point of view that our eye is at every moment the bearer, is no longer there to establish our position. We are reduced to ourselves."

Notes to Pages 104–107

35. "But if the night closes our eyes, it is in order that we may listen, not only with the ears, but also with the gills of our soul, breathing as fish do."

36. "I possess the creative pulse."

37. "[The human being] is indivisible, when all is said and done, and that is the lesson of *Connaissance de l'Est* that the faculties of the human being are never abandoned, and in particular the will.... I never lose the sense of my personality."

38. "nothing subsists on its own, but rather in an infinite relation with all other things." For another depiction of the process of *connaissance* through which we perceive the structure of the created world, see *Jardins* in Claudel (1973, 99).

39. Saint Thomas writes, "[N]ow all things are dealt with in holy teaching in terms of God, either because they are God himself or because they are relative to him as their origin and end.... Though we cannot know what God is, nevertheless this teaching employs an effect of his, of nature or of grace, in place of a definition, and by this means discusses truths about him" (1:27).

40. "I had to introduce ... Catholic dogma in the rational world and in the world that I perceived as an artist."

41. "We will not seek to understand the mechanism of things from underneath, like an engineer [on a railway] who crawls on his back under his locomotive. But we will place ourselves before the ensemble of creatures, like a critic before the product of a poet, tasting fully the thing, examining by which means he produced his effects."

42. "Syllogism is the process by which we recognize things and recognize ourselves among them."

43. "Logical inquiry already reveals to us that we can only define something ... in terms of the characteristics through which it differs from all other things."

44. "Humankind knows the world not by what it takes away from it but by what it adds: itself. By its presence, it creates the harmony [between itself and the rest of creation] that is the object of its knowledge." "It senses within itself, it possesses the very movement of which the successive horizons that spread out around it are the circumferent reporters."

45. " ... I see, although truly distant, [when] aligned by my eyes, that the greenness of a maple tree harmoniously joins that of a pine tree."

46. "this forestry text, the arborescent statement of a new *Ars poetica* of the Universe, of a new Logic."

47. "the new word, the operation resulting from the conjoined and simultaneous existence of two different things."

48. "The second Logic is like syntax that teaches the art of assembling [various elements], and this is practiced before our eyes by nature itself.... Metaphor, the fundamental iamb or relation of a grave and acute [accent], is not played only in the pages of our books: it is the autonomous art used by all that

is born." On the idea of humankind reading nature in terms of a text, see Brodeur (316, 319).

49. Claudel underscores the notion of poiesis in the section "Art poétique de l'Univers" ("*Ars poetica* of the Universe") with a note: "poïein-faire" (1957, 143).

50. "when God made man in His image, it was in His image as the Creator."

51. "I understand that everything subsists not alone, but rather in an infinite relation with all other things." Compare Madaule (1969, 17).

52. *La Poésie est un art* reviews the complex role played by metaphor in *Art poétique*: "Partout où il y a langage . . . il y a une poésie à l'état latent . . . partout où il y a attention, et surtout où il y a rapport, ce rapport secret . . . entre les choses, les personnes et les idées qu'on appelle analogie et dont la rhétorique a fait la métaphore, il y a poésie. La texture même du langage, et par conséquent de la pensée, est faite de métaphore" (Claudel, 1965, 55; "Wherever there is language . . . there is latent poetry . . . wherever there is attention, and especially wherever there is relation, the secret relation . . . between things, people, and ideas that we call analogy and from which rhetoric derives metaphor, there is poetry. The texture itself of language, and consequently of thought, is made of metaphors"). For Claudel metaphor is a formal feature of language and thought anchored by mimesis, whereas for Rimbaud *metaphora* is a psychopoetic functioning linked to poiesis.

53. "C'est ce que j'exprime en disant que toute connaissance est une 'naissance,' par une espèce de jeu de mots qui . . . est confirmé par l'étymologie: 'connaissance est une 'co-naissance.' Nous ne cessons pas de co-naître au monde" (Claudel et Amrouche 195; "This is what I mean by saying that all knowledge is a 'birth,' with a play on words that . . . etymology confirms; 'knowledge is a co-birth.' We do not cease co-birthing [in relation] to the world").

54. "Everything is defined and defining; it is defined by all of its aspects, it defines by a single aspect. It knows by what it excludes, by fact or by nature. . . . Knowledge is thus taken here in its literal sense of causation and action exercised externally, it is the effect itself traced upon other [things]."

55. "We know things by giving them the means to exert an action on our 'movement.' We know with them, we produce them in their relations with us."

56. "words are the signs that we use to name things; we *call* them, in effect, we evoke them by constituting in ourselves the state of co-birth that responds to their sensorial existence."

57. "Every 'proposition' is first of all the statement of relations, of the balance that we establish between thing[s] and ourselves, [that is], between the subject and the object."

58. For other evidence concerning the importance of Saint Thomas, see Claudel et Amrouche (65, 196).

59. "While Saint Thomas constructs with syllogism his immense edifice on the basis of revelation, Saint Bonaventura, his emulator in the fraternal order

Notes to Pages 110–112

and rival, gives back, with analogy, the inexhaustible key of discovery to poets and thinkers of the future. What an hour for humanity when truth based in reason turns to love which questions it with an incontestable face."

60. "humankind . . . produces itself in relation to God, it knows itself, engendered, in relation to its Creator. . . . As humankind knows, so it knows itself . . . by virtue of this Author, of this Master from whom it received power [to know]."

61. "[Humankind] constitutes for itself, wherever it is, a center, and has the capacity to transport this center wherever it desires." For a later elaboration of Claudelian *connaissance* in relation to God, see Claudel's *Légende de Prâkriti* (1965, 966–67).

62. Shurr restates Claudel's view of the subject's transcendent vision: "In man, [God] insufflated a spirit, a soul, and an intelligent and autonomous principle. These qualities enable man to see within himself and comprehend that which was created" (50–51).

63. "In the broad sense, *co-naître* means to exist at the same time. . . . There is harmony at every moment between all parts of creation."

6. REVEALING DIVINE ORDER: *POESIS PERENNIS*

1. Claudel asserts the continuity linking *Art poétique* and *Cinq grandes odes* in an 11 January 1908 letter to Jacques Rivière: "Je compose en ce moment la dernière des quatre *Grandes Odes* ou psaumes ou monologues où je reprends et développe en les mêlant à ma théorie de la parole et aux incidents de ma vie et présente la doctrine de mes deux traités" (qtd. in Guyard 24; "I am composing at this time the last of the four *Great Odes* or psalms or monologues, where I take up again and develop the doctrine of my two treatises, while adding to them my theory of speech and incidents from my life"). For example, the birth of Claudel's daughter Marie, born in China in 1907, is an explicit theme of the third ode, *Magnificat*, composed the same year. An 8 November 1908 letter to André Gide also links *Art poétique* and the *Odes* (Claudel et Gide 91). Critics thus generally affirm this continuity (compare to Fumet's introduction in Claudel, 1957; Fowlie 33; Maurocordato 17).

2. Claudel's notion of lyric voice linked to God recalls the early French romantic tradition traced to Lamartine that Rimbaud rejected.

3. Richard Berchan similarly reads the ode to *Les Muses* in terms of Claudel's attempt to renounce the world (and poetry) to commit to the priesthood: "At the very moment, in 1900 at Ligugé, when Claudel is ostensibly renouncing the world to become a priest, a poem emerges irrepressibly from him, a lyrical *ars poetica* which, in effect, undermines the act of renunciation. This poem has a goal of its own . . . which is to keep the poet [in Claudel] alive" (33).

4. "I had to, in sum, more or less consciously repress [imagination and

sensibility] . . . for the benefit of the rational and spiritual formation that I was pursuing at the time. . . . Thus underlying my artistic life at that time was this piercingly painful question: what awaits me . . . am I going to try monastic life? This was the problem that I tried to resolve upon my return [from China] in 1900."

5. In *Mémoires improvisés*, Claudel affirms as the inspiration of this ode a bas-relief of the Muses he had seen at the Louvre (Claudel et Amrouche 160). For an insightful recent analysis of the nine Muses and their roles in the creative process, see Hellerstein (1990, 15–29). Other noteworthy commentaries on the composition of the ode to *Les Muses* include Berchan (29); Fowlie (39–42); Guyard (32, 41); and Robichez (141).

6. "I acknowledged you all, complete council of the nine inner Nymphs! / Generative phrase! dark instrument of language and cluster of living women! / [Creative presence! Nothing would arise if you were not nine!]" (trans. in Claudel, 1967, 10).

7. "For behold, the new-made poet, overwhelmed with the outthrust of meaning / The black clamour of all life bound by the navel to the stirring of the foundations / Opens himself, the seizure / Bursting open the door, the breath of its own accord / Forcing the sundering jaws / The trembling sisterhood with one cry! / Now he can no longer be silent! That question which came from him / He has given it for ever / To the learned choir of inextinguishable Echo" (trans. in Claudel, 1967, 10).

8. A subsequent *verset* similarly underscores the autonomous genesis of the creative process: "Ainsi subitement du milieu de la nuit que mon poëme de tous côtés frappe comme l'éclat de la foudre trifourchue" (Claudel, 1957, 223; "Thus swiftly in the midst of the night where my poem strikes on all sides like flashes of three-pronged lightening [trans. in Claudel, 1967, 11]). Compare *La Source* in Claudel (1973).

9. "the poet like an instrument into which one blows."

10. "A l'origine se trouve un *acte créateur*" (Claudel, 1957, 95; "In the beginning there is a *creative act*").

11. "There is not a poet, in fact, who does not have to be inspired to create, who does not receive this mysterious breath that the Ancients called the Muse. . . . This inspiration suggests an analogy with the prophetic spirit."

12. "Oh my soul! the poem is not made of these letters which I drive in like nails, but of the white spaces left on the paper" (trans. in Claudel, 1967, 11).

13. In *La Philosophie du livre*, Claudel describes the primordial role played by intermittent silence in the creation of a poem (1965, 76, 77).

14. In *Réflexions et propositions sur le vers français*, Claudel elucidates the multifaceted notion of iambic rhythm that informs *Cinq grandes odes* (1965, 3).

15. "Verse composed of a line and a blank is this double act, this respiration through which humankind absorbs life and releases intelligible speech."

16. Fowlie links the *verset* with Claudel's cosmology in which we find an analogous iambic rhythm that informs the movement constitutive of universal

harmony (35–36). Similarly, C. N. Rigolot states that "rhythm lies at the heart of Claudel's verse as well as his universe. This is the rhythm of respiration, of the heart, of the Gregorian chants, of psalms—a rhythm revealed in verse of lengths that vary according to their emotional content" (53).

17. "The new verse is not, like the Latin phrase, only an isolated utterance. . . . It does not just exist, rather it functions. It is not only the result of poetic elaboration, it is also the living organ, the regular beat of the pump that draws sentiments and ideas from the unknown."

18. "O my soul! let us plan nothing! [O] my untamed soul, let us be free and ready, / Like the huge frail armies of swallows when they hear the voiceless summons of autumn! . . . / Let there be nothing slavish about my verses; let them be like the sea-eagle that s[w]oops on a great fish, / Nothing visible but a shining flurry of wings and the leaping spray!" (trans. in Claudel, 1967, 12).

19. "May the new language, a lake full of springs / Overflow by all outlets! . . . / The activity of the soul composed upon the tune of its own words! / The intervention of the marvellous [sic] question, the [transparent] dialogue with inexhaustible silence" (trans. in Claudel, 1967, 14).

20. "Poet, you cannot sing well / Unless your song is in measure. . . . / O grammarian within my verses! Do not seek the / [way], seek the center" (trans. in Claudel, 1967, 15).

21. "But your song, you who are Muse to the poet, / Is not the bee's bourdon, the purling spring, the bird of paradise among the clove-trees! / But as the Lord God created everything, thus you discover your joy in the possession of its name, / And as He once said in the silence ['Let there be light! And there was light'], brimming with love, you repeat and follow His naming, / Like a little child spelling it out, 'Thus it is!' O servant of God, full of grace!" (trans. in Claudel, 1967, 17).

22. "You ratify it in substance, you contemplate each thing in your heart, and try to find *the way of saying it*. / When He created the Universe, when He ordered the Game in its beauty, when He unleashed the [vast] ceremony, / Something of us was with Him, seeing all, rejoicing in His handiwork, / His watchfulness in His own day, His decree in His Sabbath! / Thus, poet when you speak, in a delectable enumeration, / Giving to each thing its name, / Like a father you mysteriously summon its essence, and / Just as you once had a part in creating it, you partake of its existence. / Every word a repetition. / Such is the song which you sing in the silence, and such the blessed harmony / Whose assemblage and dissolution you nourish within you" (trans. in Claudel, 1967, 17–18).

23. Retrospectively, Claudel upholds the passage from the ode to *Les Muses* as a statement about the grounding of his poetic discourse in metaphysics aimed at revealing a Catholic worldview (Claudel et Amrouche 162–63).

24. Compare Poulet, who closely identifies the poet with God the Father (1961, 478–79).

25. "I have discovered the secret; I know how to speak; if I wish, I know

how to tell you / What each thing *wishes* [*means*] *to say*. / I am initiated into silence; there is a living inexhaustible ceremony, there is a world to invade, an insatiable poem to fill" (trans. in Claudel, 1967, 18). Again, we remark the semantic play on the expression *vouloir dire* (to mean and to wish or mean to say).

26. "Poetry is the effect of a certain need to make, to realize with words, the idea that one had of something. It is necessary, then, that the imagination have a lively and strong idea, although at first imperfect and muddled, of the object that it proposes to realize. Moreover, it is necessary for us to have put our sensibility regarding this object in a state of desire.... The work of art is the result of the imagination in collaboration with desire.... And little by little, under this regular impulse, between the two poles of imagination and desire, the flow of words and ideas begins to spring forth."

27. "Just as prior to voice, there is breath, so too prior to expression there is the desire to express and this pressure of the soul which humankind transposes into words.... But this breath itself, this desire, is already informed by order and intelligence."

28. "It is in this sense that poetry joins prayer because it brings out the pure essence of things as creatures of God and witnesses for God."

29. "to elucidate all things, to restore their authentic signification. Such a design does not allow the poet to attribute an egotistic catharsis to his work. ... Everything in the work of art must serve.... Everything in it signifies, as does the universe, in the least of its parts."

30. "After the long reeking silence ... / Suddenly the spirit once more, suddenly inspiration ... / Here ... is the Ode, this great new Ode that comes before you" (trans. in Claudel, 1967, 23–24).

31. "For now I am free! what does it matter to me how cruelly you manage things? For I at least am free! I have discovered the secret! I at least am outside! / I no longer take my place with created things, but have my part with what makes them, the [liquid, lascivious mind] spirit which is fluid and yearns" (trans. in Claudel, 1967, 25).

32. Compare Madaule on the analogy of *l'esprit* and *l'eau* (1969, 48–49).

33. "I share the liberty of the omnipresent sea."

34. "I sense, I scent out, I [decipher], I track down, I discover by instinct / How the thing is done!" (trans. in Claudel, 1967, 27).

35. "Being man, / I know what I do. / This out-thrust, this power of birth and creation, / Are things that I use and command, / I live in the world, and my awareness ranges throughout. / I know all things, all things know themselves in me. / To each thing I bring deliverance; / Thanks to me / No thing is any longer alone, for I join it to another in my heart" (trans. in Claudel, 1967, 27).

36. "Lord, I behold it, the key which delivers / Is not that which opens, but that which shuts! / [You are here with me]. / Your will shuts it in like a wall, your power shuts it in like a fortress! / ... It is closed in, and suddenly all

things in my eyes / Have achieved proportion and distance" (trans. in Claudel, 1967, 29).

37. "I perceive clearly the ways of non-existence, but there is only one way / Of truly existing: to be you, to have my being within you!" (trans. in Claudel, 1967, 27). This verset repeats the relation of God and the universe set forth in *Art poétique:* "L'univers n'est qu'une manière totale de ne pas être ce qui est" (1957, 184; "The universe is only a complete way of not being what is," notably God).

38. "Welcome then, o world made new in my eyes, o world now one and whole! / O full Credo of things visible and invisible, I accept you with a Catholic heart" (trans. in Claudel, 1967, 29).

39. "Every being, as the work / Of Eternity is also its expression. / Eternity is here, and the things of the moment happen within it. . . . / What is given is only what is received, / And as all things have had / Their being from you, in time they restore what is eternal" (trans. in Claudel, 1967, 30–31). On the idea that divine order is perpetually re-created, see also Claudel (1957, 135–40).

40. "And I too / Have a voice, and hear the sound it makes, / . . . Thus speaks the voice with which I make eternal words out of you. I can name only the eternal. . . . / So make me wholly this voice, I who make eternal things with my voice, / Totally intelligible speech" (trans. in Claudel, 1967, 31).

41. For a later elaboration of the notion of the self synoymous with the speaking subject, see *La Légende de Prâkriti* (Claudel, 1965, 946–47).

42. "God, who breathed over chaos . . . you breathe into my nostrils the same spirit of creation and form" (trans. in Claudel, 1967, 31).

43. "The intelligible word, and speech that is truly *expressed*, and the voice that is spirit and water! . . . / Because only this is fitted to a divine measure. / Because it is measure itself, / Holy and free, all powerful and creative. . . . / [This is an invisible substance, it is the measure superior to speech]" (trans. in Claudel, 1967, 35–36). Compare "L'acte par lequel l'homme atteste la permanence des choses . . . et répète l'ordre qui l'a créée, s'appelle la parole. . . . Nommer une chose . . . c'est la produire par rapport à son principe" (1957, 101–2; "The act by which humankind attests the permanence of things . . . and repeats the order which created it, is called speech. . . . To name something . . . is to produce it in relation to its everlasting principle").

44. "My soul doth magnify the Lord. / . . . And, meeting you, I was like a wrestler who yields, / Not because he thinks himself weak, but because his opponent is stronger. / You called me by my name / Like one who knew it, you chose me from among all those of my generation" (trans. in Claudel, 1967, 37–38).

45. "And, out of this spirit and sound which you have placed within me . . . / May the sound have a voice, and the voice within me find words! / Amidst the whole universe which stammers, may I make ready my heart like a man who knows what it is that he has to say. . . . / Only let me find the right words,

only let me breathe / Those words from my heart, having found them, and then die, having spoken them, and let my head fall . . . / like an aged priest who dies in the act of consecration" (trans. in Claudel, 1967, 38–40). Compare Hellerstein (1990, 58).

46. "[E]ternity alone would suffice for the task that has been given me. / And I know the responsibility is mine, and I believe in my master just as he does in me. / I have faith in your word, and have no need to see your promise on paper. / For this we break the bondage of dreams, and tread the idols underfoot, and embrace the cross with the cross. / For the image of death creates death, and imitation of life / Creates life, and the vision of God engenders life eternal" (trans. in Claudel, 1967, 41–42).

47. "it is not this body alone that I must be master of, but the whole brute world, and provide / The means to understand and dissolve and assimilate it / Within you and no longer see anything / Resistant to your light that is within me. / For there are those who see and hear by the eyes and ears, / But I see and listen by the spirit alone. / I will see with this dark light!" (trans. in Claudel, 1967, 43). Compare 1 Cor. 13.12.

48. For a comprehensive statement linking verbal art and Catholicism, see *L'Art et la foi*, in which Claudel rejects the doctrine of art for art's sake (1965, 66, 67)—precisely the poetics we find in Rimbaud, however.

49. "Dialogue between the poet and the Muse who little by little becomes Grace. He tries to drive her back, commanding her to leave him to his human duties; he offers to give her, instead of his soul, the whole universe which he is about to recreate through intelligence and the word" (trans. in Claudel, 1967, 53).

50. "Ah, I am drunk, given up to the god! I hear a voice within me, a / rhythm gathering speed. . . . / What do all these men matter to me now? It was not for them I was made, but for the / Transport of this holy measure! / Cry of the muted trumpet! Muffled drumming on the tun of excess! / What do any of them matter to me? This rhythm alone! What does it matter whether or not they follow me, whether or not they listen? / The great wings of poetry unfold" (trans. in Claudel, 1967, 54).

51. Hellerstein, in her paradigm of poetic voice in *Cinq grandes odes*, relates identifications of the poet with feminine and masculine roles in (pro)creation, that is, anima and animus, to the mystical union in Platonic terms, which involves a return to a former androgynous state (1990, 60–76; esp. 71, 73).

52. "And because I am a little drunk, so that sometimes another word comes, / In the way that you like instead of the right one, / Let me have it out with you, / Let me drive you back in this strophe before, with a feline cry, you spring on me again like a wave. / Go a little away from me! Let me do what I want a little. / . . . At least let me do what I want with my piece of paper, and accomplish with studious art / My task like those who have one" (trans. in Claudel, 1967, 54–55).

53. "I say in my turn that nothing is made in nature without design and

Notes to Pages 128–130

purpose towards man, / And, as the light is made for his eyes, and sound for his ears, so all things are made for analysis by his intelligence, / Which is continous with the intelligence that remakes them from the recovered element. . . . / And I can speak, being continuous with all silent things, / Words which in their place are intelligence and will. / I shall sing the great song of man set free from chance" (trans. in Claudel, 1967, 56).

54. "Reason does not reach me, you will not, no will not do with me what you like; I sing and dance" (trans. in Claudel, 1967, 57).

55. "Fool, don't argue, make use of this golden hour! . . . discover the huge divine laughter" (trans. in Claudel, 1967, 57).

56. "You call me the Muse and my other name is Grace."

57. "Do not permit this Muse to come, and to tempt me as if I were a young man, / Not with a song nor with the beauty of her countenance" (trans. in Claudel, 1967, 60).

58. "Death of myself, and of all things, in which I must suffer creation" (trans. in Claudel, 1967, 62).

59. "It is *you* I ask for. / Liberator of men, reuniter of images and cities! / Liberate yourself! Reuniter of all men, join yourself again to yourself! / Be one spirit! One sole intention!" (trans. in Claudel, 1967, 64).

60. "In order to contain the world the poet must himself be closed, like the universe itself, which God has made inexhaustible and complete" (trans. in Claudel, 1967, 67).

61. "My prime duty is to God, and to the task he has given me to perform, which is to bring everything together within him" (trans. in Claudel, 1967, 67).

62. "Once I knew passion, but now I know only the passion of patience and the desire / To know God in his fixity, and to find truth by attention and each thing that is all the others by recreating it with its intelligible name in my thought" (trans. in Claudel, 1967, 69).

63. "I want to create the world of God again. . . . The Word of God is the way that God gives himself to [hu]mankind. / The created word is the way by which all created things are given to [hu]man[kind]" (trans. in Claudel, 1967, 70).

64. "the Word *par excellence*, the transcendent Word, the Word that is God, the Word that is with God, the Word 'to be.' "

65. "to restore God in His creation and creation in God with the help of the Word that was so generously given to the poet." "It is with . . . his Word that the poet returns the world to God."

66. "O point on all sides around me, where indivisible frontiers meet! seamless universe! world inexhaustible and closed! / . . . O Lord God, nothing exists except as an image of your perfection!" (trans. in Claudel, 1967, 70–71). For a more comprehensive statement on the trace of the infinite in the finite, see *Art poétique* (Claudel, 1957, 194).

67. "Blessed be God, who does not leave his works unfinished, / And who has made me a *complete* man, in the image of his own perfection. / And I am

able to understand, being able to grasp and to measure. / You have placed within me relationship and proportion / Once and for always. . . . / Poet, I have found the unit of measure. I can measure the universe, for I am its image" (trans. in Claudel, 1967, 73–74). "[I]t is I who give [nature] its meaning; each thing within me becomes / Eternal in the notion I have of it" (76–77). Ruth N. Horry confirms the Catholic worldview in Claudel: "Claudel begins with the premise that each thing or being in creation is a partial image of God. He, as poet, by involving himself with the world of matter was reaching toward God" (5–6); "Claudel thus believes that the material macrocosm of the universe is implanted in the immaterial microcosm that is the soul of man" (51).

68. "our imaginations cannot add a single term to this Number ecstatic before your Unity" (trans. in Claudel, 1967, 78).

69. Implicitly distinguishing Claudel from Rimbaud, Raymond states that "[nous] n'allons pas voir . . . en Claudel un poète inconscient qui vaticine dans les ténèbres. . . . Cette poésie claudélienne, quoi qu'on ait dit et quoi qu'il semble d'abord, vise, par des voies parfois étranges et difficiles, à une intelligibilité supérieure" (207–8; "[we] are not going to see . . . in Claudel an unconscious poet who makes blind prophesies. . . . Claudelian poetry, whatever one has said and whatever it may seem initially to be, aims, in sometimes strange and difficult ways, to attain superior intelligibility").

70. For a different staging of Claudel's "corrective" response to Rimbaldian symbolism, see Whitaker (1972).

WORKS CONSULTED

Abastado, Claude. "Ecriture automatique et instance du sujet." *Revue des Sciences Humaines* 56.184 (1981): 59–75.

Ahearn, Edward. J. "Explosions of the Real: Rimbaud's Ecstatic and Political Subversions." *Stanford French Review* 9.1 (Spring 1985): 71–81.

Antoine, Gerald. "Parabole d'Animus et d'Anima: pour faire mieux comprendre certaines oeuvres de Paul Claudel." *Travaux de linguistique et de littérature* 13.2 (1975): 705–23.

Archard, David. *Consciousness and the Unconscious*. La Salle, IL: Open Court, 1984.

Aristotle. *The Metaphysics*. 1933. Trans. Hugh Tredennick. Cambridge, MA: Harvard UP, 1947.

———. *The Rhetoric and the Poetics of Aristotle*. Trans. W. Rhys Roberts and Ingram Bywater, reprinted from the Oxford Translation of Aristotle. Toronto: Random, 1954.

Arlow, Jacob A. "Metaphor and the Psychoanalytic Situation." *The Psychoanalytic Quarterly* 48 (1979): 363–85.

Aubin, H. "Le cas Rimbaud." *Evolution psychiatrique* 15 (1955): 329–47.

Autrand, Michel. "Claudel, poète de la négation." *Europe* 635 (mars 1982): 124–36.

Auvinet, Louis-François Philippe. *Aspects psychologiques d'Arthur Rimbaud*. Bordeaux: Th. Médicale, 1941.

Baillarger, Jules. *Des hallucinations, des causes qui les produisent, et des maladies qu'elles caractérisent*. Paris, 1844.

Bakhtin, Mikhail. *The Dialogic Imagination*. Ed. Michael Holquist. Trans. Caryl Emerson and Michael Holquist. Austin: U of Texas P, 1981.

Balakian, Anna. *Literary Origins of Surrealism*. New York: King's Crown, 1947.

Bandelier, Danielle. *Se dire et se taire: L'écriture d'Une saison en enfer d'Arthur Rimbaud*. Neuchâtel: Baconnière, 1988.

Bär, Eugène. "The Language of the Unconscious According to Jacques Lacan." *Semiotica* 3.3 (1971): 241–68.

Baudelaire, Charles. *Oeuvres complètes*. 2 tomes. Ed. Claudel Pichois. Paris: Gallimard, 1961–76.

Baudry, Jean-Louis. "Le texte de Rimbaud." *Tel Quel* 35 (Automne 1968): 46–63.

———. "Le texte de Rimbaud." *Tel Quel* 36 (Hiver 1969): 33–53.

Bays, Gwendolyn. *The Orphic Vision: Seer Poets from Novalis to Rimbaud*. Lincoln: U of Nebraska P, 1964.

———. "Rimbaud—Father of Surrealism?" *Yale French Studies* 31 (1964): 45–51.

Becker, Aimé. "Saint Augustin et Paul Claudel: La rencontre du Dieu vivant." *Augustinus* 32 (1987): 455–74.

Béguin, Albert. *L'Ame romantique et le rêve*. Paris: José Corti, 1939.

Belaval, Yvon. "Poésie et psychanalyse." *Cahiers de L'Association Internationale des Etudes Françaises* 7 (1955): 5–22.

Benveniste, Emile. *Problèmes de linguistique générale*. Paris: Gallimard, 1966.

———. *Problems in General Linguistics*. Trans. Mary Elizabeth Meek. Coral Gables: U of Miami P, 1971.

Berchan, Richard. "Paul Claudel's 'Ode to the Muses': Reflexions on the Role of a Poem in the Creation of its Author." *Claudel Studies* 1.1 (1972): 28–35.

Berrichon, Paterne. "Rimbaud et Claudel." *Mercure de France* 16 jan. 1912: 445–46.

Bersani, Leo. "Rimbaud's Simplicity." *A Future for Astyanax: Character and Desire in Literature*. Boston: Little, 1969. 230–58.

Bivort, Olivier. "Le tiret dans les *Illuminations*." *Parade sauvage* 8 (sept. 1991): 2–8.

Black, Max. *Models and Metaphors*. Ithaca, NY: Cornell UP, 1962.

Blanchet, André. "L'Elaboration par Claudel de son article sur Rimbaud." *Revue d'Histoire Littéraire de la France* 67 (1967): 759–75.

Blanchot, Maurice. "L'Autre Claudel." *La Nouvelle Revue Française* 1 sept. 1955: 404–23.

———. *L'Espace littéraire*. Paris: Gallimard, 1955.

———. *La part du feu*. Paris: Gallimard, 1949.

Bloom, Harold. *Agon*. New York: Oxford UP, 1982.

———. *The Anxiety of Influence: A Theory of Poetry*. New York: Oxford UP, 1973.

———. *The Breaking of the Vessels*. Chicago: U of Chicago P, 1982.

———. *A Map of Misreading*. New York: Oxford UP, 1975.

———. *Poetry and Repression*. New Haven and London: Yale UP, 1976.

Bodenham, C. H. L. "Arthur Rimbaud: Poetry and After." *Modern Language Review* 77.2 (1982): 294–309.

———. "Rimbaud's 'Poétique sensationniste' and Some Nineteenth-century Medical Writing." *French Studies* 38 (Jan. 1984): 32–39.

Bonaventura, Saint. *The Mind's Road to God*. Trans. George Boas. New York: Liberal Arts, 1953.

Bonnefis, Philippe. "Onze notes pour fragmenter un texte de Rimbaud." *Littérature* 11 (oct. 1973): 46–67.

Bonnefoy, Yves. *Rimbaud*. Paris: Seuil, 1961.

———. *Rimbaud*. Trans. Paul Schmidt. New York: Harper & Row, 1973.

Bouillane de Lacoste, Henri de. *Rimbaud et le problème des Illuminations*. Paris: Mercure de France, 1949.

Works Consulted

Bowie, Malcolm. *Freud, Proust, and Lacan: Theory as Fiction.* Cambridge: Cambridge UP, 1987.

Breton, André. *La clé des champs.* Hollande: Pauvert, 1967.

———. *Manifestes du surréalisme.* Paris: Gallimard, 1963.

———. *Les pas perdus.* Paris: Gallimard, 1924.

———. *Point du jour.* Paris: Gallimard, 1970.

———. "Situation surréaliste de l'objet." *Position politique du surréalisme.* Paris: Pauvert, 1971. 22–30.

Brodeur, Léo A. *Le corps-sphère: clef de la symbolique claudélienne.* Québec, Canada: Cosmos, 1970.

Brosman, Catharine Savage. "The Comparative Attitudes of Gide and Claudel Towards Rimbaud." *Claudel Studies* 4.1 (1977): 19–37.

Bugliani, Ann. "The Role of Hearing and the Voice in Claudel's Works." *Claudel Studies* 2.1 (1975): 43–49.

Chambers, Ross. "Mimesis and Symbolisation: A Question in Rimbaud Criticism." *Australian Journal of French Studies* 11.1 (Jan.–Apr. 1974): 54–64.

Chase, Cynthia. "Transference as Trope and Persuasion." *Discourse in Literature and Psychoanalysis.* Ed. Shlomith Rimmon-Kenan. London: Methuen, 1987. 211–32.

Cirlot, J. E. *A Dictionary of Symbols.* Trans. Jack Sage. 1962. New York: Philosophical Library, 1971.

Claisse, Bruno. *Rimbaud ou 'le dégagement rêvé.'* Charleville, France: Musée-Bibliothèque Arthur Rimbaud, 1990.

Clark, Herbert H., and Susan E. Haviland. "Psychological Processes as Linguistic Explanation." *Explaining Linguistic Phenomena.* Ed. David Cohen. Washington: Hemisphere; New York: Wiley, 1974. 91–124.

Claudel, Paul. *Connaissance de l'Est.* Ed. Gilbert Gadoffre. Paris: Mercure de France, 1973.

———. *The East I Know.* Trans. Teresa Frances and William Rose Benét. New Haven: Yale UP, 1914.

———. *Five Great Odes.* Trans. Edward Lucie-Smith. London: Rapp & Carroll, 1967.

———. "Lettres inédites à Maurice Pottecher." *Cahiers Paul Claudel* 1. Paris: Gallimard, 1959. 68–111.

———. *Oeuvre poétique.* Intro. Stanislas Fumet. Paris: Gallimard, 1957.

———. *Oeuvres complètes.* 29 tomes. Paris: Gallimard, 1954–86.

———. *Oeuvres en prose.* Ed. Jacques Petit et Charles Galpérine. Paris: Gallimard, 1965.

Claudel, Paul, et Jean Amrouche. *Mémoires improvisés.* Paris: Gallimard, 1954.

Claudel, Paul, et André Gide. *Correspondance 1899–1926.* Préface Robert Mallet. Paris: Gallimard, 1949.

Coates, Paul. *Words after Speech: A Comparative Study of Romanticism and Symbolism.* New York: St. Martin's, 1986.

Collier, Peter. "Lectures de *Mémoire*." *Parade sauvage* 2 (1990): 60–73.
Condillac, Etienne Bonnet de. *Essai sur l'origine des connaissances humaines*. Paris, 1803.
Cournut, Jean. "L'ombre de l'objet et la représentation du mot." *Revue Française de Psychanalyse* 69 (mai–juin 1986): 871–74.
Culler, Jonathan. "Reading Lyric." *Yale French Studies* 69 (1986): 98–106.
———. *Structuralist Poetics*. Ithaca, NY: Cornell UP, 1975.
Davidson, Donald. "What Metaphors Mean." *Critical Inquiry* 5.1 (1978): 31–47.
Davies, Margaret. "Le thème de la voyance dans 'Après de déluge,' 'Métropolitain,' et 'Barbare'." *Revue des Lettres Modernes* 323–26 (1971): 19–39.
Delahaye, Ernest. *Les Illuminations et Une Saison en enfer*. Paris: Messein, 1927.
Delattre, Jean-Luc. *Le déséquilibre mental d'Arthur Rimbaud*. Paris: Le François, 1928.
De Man, Paul. "The Epistemology of Metaphor." *Critical Inquiry* 5.1 (1978): 13–30.
———. *The Rhetoric of Romanticism*. New York: Columbia UP, 1984.
Derrida, Jacques. *L'écriture et la différence*. Paris: Seuil, 1967.
———. *Marges de la philosophie*. Paris: Minuit, 1972.
Dillman, Karin. *The Subject in Rimbaud, from Self to "Je."* New York: Lang, 1984.
Dumarsais, César Chesneau. *Les tropes*. Intro. Gérard Genette. 1818. Genève: Slatkine, 1967.
Eco, Umberto. *The Aesthetics of Thomas Aquinas*. Trans. Hugh Bredin. Cambridge, MA: Harvard UP, 1988.
———. "Metaphor." *Semiotics and the Philosophy of Language*. Bloomington: Indiana UP, 1984. 87–129.
———. "The Semantics of Metaphor." *The Role of the Reader: Explorations in the Semiotics of Texts*. Bloomington: Indiana UP, 1979. 67–89.
———. *A Theory of Semiotics*. Bloomington: Indiana UP, 1976.
Eigeldinger, Marc. "L'intertextualité mythique dans les 'Illuminations.'" *Cahiers de l'Association Internationale des Etudes Françaises* 36 (1984): 253–72.
———. "Notes sur la poétique de la voyance." *Revue des Sciences Humaines* 64.193 (jan.–mar. 1984): 25–28.
———. "La voyance avant Rimbaud." *Lettres du voyant*. Ed. Gérald Schaeffer. Genève: Droz, 1975.
Elam, Keir. *The Semiotics of Theatre and Drama*. London: Methuen, 1980.
Engell, James. *The Creative Imagination: Enlightenment to Romanticism*. Cambridge, MA: Harvard UP, 1981.
Erwin, John F. "Claudel and the Lesson of Mallarmé: The Theme of Absence." *L'Esprit Créateur* 13.1 (Spring 1973): 44–54.
Etiemble, René. *Structure du mythe*. Paris: Gallimard, 1952. Tome 2 du *Mythe de Rimbaud*. 5 tomes. 1952–67.
Felman, Shoshana. *La folie et la chose littéraire*. Paris: Seuil, 1978.

———. *Literature and Psychoanalysis: The Question of Reading, Otherwise*. Baltimore: Johns Hopkins UP, 1982.
———. "On Reading Poetry: Reflections on the Limits and Possibilities of Psychoanalytical Approaches." *The Literary Freud: Mechanisms of Defense and the Poetic Will*. Ed. Joseph Smith. New Haven: Yale UP, 1980.
———. "Tu as bien fait de partir, Arthur Rimbaud: Poésie et modernité." *Littérature* 11 (1973): 3–21.
———. *Writing and Madness*. Trans. Martha Noel Evans and Brian Massumi. Ithaca, NY: Cornell UP, 1985.
Fondane, Benjamin. *Rimbaud le voyou*. Paris: Complexe, 1990.
Fontanier, Pierre. *Les figures du discours*. Intro. Gérard Genette. Paris: Flammarion, 1977.
Forrester, John. *Language and the Origins of Psychoanalysis*. New York: Columbia UP, 1980.
———. "Psychoanalysis or Literature?" *French Studies* 35 (Apr. 1981): 170–79.
Fowlie, Wallace. *Paul Claudel*. London: Bowes & Bowes, 1957.
Freadman, Anne. "A Reading of 'Mystique.' " *Australian Journal of French Studies* 11.1 (Jan.–Apr. 1974): 65–82.
Fretet, Jean. *L'Aliénation poétique*. Paris: Janin, 1946.
Freud, Sigmund. *The Standard Edition of the Complete Psychological Works of Sigmund Freud*. Ed. and trans. James Strachey. 24 vols. London: Hogarth, 1953–74.
Friedrich, Hugo. *The Structure of Modern Poetry*. Evanston, IL: Northwestern UP, 1974.
Frohock, W. M. *Rimbaud's Poetic Practice: Image and Theme in the Major Poems*. Cambridge, MA: Harvard UP, 1963.
Gadoffre, Gilbert. "Les trois sources de l'analogie claudélienne." *French Studies* 13 (Apr. 1959): 135–45.
Genette, Gérard. *Figures II*. Paris: Seuil, 1969.
———. *Figures: essais*. Paris: Seuil, 1966.
———. *Figures III*. Paris: Seuil, 1972.
Glauser, Alfred. *Le poème-symbole*. Paris: Nizet, 1967.
———. *La poétique de Hugo*. Paris: Nizet, 1978.
Gleize, Jean-Marie. "D'ailleurs il n'y a rien à voir là-dedans." *Revue des Sciences Humaines* 64.193 (1984): 33–37.
———. *Poésie et figuration*. Paris: Seuil, 1983.
Godfrey, Sima. "The Anxiety of Anticipation: Ulterior Motives in French Poetry." *Yale French Studies* 66 (1984): 1–26.
Greenburg, Wendy Nicolas. *The Power of Rhetoric: Hugo's Metaphor and Poetics*. New York: Lang, 1985.
Groupeμ: Dubois, Jacques, et al. *Rhétorique générale*. Paris: Larousse, 1970.
Guillemin, Henri. "Claudel avant sa 'conversion'." *Revue de Paris* (mai–août 1955): 89–100.

———. "Claudel jusqu'à sa 'conversion'." *Revue de Paris* (jan.–avr. 1955): 20–30.

Gumpel, Lisolette. *Metaphor Reexamined*. Bloomington: Indiana UP, 1984.

Guyard, Marius-François. *Recherches claudéliennes: autour des 'Cinq grandes odes.'* Paris: Klincksieck, 1963.

Guyaux, André. "L'Autre et le rêve." *Cahiers de l'Association Internationale des Etudes Françaises* 36 (1978): 223–38.

———. *Duplicités de Rimbaud*. Paris-Genève: Champion-Slatkine, 1991.

———. *Poétique du fragment*. Neuchâtel: Baconnière, 1985.

———. "Trente répliques à 'Je est un autre' petite phrase." *Revue des Sciences Humaines* 64.193 (1984): 39–43.

Hackett, C. A. *Rimbaud: A Critical Introduction*. Cambridge, MA: Harvard UP, 1981.

———. " 'Une saison en enfer': frénésie et structure." *Revue des Lettres Modernes* 370–73 (1973): 7–15.

Harries, Karsten. "Metaphor and Transcendence." *Critical Inquiry* 5.1 (1978): 73–90.

Haskell, Robert, ed. *Cognition and Symbolic Structures: The Psychology of Metaphoric Transformation*. Norwood, NJ: Allex, 1987.

Hausman, Carl R. *Metaphor and Art: Interactionism and Reference in the Verbal and Nonverbal Arts*. Cambridge: Cambridge UP, 1989.

Hawkes, Terence. *Metaphor*. 1972. London: Methuen, 1986.

———. *Structuralism and Semiotics*. Berkeley: U of California P, 1977.

Heidegger, Martin. *Poetry, Language, and Thought*. New York: Harper & Row, 1971.

Hellerstein, Nina. *Mythe et structure dans les Cinq grandes odes de Paul Claudel*. Paris: Diffusion des Belles Lettres, 1990.

———. "The Oriental Legends and Their Role in Claudel's 'Connaissance de l'Est.' " *Claudel Studies* 1.2 (1973): 36–45.

Hester, Marcus. *The Meaning of Poetic Metaphor*. Paris: Mouton, 1967.

Heyndels, Ralph. "A partir de Rimbaud aujourd'hui: 'Après le déluge'." *Littérature* 11 (oct. 1983): 120–28.

Heynick, Frank. *Language and its Disturbances in Dreams: The Pioneering Work of Freud and Kraepelin Updated*. New York: Wiley, 1993.

Hill, John Spencer, ed. *The Romantic Imagination: A Casebook*. London: MacMillan, 1977.

Hillman, James. "Further Notes on Image." *Spring* (1978): 152–82.

———. "An Inquiry into Image." *Spring* (1977): 62–88.

Horry, Ruth N. *Paul Claudel and Saint-John Perse*. Chapel Hill: U of North Carolina P, 1971.

Hosek, Chaviva, and Patricia Parker, eds. *Lyric Poetry: Beyond New Criticism*. Ithaca, NY: Cornell UP, 1985.

Houston, John Porter. *French Symbolism and the Modernist Movement*. Baton Rouge: UP of Louisiana, 1980.

Works Consulted

———. *Patterns of Thought in Rimbaud and Mallarmé*. Lexington: French Forum, 1986.

Hubert, Renée Riese. "The Use of Reversals in Rimbaud's Illuminations." *L'Esprit Créateur* 9.1 (1969): 9–17.

Imbs, Paul, ed. *Trésor de la langue française: dictionnaire de la langue du XIXe et du XXe siècle (1709–1960)*. 16 tomes. Paris: Centre national de la recherche scientifique, 1971–94.

Izambard, Georges. *Rimbaud tel que je l'ai connu*. Paris: Mercure de France, 1963.

Jakobson, Roman. "Linguistics and Poetics." *Style in Language*. Ed. Thomas Seboek. Cambridge: Cambridge UP, 1960. 350–77.

———. "Two Aspects of Language and Two Types of Aphasic Disturbances." *Fundamentals of Language*. Roman Jakobson and Morris Halle. The Hague: Mouton, 1956. 55–87.

Jaynes, Julian. *The Origin of Consciousness in the Breakdown of the Bicameral Mind*. Boston: Houghton, 1976.

Jeancolas, Claude. *Le dictionnaire Rimbaud*. Paris: Balland, 1991.

Jouve, Raymond. *Comment lire Paul Claudel*. Paris: Editions "Aux Etudiants de France," 1946.

Jung, Carl G. *The Spirit in Man, Art, and Literature*. The Collected Works of C. G. Jung. Trans. R. F. C. Hull. Vol. 15. Princeton: Princeton UP, 1966.

———. *Two Essays on Analytical Psychology*. The Collected Works of C. G. Jung. Trans. R. F. C. Hull. Vol. 7. New York: Bollingen, 1953.

Jutrin, Monique. "Parole et silence dans 'Une saison en enfer': l'expérience du moi divisé." *Revue des Lettres Modernes* 445–49 (1976): 7–23.

Kalb, Henry E. "Motifs and Figures in Claudel's First 'Ode.' " *Claudel Studies* 2.1 (1975): 35–42.

Kelly, Bernard. *The Metaphysical Background of Analogy*. London: Aquin, 1958.

Kentner, Susan. "Toward a Rhetoric of Translation: The Problem of Metaphor in Rimbaud's Prose Poetry." Diss. U of Chicago, 1981.

Kittang, Atle. *Discours et jeu: essai d'analyse des textes d'Arthur Rimbaud*. Bergen: Universitetsforlaget, 1975.

Kittay, Eva Feder. *Metaphor: Its Cognitive Force and Linguistic Structure*. Oxford: Clarendon, 1987.

Klein, David B. *The Unconscious: Invention or Discovery*. Santa Monica, CA: Goodyear, 1977.

Kott, Jan. *The Bottom Translation: Marlowe and Shakespeare and the Carnival Tradition*. Evanston, IL: Northwestern UP, 1987.

Kristeva, Julia. *Desire in Language: A Semiotic Approach to Literature and Art*. New York: Columbia UP, 1980.

———. *Revolution in Poetic Language*. New York: Columbia UP, 1984.

Lacan, Jacques. *Ecrits*. Paris: Seuil, 1966.

———. *The Four Fundamental Concepts of Psycho-analysis*. Ed. Jacques-Alain Miller. Trans. Alan Sheridan. London: Hogarth and the Institute of Psycho-analysis, 1977.

―――. *The Language of the Self: The Function of Language in Psychoanalysis*. Trans. Anthony Wilden. Baltimore: Johns Hopkins UP, 1968.
―――. *Le séminaire: les psychoses*. Paris: Seuil, 1981.
Lacose, Jean, Gilles Marcotte, et Dominique Noguez. *Rimbaud*. Ville la Salle, Québec: Hurtubise, 1993.
Lakoff, George, and Mark Johnson. *Metaphors We Live By*. Chicago: U of Chicago P, 1980.
Lakoff, George, and Mark Turner. *More Than Cool Reason: A Field Guide to Poetic Metaphor*. Chicago: U of Chicago P, 1989.
Lalande, André. *Vocabulaire technique et critique de la philosophie*. Paris: PUF, 1988.
Lapeyre, Paule. *Le vertige de Rimbaud: clé d'une perception poétique*. Neuchâtel: Baconnière, 1981.
Laplanche, Jean, et Serge Leclaire. "The Unconscious: A Psychoanalytic Study." *Yale French Studies* 48 (1972): 118–202.
Laplanche Jean, and J.-B. Pontalis. *Vocabulaire de la psychanalyse*. Paris: PUF, 1967.
Lawler, James. *The Language of French Symbolism*. Princeton: Princeton UP, 1969.
Lefèvre, Frédéric. *Les sources de Paul Claudel*. Paris: LeMercier, 1927.
Levins, Samuel. *Metaphoric Worlds: Conceptions of a Romantic Nature*. New Haven: Yale UP, 1988.
Littré, Emile. *Dictionnaire de la langue française*. Paris: Hachette, 1874.
Lodge, David. *The Modes of Modern Writing*. Ithaca, NY: Cornell UP, 1977.
Lucas, Frank. *The Decline and Fall of the Romantic Ideal*. 1936. New York: Macmillan, 1937.
Lucie-Smith, Edward. "The *Cinq grandes odes* of Paul Claudel." *Claudel: A Reappraisal*. Ed. Richard Griffiths. London: Rapp & Whiting, 1968. 79–90.
Lyotard, François. *Discours, figure*. Paris: Klincksieck, 1971.
MacCabe, Colin, ed. *The Talking Cure: Essays in Psychoanalysis and Literature*. New York: St. Martin's, 1981.
MacCombie, John. *The Prince and the Genie: A Study of Rimbaud's Influence on Claudel*. Boston: U of Massachusetts P, 1972.
Madaule, Jacques. "Baudelaire et Claudel." *Europe* 456–57 (avr.–mai 1967): 197–204.
―――. *Claudel et le dieu caché*. Paris: Brouwer, 1969.
―――. *Le génie de Paul Claudel*. Paris: Brouwer, 1933.
Mallarmé, Stéphane. *Oeuvres complètes*. Paris: Gallimard, 1945.
―――. *Propos sur la poésie*. Monaco: Rocher, 1946.
―――. *Vers et prose*. Paris: Garnier & Flammarion, 1977.
Marcotte, Gilles. *La prose de Rimbaud*. Montréal: Primeur, 1983.
Marie, Charles P. "Les possédés de transcendance: Maurice Clavel, Pierre Henri Simon, Paul Claudel." *Claudel Studies* 3.1 (1976): 37–47.

Works Consulted

Matucci, Mario. "De Baudelaire à Rimbaud: le chemin de la voyance." *Cahiers de l'Association Internationale des Etudes Françaises* 36 (1984): 239–51.

Maurocordato, Alexandre. *L'Ode de Paul Claudel: essai de phénoménologie littéraire.* Paris: Lettres Modernes, 1974.

McNeil, Lynda D. *Recreating the World/Word: The Mythic Mode as Symbolic Discourse.* Albany: State U of New York P, 1992.

Mellard, James M. *Using Lacan, Reading Fiction.* Urbana: U of Illinois P, 1991.

"Métaphore." *Encyclopédie de Diderot et d'Alembert.* Tome 10. Ed. Franco Maria Ricci. Neuchâtel, 1765.

Miall, David S., ed. *Metaphor: Problems and Perspectives.* Brighton, Sussex: Harvester, 1982.

Michelet, Jules. *Oeuvres complètes.* 4 tomes. Ed. Paul Viallaneix. Paris: Flammarion, 1971.

Miel, Jan. "Jacques Lacan and the Structure of the Unconscious." *Yale French Studies* 36–37 (1966): 104–11.

Millet-Gérard, Dominique. "Anima et la sagesse: Pour une poétique comparée de l'exégèse claudélienne." *L'Information littéraire* 40.1 (1988): 22–25.

Minahen, Charles D. " 'Tourbillons de lumière': The Symbolism of Rimbaud's Illuminating Vortices." *Stanford French Review* 9 (Winter 1985): 351–64.

Moller, Lis. *The Freudian Reading.* Philadelphia: U of Pennsylvania P, 1991.

Mooij, J. J. A. *A Study of Metaphor.* Amsterdam: North-Holland, 1976.

Morace, Robert. "Dialogues and Dialogics." *Modern Language Studies* 23.3 (Summer 1993): 73–91.

Morisot, Jean-Claude. *Claudel et Rimbaud: étude de transformations.* Paris: Lettres Modernes, 1976.

Nagy, Moses M. "Christmas 1886: A Day of Transfiguration of Claudel." *Claudel Studies* 14.1–2 (1987): 3–7.

———. "Claudel's Conversion: The Beginning of his Apostleship." *Claudel Studies* 6.1 (1978): 5–15.

Nakaji, Yoshikazu. "Barbare: une lecture." *Parade sauvage* 8 (sept. 1991): 117–25.

Nerval, Gérard. *Oeuvres.* Paris: Pléiade, 1961.

Nietzsche, Friedrich. *The Complete Works of Friedrich Nietzsche.* 18 vols. Ed. Oscar Levy. London: Darien. 1909–13.

Paliyenko, Adrianna M. "Margins of Madness and Creativity." *Dreams in French Literature.* Ed. Tom Conner. Amsterdam: Rodopi, 1995. 173–98.

Palombo, Stanley. "The Cognitive Act in Dream Construction." *American Academy of Psychoanalysis* 8 (1980): 186–201.

———. "The Genius of the Dream." *American Journal of Psychoanalysis* 43 (1983): 301–13.

Parker, Patricia A. "The Metaphorical Plot." *Metaphor: Problems and Perspectives.* Ed. David S. Miall. Brighton, Sussex: Harvester, 1982. 133–57.

Peckham, Morse. "Metaphor: A Little Plain Speaking on a Weary Subject."

The Triumph of Romanticism. Columbia: U of South Carolina P, 1970. 401–20.

Perloff, Marjorie. *The Poetics of Indeterminacy: Rimbaud to Cage*. Boston: Northwestern UP, 1983.

Peschel, Enid Rhodes. *Flux and Reflux: Ambivalence in the Poems of Arthur Rimbaud*. Genève: Droz, 1977.

Petralia, Franco. "Le Rimbaud de Claudel." *Revue des Langues Vivantes* 22.3 (1956): 214–35.

Phelan, Gerald Bernard. *Saint Thomas and Analogy*. Milwaukee: Marquette UP, 1973.

Pinquet, Maurice. "Le Rimbaud d'André Suarès." *Société Japonaise de Langue et Littérature Française* 4(1964): 93–104.

Plato. *The Republic of Plato*. Trans. Francis MacDonald Cornford. Oxford: Clarendon, 1941.

Plessen, Jacques. "Deux fois Rimbaud." *Littérature* 11 (oct. 1973): 102–9.

———. "La métaphore chez Rimbaud." *Travaux de linguistique et de littérature* 21 (1983): 199–214.

———. *Promenade et poésie: l'expérience de la marche et du mouvement dans l'oeuvre de Rimbaud*. La Haye: Mouton, 1967.

Poulet, Georges. *Les métamorphoses du cercle*. Paris: Plon, 1961.

———. "Oeuf, semence, bouche ouverte, zéro." *La Nouvelle Revue Française* 1 sept. 1955: 445–66.

———. *La poésie éclatée: Baudelaire-Rimbaud*. Paris: PUF, 1980.

Preminger, Alex, ed. *Princeton Encyclopedia of Poetry and Poetics*. Princeton: Princeton UP, 1974.

Pringent, Christian. "Pour l'amour d'un porc." *Revue des Sciences Humaines* 64.193 (1984): 63–67.

Printemps. *Le Grand Jeu*. 3 tomes. 1928–30. Paris: Herne, 1968.

Ragland-Sullivan, Ellie. *Jacques Lacan and the Philosophy of Language*. Urbana: U of Illinois P, 1986.

Rand, Nicolas, and Maria Torok. "Questions to Freudian Psychoanalysis: Dream Interpretation, Reality, Fantasy." *Critical Inquiry* 19 (Spring 1993): 567–94.

Ray, Lionel. *Arthur Rimbaud*. Paris: Seghers, 1976.

Raybaud, Antoine. *Fabrique d'Illuminations*. Paris: Seuil, 1989.

Raymond, Marcel. *De Baudelaire au surréalisme: essai sur le mouvement poétique contemporain*. Paris: Corrêa, 1934.

Reich, Zdenko. "Préface à une étude sur la métaphore." *Le surréalisme au service de la révolution*. 5 (15 mai 1933): 25–27.

Rémond, René. "1886: l'idéologie dominante." *Paul Claudel et la conversion*. Ed. Gerald Antoine. Le Rocher: Cahiers, 1986. 62–66.

Renéville, Rolland de. *Rimbaud le voyant*. 1929. Vanves: Thot, 1985.

Rice, Donald, and Peter Schofer. *Rhetorical Poetics: Theory and Practice of Fig-*

Works Consulted

ural and Symbolic Reading in Modern French Literature. Madison: U of Wisconsin P, 1983.

Richard, Jean-Pierre. *Poésie et profondeur*. Paris: Seuil, 1955.

Richards, I. A. *The Philosophy of Rhetoric*. Oxford: Oxford UP, 1936.

Ricoeur, Paul. "Imagination et métaphore." *Psychologie médicale* 14.12 (1982): 1883–87.

———. *La métaphore vive*. Paris: Seuil, 1975.

———. "The Metaphorical Process as Cognition, Imagination, and Feeling." *Critical Inquiry* 5.1 (1978): 143–59.

———. *The Rule of Metaphor*. Trans. Robert Czerny. Toronto: U of Toronto P, 1984.

Rifelj, Carol de Dobay. *Word and Figure*. Columbus: Ohio State UP, 1987.

Riffaterre, Michael. *Semiotics of Poetry*. Bloomington: Indiana UP, 1978.

———. "Sur la sémiotique de l'obscurité en poésie: 'Promontoire' de Rimbaud." *French Review* 55.5 (avr. 1982): 625–32.

Rigolot, C. N. "The Symbol of the Circle and the Center in the Works of Paul Claudel." *Claudel Studies* 1.2 (1972): 47–57.

Rimbaud, Arthur. *Illuminations*. Trans. Louise Varèse. New York: New Directions, 1946.

———. *Illuminations: suivi de correspondence* (1873–1891). Préface Jean-Luc Steinmetz. Paris: Flammarion, 1989.

———. *Oeuvres*. Intro. Suzanne Bernard et André Guyaux. Paris: Garnier, 1983.

———. *Oeuvres complètes*. Intro. Antoine Adam. Paris: Gallimard, 1972.

———. *Oeuvres de Arthur Rimbaud*. Préface Paul Claudel. Paris: Mercure de France, 1947.

———. *Rimbaud: Complete Works, Selected Letters*. Trans. Wallace Fowlie. Chicago: U of Chicago P, 1966.

———. *A Season in Hell*. Trans. Louise Varèse. New York: New Directions, 1945.

———. *A Season in Hell and Illuminations*. Trans. Bertrand Mathieu. Brockport, NY: BOA, 1991.

Rimbaud, Isabelle. "Rimbaud mystique." *Mercure de France* 16 juin 1914: 699–713.

Rincé, Dominique. *Baudelaire et la modernité poétique*. Paris: PUF, 1984.

Rivière, Jacques. "Rimbaud." *La Nouvelle Revue Française* 12 (juil.–sept. 1914): 5–48; 209–30.

Robichez, Jacques. "Ordre et désordre dans les 'Cinq Grandes Odes.'" *Travaux de linguistique et de littérature* 17 (1979): 139–44.

Rogers, Robert. *Metaphor: A Psychoanalytic View*. Berkeley: U of California Press, 1978.

Ross, Kristin. *The Emergence of Social Space: Rimbaud and the Paris Commune*. Minneapolis: U of Minnesota P, 1988.

Rousseau, Jean Jacques. *Essai sur l'origine des langues*. Tome 2. *Oeuvres complètes*. 22 tomes. Paris, 1824.
Ruchon, François. *Jean-Arthur Rimbaud*. Paris: Ancienne Honoré Champion, 1929.
Sacchi, Sergio. " 'Barbare' de Rimbaud: de la métaphore au mythe." *Etudes Françaises* 1 (1992): 92–103.
Saussure, Ferdinand de. *Cours de linguistique générale*. Paris: Payot, 1980.
Schofer, Peter, and Donald Rice. "The Rhetoric of Displacement and Condensation." *Pre/Text* 3 (1982): 9–29.
Schwab, Gabriele. "Genesis of the Subject, Imaginary Functions, and Poetic Language." *New Literary History* 15 (1984): 453–74.
Shelley, Percy Bysshe. *A Defence of Poetry*. New York: Bobbs-Merrill, 1965.
Shurr, Georgia Hooks. "Claudel's Religion: The Critics and Some Conclusions." *Claudel Studies* 2.1 (1975): 50–63.
Silverman, Kaja. *The Subject of Semiotics*. New York: Oxford UP. 1983.
Skura, Meredith. *The Literary Use of the Psychoanalytic Process*. New Haven: Yale UP, 1981.
Spector, Jack J. *The Aesthetics of Freud: A Study in Psychoanalysis and Art*. New York: Praeger, 1973.
Spire, André. "Baudelaire esthéticien." *Europe* 456–57 (avr.–mai 1967): 79–99.
Starkie, Enid. *Arthur Rimbaud*. New York: Norton, 1939.
States, Bert. *The Rhetoric of Dreams*. Ithaca, NY: Cornell UP, 1988.
Steinmetz, Jean-Luc. *Arthur Rimbaud: une question de présence*. Paris: Tallandier, 1991.
———. *La poésie et ses raisons*. Paris: Corti, 1990.
Tamba, Irène. "Pour une approche énonciative du sens métaphorique." *Travaux de linguistique et de littérature* 21 (1983): 175–85.
Thom, Martin. "The Unconscious Structured as a Language." *The Talking Cure: Essays in Psychoanalysis and Literature*. Ed. Colin MacCabe. New York: St. Martin's, 1981. 1–44.
Thomas Aquinas, Saint. *Summa Theologiae*. Preface Thomas Gilby. 60 vols. New York: McGraw, 1964–66.
Thomas, Owen. *Metaphor and Related Subjects*. New York: Random, 1969.
Todorov, Tzvetan. "A Complication of Text: The *Illuminations*." *French Literary Theory Today*. Ed. Tzvetan Todorov. Cambridge: Cambridge UP, 1982. 223–37.
———. "Les *Illuminations*." *Les genres du discours*. Paris: Seuil, 1978. 204–20.
———. *The Poetics of Prose*. Trans. Richard Howard. Intro. Jonathan Culler. Ithaca, NY: Cornell UP, 1977.
———. "Poetry Without Verse." *The Prose Poem in France*. New York: Columbia UP, 1983. 60–78.
———. "Remarques sur l'obscurité." *Rimbaud: le poème en prose et la traduction poétique*. Ed. Sergio Sacchi. Tübingen: Narr, 1988. 11–17.
———. *Théories du symbole*. Paris: Seuil, 1977.

———. *Theories of the Symbol*. Trans. Catherine Porter. Ithaca, NY: Cornell UP, 1982.

Tourangeau, Roger. "Metaphor and Cognitive Structure." *Metaphor: Problems and Perspectives*. Ed. David S. Miall. Brighton, Sussex: Harvester, 1982. 14–35.

Tracy, David. *The Analogical Imagination: Christian Theology and the Culture of Pluralism*. New York: Crossroad, 1989.

Trilling, Lionel. *The Liberal Imagination*. New York: Scribner's, 1950.

Turbayne, Colin. *The Myth of Metaphor*. New Haven: Yale UP, 1962.

Verlaine, Paul. *Fêtes galantes; La bonne chanson; Romance sans paroles; Ecrits sur Rimbaud*. Paris: Garnier Flammarion, 1976.

———. *Oeuvres en prose*. Paris: Gallimard, 1972.

Vico, Giambattista. *The New Science of Giambattista Vico*. Trans. Thomas Bergin and Max Harold Firsch. Ithaca, NY: Cornell UP, 1948.

Waugh, Linda. "The Poetic Function and the Nature of Language." *Verbal Art, Verbal Sign, Verbal Time*. Ed. Krystyna Pomorska and Stephen Rudy. Minneapolis: U of Minnesota P, 1985. 143–68.

Weber, Samuel. *Return to Freud: Jacques Lacan's Dislocation of Psychoanalysis*. Cambridge: Cambridge UP, 1991.

Whitaker, Marie-Joséphine. "La 'clameur noire' d'une poétique inspirée." *Poétique* 18.74 (avr. 1988): 233–48.

———. "L'Influence de Rimbaud sur Claudel." *Cahiers du centre d'études théologiques de Caen* 1 (1987): 13–24.

———. *La structure du monde imaginaire de Rimbaud*. Paris: Nizet, 1972.

White, Hayden. "The Real, the True, and the Figurative in the Human Sciences." *Profession* (1992): 15–17.

Wilson, Colin. *Poetry and Mysticism*. London: Hutchinson, 1970.

Wing, Nathaniel. "The Autobiography of Rhetoric: On Reading Rimbaud's 'Une saison en enfer.'" *French Forum* 9.1 (Jan. 1984): 42–58.

———. *Present Appearances: Aspects of Poetic Structure in Rimbaud's 'Illuminations.'* University, MS: Romance, 1974.

Wolff, Edgar. "Arthur Rimbaud, fut-il schizophrène?" *Annales Médico-Psychologiques* 114.11 (oct. 1956): 443–44.

Yuasa, Hiroo. "La tentative de 'je-autre' ou l'approche de l'inconnu." *Rimbaud multiple*. Ed. Alain Borer. Paris: Touzot, 1985. 228–44.

INDEX

Adam, Antoine, 147n.53, 155n.14, 169nn. 46, 48
Adieu, 12
Aesthetics and metaphysics, 105–10, 114–16, 118, 119, 125–26; and Claudel's revisionism, 12–13, 14
Alchimie du verbe (*Une Saison en enfer*), 58–59, 61
Amrouche, Jean, 95, 107
Analogy (*see also* Claudelian metaphor): Aristotelian and Thomist, 20–21, 103, 105–7, 109–10; and Freudian dreamwork, 26–27
Anima and animus, 14–18, 127
Après le déluge (*Illuminations*), 71–74, 78
Aquinas, Saint Thomas, 97, 103, 105–6, 109–10
Aristotle, 20–23, 27, 97, 135, 136; on analogy, 20–21, 103, 105–7, 109
Art poétique (Claudel), 2, 97, 100, 111, 125; divine inspiration in, 19, 106, 107–8, 110; metaphor in, 9, 94, 98, 105–10, 114
Ascesis, psychical, 10, 39, 43, 91; and Orphic myth, 45–46, 50–51
Aube (*Illuminations*), 68–71
Aurélia (Nerval), 70
Autonomous creative impulse. *See* Creative impulse; Divine inspiration

Baillarger, Jules, 59, 165n.22
Bakhtin, Mikhail, 63–64
Banville, Théodore, 36, 37–38, 39
Barbare (*Illuminations*), 74–76, 78, 86–91
Barrès, Maurice, 94
Baudelaire, Charles, 40, 94, 142n.13, 145n.36; call to arms by, 33, 39, 100; and Rimbaud compared, 47–48, 49, 54, 63, 73, 155n.14
Baudry, Jean-Louis, 167n.33, 168n.41, 170n.59

Bays, Gwendolyn, 157n.35
Benveniste, Emile, 43, 64, 65, 73, 76–77; on *Aube*, 70; on *Parade*, 66, 67, 71
Berchan, Richard, 177n.3
Berrichon, Paterne, 6, 143n.15
Beyond the Pleasure Principle (Freud), 37
Bivort, Olivier, 167n.31
Blanchet, André, 7
Bloom, Harold, 3, 12, 36, 37, 157n.32; on Prometheus complex, 46–47; on *tessera*, 9
Bonaventura, Saint, 102–4, 110
Bonnefis, Philippe, 166n.30
Bonnefoy, Yves, 144n.24
Booz endormi (Hugo), 31–32
Bottom (*Illuminations*), 80–84, 90; desire in, 81, 82, 84–86
Bouillane de Lacoste, Henri de, 8, 159n.47
Breton, André, 61, 91, 155n.17
Brosman, Catharine Savage, 143n.18
Burdeau, Auguste, 105

Ça et là (*Connaissance de l'Est*), 100
Cathédrale, La (Huysmans), 103
Catholicism: in *Cinq grandes odes*, 114, 118, 122–23, 125–26, 130; and Claudel's conversion, 2, 7, 13–14, 94, 143n.19, 146n.46; and Claudel's misreading of Rimbaud, 2, 4–5, 14, 91–92; and *connaissance*, 101; mystical lyricism as assertion of, 93–94, 119–20, 122–23; surrealist rejection of, 91–92
Catholic renaissance, 91, 94
Chateaubriand, François-René de, 35
Cinq grandes odes (Claudel), 15, 111–14; and Claudel's revisionism, 2, 8, 9, 10, 14, 15; *La Maison fermée*, 111, 112, 128–30; *La Muse qui est la Grâce*, 126–28; *L'Esprit et l'eau*, 120–23;

199

Cinq grandes odes (Claudel) (*continued*)
  Magnificat, 123–26, 177n.1; metaphoric structure of, 9, 13, 94–95, 114–16, 117, 129–31; self-surrender in, 8, 110, 112, 115, 128–29; subjective vs. mystical lyricism in, 116–19, 123, 128
Claisse, Bruno, 170n.55
Claudel, Marie, 177n.1
Claudel, Paul (*see also Art poétique; Cinq grandes odes;* Claudelian metaphor; *Connaissance; Connaissance de l'Est;* Mystical lyricism): conversion of, 2, 6–7, 13–14, 94, 143n.19, 146n.46; vocation of, 2, 112, 125
Claudelian metaphor, 117, 122, 123, 125; as basis of Claudel's metaphysics, 93–95, 98–100, 106–9, 129–31; and Claudel's misreading of Rimbaud, 9, 11–13, 33–34, 96; influences on, 9, 97–98, 102–3, 105–7, 109–10; and rhythm, 99–100, 104, 106, 114–16; and sensory knowledge, 99–102, 103–4, 105–6
Cognition, 22–24, 30, 32–33, 79
Cohen, Jean, 137
Condensation, 29–30, 31, 32, 60, 81; in *Barbare*, 89, 90
Condillac, Etienne Bonnet de, 138–39
Connaissance, 9–12, 79, 101, 108–9, 110; in *Cinq grandes odes*, 115, 117–18, 122, 123, 125, 130; influences on, 97–98, 103, 105–7; and sensory observation, 99–102, 103–4
Connaissance de l'Est (Claudel), 2, 8, 10, 94; mystical order in, 98–100, 101–2, 103–4; realism in, 95–96; symbolism in, 96–98
Connaissance du monde et de soi-même (*Art poétique*), 105
Connaissance du temps (*Art poétique*), 105–6, 107
Contiguity (*see also* Metonymy), 11, 25, 80, 107; in dreamwork, 26, 28–29, 31
Creative impulse (*see also* Divine inspiration; Poet-as-willful-creator; Poiesis), 6–8, 10, 33–34; and anima and animus, 15–18, 127; in *Illuminations*, 62, 73, 76, 80, 88, 89; and poetics of hallucination, 58–59; unconscious Other as source of, 36–37, 39, 41–46, 61; and universal language, 47–48, 49

Decline and Fall of the Romantic Ideal, The (Lucas), 35
Deictics, 65, 71, 75
De L'Allemagne (de Staël), 35
Délires (*Une Saison en enfer*), 15, 16, 57
Demeny, Paul, seer letter to. See *Lettres du voyant*
Dérivation, La (*Connaissance de l'Est*), 96
Dernier salut à Arthur Rimbaud, Un (Claudel), 18–19
Derrida, Jacques, 140
Desbordes-Valmore, Marceline, 35
Desire, 8, 68, 77, 118–19; in *Bottom*, 81, 82, 84–86; sublimation of, 110, 111–12, 115–17, 128, 129
Dialogism, 35, 62–66, 76–77; and anima and animus, 15–18, 127; in *Après le déluge*, 71–74; in *Aube*, 68–71; in *Barbare*, 74–76, 86; in *Cinq grandes odes*, 15, 115–16, 126–28; in *Lettres du voyant*, 39, 42, 43–44, 46, 74; and oneiric writing, 77–80; in *Parade*, 66–68, 71; in *Une saison en enfer*, 49–50, 54–57
Dillman, Karin, 41, 43
Discontinuity, in *Illuminations*, 77–78, 86–87
Discourse. See Language
Displacement, 27, 28, 29–30, 31, 32; in *Aube*, 70; in *Bottom*, 81
Divine inspiration, 93–95, 111–12, 119–20; anima as, 16–18, 127; in *Art poétique*, 19, 106, 107–8, 110; and Claudel's misreading of Rimbaud, 6–8, 10, 14, 16–19, 131; in *Connaissance de l'Est*, 98–100, 101–2, 103–4; and divine rhythm, 99–100, 104, 114–16; in *La maison fermée*, 129–30; in *La Muse qui est la Grâce*, 126, 128; in *L'Esprit et l'eau*, 120–23; in *Magnificat*, 124–25; Muses identified with, 112–14; vs. poet-as-willful-creator, 14, 111, 116–19, 121–22
Dreamwork (*see also* Oneiric writing), 26–30, 59, 70, 72–73, 79–80, 81; Lacan

Index

on, 30–33, 151n.20; and universal language, 49
Dumarsais, César Chesneau, 135–37

Eco, Umberto, 149n.3
Ego self, 16, 43, 45
Eigeldinger, Marc, 41, 48, 166n.27
Entrée de la Terre, L' (*Connaissance de l'Est*), 173n.17
Ephebe, 3
Esprit et l'eau, L' (*Cinq grandes odes*), 120–23, 125–26
Esquirol, Jean-Etienne, 59
Essai sur l'origine des connaissance humaines (Condillac), 138–39
Essai sur l'origine des langues (Rousseau), 139–40
Etiemble, René, 144n.30, 146n.50

Figures. *See* Tropes
First-person narration, 49, 54, 55, 62–63; in *Illuminations*, 65, 67–70, 72, 74–76, 89
Flaubert, Gustave, 96, 98
Fleuve, Le (*Connaissance de l'Est*), 173n.20
Fontanier, Pierre, 135, 136–37
Form, and formlessness, 48–49, 87, 89–90
Forrester, John, 32
Fowlie, Wallace, 85, 95, 145n.36, 147n.60, 163n.8, 171n.2; on Claudelian metaphor, 107–8, 171n.3, 178n.16
Freadman, Anne, 166–67n.30
Free association, 27, 28, 30
Fretet, Jean, 57
Freud, Sigmund, 26–30, 33, 46, 49, 80; on condensation, 27, 29–30, 81; on creativity, 154n.4; on opposites, 30, 85; on repression, 37, 156n.32
Friedrich, Hugo, 62, 92, 142n.13
Frohock, W. M., 162n.79

Gadoffre, Gilbert, 103
Genette, Gérard, 137
Grand Jeu, Le, 91
Gumpel, Liselotte, 149n.8
Guyaux, André, 167n.36, 169n.47

Hallucination, poetics of (*see also* Oneiric writing), 37, 57–61, 77
Hellerstein, Nina, 95, 182n.51
Heterogeneous subject. *See* Split subject
Heynick, Frank, 152n.34
Hölderlin, Friedrich, 79
Horry, Ruth N., 184n.67
Houston, John Porter, 48, 169n.51
Hugo, Victor, 31–32, 35, 62, 111; and divine order, 96, 97, 101
Huysmans, Joris-Karl, 103

Idealism, 5, 19, 97–98, 111, 123
I is an Other. *See Je est un autre*
Illuminations (Rimbaud), 4, 27, 36–37, 44, 62–66, 77–80; *Aprés le déluge*, 71–74, 78; *Aube*, 68–71; *Barbare*, 74–76, 78, 86–91; *Bottom*, 80–86, 90; and Claudel's conversion, 2, 13–14, 143n.19, 146n.46; hallucination in, 37, 57; *Parade*, 66–68, 71, 77; supernatural in, 2, 5, 9, 19, 91; and *Une saison en enfer*, 8–9, 12, 50, 55, 62–63; universal language in, 49
Immanence, 8, 10, 41, 45–46, 131
Impossible, L' (*Une saison en enfer*), 53–54
Inconnu. *See* Unknown, the
Influence (*see also* Revisionism), 3–4, 37–40; on Claudelian metaphor, 9, 97–98, 102–3, 105–7, 109–10
Interpretation of Dreams, The (Freud), 29, 31, 150n.16, 151n.20, 153n.37
"Introduction à un poème sur Dante" (Claudel), 93
Izambard, Georges, 39, 41, 42, 44

Jakobson, Roman, 24–26
Jeancolas, Claude, 169nn. 47, 54
Je est un autre (*see also* Split subject), 17, 30, 35, 41–42, 52; and dialogism, 42, 43–44, 63–64; and mental alienation, 76; and poetics of hallucination, 60
Jeunesse (*Illuminations*), 77, 86
Johnson, Mark, 149n.5
Jouve, Raymond, 129
Jung, Carl G., 17, 127
Jutrin, Monique, 50–51, 52

Index

Kittang, Atle, 41, 167n.33
Kittay, Eva Feder, 149n.6
Kott, Jan, 82, 169n.48
Kristeva, Julia, 64, 70–71, 73, 75–76, 152n.27
Kronos, 169n.50

Lacan, Jacques, 26, 64, 119, 153n.1, 162n.3; on dreamwork, 30–33, 151n.20; on split subject, 10, 15, 43–44, 52, 53
Lacose, Jean, 55
Lakoff, George, 149n.5
Lamartine, Alphonse de, 35, 39, 62, 111
Lampe et la cloche, La (*Connaissance de l'Est*), 103–4
Language (*see also* Signifier and signified): bipolar model of, 25, 151n.24; and *connaissance*, 108–9; genesis of, 23–24, 135–36, 138–40; and lack, 119; and the Muses, 113; quotidian vs. poetic, 21, 23–25, 107, 135–36, 138–39; as source of split subject, 51–52, 53–54; universal, 47–49
Laplanche, Jean, 26
Lautréamont, Compte du, 49, 54, 63
Lawler, James, 164n.12
Leclaire, Serge, 26
Lefèvre, Frédéric, 141n.7
Lettre à l'Abbé Bremond sur l'inspiration poétique (Claudel), 119
Lettres du voyant (Rimbaud), 43–45, 62–63, 67–68, 74; and objective poetry, 36, 37, 40–43, 62; and Orphic and Promethean myths, 45–47; on Romanticism, 37–40; and universal language, 47–49
Leuret, François, 59
Littré, Emile, 63, 76
Loi Falloux, 94
Lucas, Frank, 35
Lucie-Smith, Edward, 4

MacCombie, John, 141n.4
Ma conversion (Claudel), 7, 13
Magnificat (*Cinq grandes odes*), 123–26, 177n.1

Maison fermée, La (*Cinq grandes odes*), 111, 112, 128–30
Mallarmé: La Catastrophe d'Igitur (Claudel), 97–98
Mallarmé, Stéphane, 4, 5, 96, 97–98, 114, 145n.36
Mallet, Roger, 95
Marée de Midi, La (*Connaissance de l'Est*), 100
Massis, Henri, 116
Materialism, 2, 5, 13, 19, 96, 97
Materialist mysticism, 11–12
Mathieu, Bertrand, 163n.8
Matin (*Une saison en enfer*), 53
Maury, Alfred, 59
Mauvais sang (*Une saison en enfer*), 51–53, 55, 57, 58
Méditations poétiques (Lamartine), 35
Mémoires improvisés (Claudel et Amrouche), 95, 105, 178n.5
Mental alienation, 57–58, 70, 76, 86
Metaphor (*see also* Analogy; Claudelian metaphor; Metonymy): and Claudel's misreading of Rimbaud, 9, 11–13, 33–34, 96; as cognitive process, 22–24, 30, 32–33; and Freudian dreamwork, 26–30, 80, 81; and genesis of language, 23–24, 135–36, 138–40; Lacanian view of, 26, 30–33; mimetic function of, 20–21, 136–37; neoclassical view of, 135–38; and oneiric writing, 78–80; and poetics of hallucination, 60–61; in poetic vs. quotidian language, 21, 23–25, 107, 135–36, 138–39; poietic function of, 22–24, 29–30, 32–33, 136–37; and repression, 157n.32; structural linguistic view of, 24–26, 29, 31, 32, 151n.24
Metaphora. *See* Metaphor
Metaphysics. *See* Aesthetics and metaphysics; *Connaissance*; Mystical lyricism
Metaphysics, The (Aristotle), 103, 105
Metonymy, 11, 12, 31–33, 102, 107; in *Barbare*, 86, 87–88, 90–91; and bipolar model of language, 25–26, 151n.24; in *Bottom*, 84, 85; Dumarsais on, 136; and oneiric writing, 78–80; and poetics of hallucination, 60

Index

Michelet, Jules, 150n.11, 170n.55
Midsummer Night's Dream, A (Shakespeare), 80, 82
Mimesis (*see also* Analogy), 20–21, 28, 36, 60, 79; in *Art poétique*, 106, 107; in *Cinq grandes odes*, 117, 123, 125, 130–31; in neoclassical debate, 136–37
Misprision. *See* Revisionism
Morisot, Jean-Claude, 1–2
Muse qui est la Grâce, La (*Cinq grandes odes*), 15, 16–17, 111, 119, 126–28
Muses, Les (*Cinq grandes odes*), 16–17, 111–14, 125; divine rhythm in, 114–16; subjective vs. mystical lyricism in, 116–19
Musset, Alfred de, 35, 39
Mystical lyricism (*see also Cinq grandes odes*), 1, 2, 11–12, 18, 110; as assertion of Catholicism, 93–94, 119–20, 122–23; in *Connaissance de l'Est*, 98–100, 101; metaphor as basis of, 93–95, 129–31; and subjective idealism, 97–98, 111, 123
Mysticism: attributed to Rimbaud, 6–7, 11–12; and universal soul, 47–48

Nagy, Moses, 142n.7
Neoclassicism, 135–38
Nerval, Gérard de, 49, 54, 63, 70, 76
New Science (Vico), 23–24
Nuit de l'enfer (*Une saison en enfer*), 55–57

Objective poetry, 36, 37, 39, 40–43, 50; in *Illuminations*, 62–63, 70–71, 76
Oneiric writing (*see also* Hallucination, poetics of), 77–80; in *Barbare*, 86–91; in *Bottom*, 80–86, 90
Orphic myth, 45–46, 47, 50–51, 56, 157n.34
Other, the. *See* Dialogism; Split subject; Unconscious Other

Palombo, Stanley, 151n.17
Parabole d'Animus et d'Anima pour faire comprendre certaines poésies d'Arthur Rimbaud (Claudel), 14–15
Parade (*Illuminations*), 66–68, 71, 77
Parataxis, 29, 77, 78

Parker, Patricia, 148n.1
Parnasse contemporain, Le, 38
Parnassianism, 38–40, 42
Péguy, Charles-Pierre, 94
Perse, Marie-René, 94
Personal lyricism (*see also* Subjective poetry), 35, 39, 42, 128
Petralia, Franco, 1, 12, 142n.12, 144n.24, 147n.52
Phelan, Gerald, 109
Philosophie du livre, La (Claudel), 178n.13
Poésie au XIXe siècle, La (Claudel), 145n.41
Poésie est un art, La (Claudel), 102–3, 176n.52
Poesis perennis, 93, 101, 106, 114, 115, 130
Poet: aspiring vs. strong, 3, 36, 37; as priest, 2, 112, 117–18, 125
Poet-as-mystic. *See* Divine inspiration
Poet-as-seer. *See Lettres du voyant*; Voyance
Poet-as-willful-creator, 7, 10, 14, 111, 116, 156n.31; animus as, 15; in *Les Muses*, 118–19; in *L'Esprit et l'eau*, 121–22; of poetics of hallucination, 58–59; and Prometheus complex, 46–47
Poetics (Aristotle), 20–22, 27
Poetic voice. *See* Voice
Poetry and Repression (Bloom), 36
Poiesis (*see also* Creative impulse; Divine inspiration), 36, 46, 74, 105; as aspect of metaphor, 22–24, 29–30, 32–33, 136–37; Claudelian metaphor as, 107–9, 129–31; and dreamwork, 28–30, 79–80; and poetics of hallucination, 60; and universal language, 48, 49
Porc, Le (*Connaissance de l'Est*), 95–96
Positivism. *See* Materialism
Postmodernism, 8, 11, 23, 33
Postromanticism, 33
Poststructuralism, 22–24, 25, 31, 55
Pottecher, Maurice, 3
Poulet, Georges, 44, 156n.31, 179n.24
Priest, poet as, 2, 112, 117–18, 125
Promeneur, Le (*Connaissance de l'Est*), 101–2, 103

Index

Prometheus complex, 46–47
Psychiatry, nineteenth-century, 59, 165n.22
Psychical ascesis. *See* Ascesis, psychical
Psychopoetics, 23, 26, 60–61, 96, 149n.4

Ragland-Sullivan, Ellie, 32, 80, 152n.29, 156n.24
Raymond, Marcel, 184n.69
Realism, 95–96, 98
Réflexions et propositions sur le vers français (Claudel), 114–15
Religion et poésie (Claudel), 101
Renard, Jules, 95
René (Chateaubriand), 35
Renéville, Rolland de, 47, 146n.50, 158n.43, 168n.39
Rêves (*Connaissance de l'Est*), 98
Revisionism, 3–6, 11–14, 91–92, 131–32; and anima and animus, 14–18; of Aristotle and Aquinas, 103, 105–7, 109–10; of creative impulse in Rimbaud, 6–8, 10, 33–34; and Prometheus complex, 46–47; of Rimbaud's *voyance*, 9–11, 18–19; of Romanticism, 36–40, 42, 58–59, 62
Rhetoric (Aristotle), 20, 22
Rigolot, C. N., 179n.16
Rimbaud, Arthur (*see also Illuminations; Lettres du voyant; Saison en enfer, Une*): chronology of works of, 8–9, 12, 62–63, 158n.47; mental health of, 57, 76; supposed conversion of, 2, 7, 13, 14, 19
Rimbaud, Isabelle, 13, 14, 19
"Rimbaud de Claudel, Le" (Petralia), 1
Rivière, Jacques, 4–5, 13, 155n.17, 177n.1
Romanticism, 35–37, 111, 135, 138–40; Rimbaud's revision of, 36–40, 42, 58–59, 62
Ronsard, Pierre de, 38
Ross, Kristin, 167n.33
Rousseau, Jean Jacques, 139–40

Saint Denys, Hervey de, 59
Saison en enfer, Une (Rimbaud), 8–9, 12–13, 19, 44; and Claudel's conversion, 6–7, 146n.46; dialogic voice in, 49–50, 54–57; negation of God in, 14, 51–53; as Orphic descent, 50–51, 56; poetics of hallucination in, 57, 58–59; speechlessness in, 16, 51–52, 53, 58–59; subject in process in, 53–54, 62
Sapienza poetica, 23–24, 48, 49, 139
Schizophrenia, 58, 77, 79
Seer letters. *See Lettres du voyant*
Self. *See* Speaking subject; Split subject; Subject
Shakespeare, William, 80, 82
Shurr, Georgia Hooks, 177n.62
Signifier and signified, 10–11, 23, 24, 50, 98, 107; and *connaissance*, 108, 109; and dreamwork, 27, 28, 29–32, 79–80; and oneiric writing, 78, 79–80, 85–86; and poetics of hallucination, 57–58, 59–60, 61
Silverman, Kaja, 33
Skura, Meredith, 150n.15, 158n.42
Soleil et chair (Rimbaud), 158n.41
Soul, universal, 47–49
Speaking subject (*see also* Dialogism; Divine inspiration), 10, 16, 38, 40, 41–45, 49; alienated by language, 51–52, 53–54; and *metaphora*, 24; and realism, 95–96
Split subject (*see also* Dialogism; Unconscious Other), 12, 35, 111; and animus and anima, 15–18, 127; in *Bottom*, 82–83; language as source of, 51–52, 53–54; in *Lettres du voyant*, 39, 41–45, 48, 62–63; and Orphic myth, 50–51, 56; and poetics of hallucination, 57–61; and Romanticism, 36–37, 40
Staël, Germaine de, 35
Starkie, Enid, 41, 42
States, Bert, 153n.36
Structural linguistics, 24–26, 29, 31, 32, 151n.24
Suarès, André, 141n.1
Subject (*see also* Speaking subject; Split subject; Unified subject): Lacanian, 10, 15, 43–44, 52, 53; modern, 38, 62; postmodern, 8, 23, 33; in process, 53–54, 62; Romantic, 35–37, 58–59, 62
Subjective idealism, 36, 41, 97–98, 111, 123

Index

Subjective poetry, 35–36, 39, 62; in *Cinq grandes odes*, 116, 118–19, 123, 128; and objective poetry, 41, 42–43, 63–64, 65, 70–71
Sujet de l'énoncé/l'énonciation, 64–65, 67, 68, 70, 71, 76; Claudel's unification of, 96–97
Summa Theologiae (Aquinas), 103, 105
Supernatural, the, 2, 5–6, 9, 13–14, 19, 91
Sur la cervelle (*Connaissance de l'Est*), 99, 104
Surrealism, 6, 12, 31, 91–92, 145n.40, 168n.40
Swedenborg, Emanuel, 47–48
Syllogism, 105–6, 110
Symbolic order of language, 41, 52, 53, 64; and dreamwork, 28, 30, 32
Symbolism, 96–97, 98

Tamba, Irène, 150n.8
Temple de la conscience, Le (*Connaissance de l'Est*), 99
Tessera, 9
Third-person narration, 63, 70, 71, 72–73, 74–75, 89
Thom, Martin, 152n.30
Todorov, Tzvetan, 57–58, 79, 137, 150n.16, 170n.58
Traité général des figures du discours (Fontanier), 136–37
Transcendence (*see also* Divine inspiration), 35, 41, 45–46, 47–48, 131; in *Connaissance de l'Est*, 97, 98–99
Transference, 21–22, 26, 27–30
Tropes, 24, 26, 27, 29, 135–37

Unconscious, the (*see also* Unconscious Other): in Freudian dreamwork, 26, 29–30; Lacanian view of, 30–32; and Orphic myth, 45–46, 47; and poetics of hallucination, 57–58, 59–61; and universal soul, 47, 49
Unconscious Other (*see also* Dialogism), 33–34, 53, 111, 126, 128; and animus and anima, 15–16; in *Après le déluge*, 73–74; in *Aube*, 69–70; in *Barbare*, 76, 87, 90–91; in *Bottom*, 80, 82, 83–85,

90; Claudel's misreading of, 4–6, 10, 91–92, 131, 132; and discontinuous narrative voice, 77, 87; and Orphic myth, 45–46, 47, 50–51, 56, 157n.34; in *Parade*, 67–68; and poetics of hallucination, 58; and Prometheus complex, 46–47; and Romanticism, 38, 39; as source of creative impulse, 36–37, 39, 41–46, 61; and universal language, 49
Underwood, Vernon, 169n.52
Unified subject (*see also Cinq grandes odes*), 35, 93; and Claudel's misreading of Rimbaud, 12, 16, 17–18; in *Connaissance de l'Est*, 95–97, 98–99, 102, 104
Universal language, 47–49
Unknown, the (*see also* Unconscious, the; Unconscious Other): and cultivation of the psyche, 39, 59; and dreamwork, 29–30; psychical vs. religious, 4, 5–6, 33–34

Varèse, Louise, 85, 163n.8
Verlaine, Paul, 12, 55, 62, 147n.53, 158n.47
Vico, Giambattista, 23–24, 138, 139
Voice (*see also* Dialogism; Divine inspiration; First-person narration; Subject): and Claudel's revisionism, 8–11, 15–18; loss of, 16, 51–52, 53, 58–59; self-surrender of, 2–3, 8, 110, 111–12, 115–17, 128–29; third-person, 63, 70, 71, 72–73, 74–75, 89
Voyance (*see also Lettres du voyant*), 9–11, 18–19, 33, 154n.12; Claudelian, 100–102, 117; and Romanticism, 36, 39–40
Voyelles (Rimbaud), 59

Waugh, Linda, 150n.13
Weber, Samuel, 150n.16, 152n.30
Whitaker, Marie-Joséphine, 18, 142n.9
White, Hayden, 150n.15
Wing, Nathaniel, 36–37, 53–54, 163n.6

Zola, Emile, 96, 98

Adrianna M. Paliyenko is an associate professor of French at Colby College, where she teaches language and literature with a focus on nineteenth-century poetry, women writers, and artistic relations. Her essays have appeared in *Claudel Studies*, *Nineteenth-Century French Studies*, *French Forum*, *Romance Quarterly*, and *Romanic Review*. Her current research focuses on the recovery of women's poetic writing in nineteenth-century France to consider the emergence of female psychology before Freudian psychoanalysis.